As I Remember

90 years in the 1900s: 1900–1990

47 years in Road Transport: 1921–1968

As I Remember

by Harold Bridges O.B.E. K. St. J.

Copyright, © Harold Bridges, A.I.R. 90, Luneside, Burrow, 1992.

Published by Harold Bridges, A.I.R. 90, Luneside, Burrow, via Carnforth LA6 2RJ.
Typeset in 10½/12 Times and designed by Carnegie Publishing Ltd., Preston.
Printed and bound in the UK by The Alden Press, Oxford.

ISBN 0-9519713-0-1

As I Remember

90 years in the 1900s: 1900–1990

47 years in Road Transport: 1921–1968

Harold Bridges O.B.E. K. St. J.

with a foreword by R. N. Hardy

Dedicated to Alice Lewis Vale
1917–1924
My Wife 1924–1977

Contents

Foreword

The story of Harold Bridges is one which will interest and inspire many people from all walks of life and of any age. He was born in 1900 and his life has spanned the century following. To have written his autobiography at the age of 90 has given him a unique perspective and is a tribute to his single-mindedness and ability.

Harold gives as his main reason for writing this book his wish to support and raise funds for the Harold Bridges Foundation and the Road Haulage Association Benevolent Fund. The former charitable Foundation was set up by Harold in 1963 and, through the donations it makes to other charitable organisations, benefits countless individuals each year. All the net proceeds from the sales of *As I Remember* will thus be donated for charitable purposes.

As I Remember is a very personal story of Harold's life, of its successes, its sadnesses, and perhaps above all its achievements, as the following pages will reveal.

R. N. Hardy
Lytham, May 1992

Chapter One

Early Life

FOR the past twenty years relations, friends and acquaintances have been telling me that I should write my life story. What a task to start at nearly 89 years of age, more particularly as there is so much to tell: happiness, sorrow, boredom and adventure; excitement, failure, success, scheming and planning, good luck – not so good luck – and, the greatest of all, to love and be loved for sixty long years, 53 of happy marriage to my dear Alice, to whom I dedicate my efforts.

I suppose in a life story one should begin at the earliest possible date in my life: the 11th May 1900 when, I am told, a boy 8lbs in weight was born at Keepers Cottage, Lodge Lane', Warton, near Lytham, Lancashire, to Elizabeth and Henry Hipkins Bridges, gamekeeper to Captain Wykeham Clifton of Warton Hall, near Lytham. Needless to say, I do not remember this event, but my birth certificate does indicate that it is correct! Dad and Mother decided to call me Harold. Why, I don't know, as there does not appear to be any Harold in earlier generations, and when, in later years, I asked, 'Why Harold?' Dad said there was only one King Harold and he died facing the enemy. So much for that. Captain Wykeham Clifton was an old soldier and Crimean War veteran, and I was told later that, as I was born the day before Mafeking was relieved in the South African Boer War, the Captain wanted me to be called Mafeking Bridges. Dad thought this would be a daft name and would not agree, but he told me later that, if he had agreed, the Captain would have put £25 into the Fylde Water Board for me which was to pay 5% compound interest for twenty years, when it would be repaid with all the interest earned. This would have been in 1921, and when my story gets to 1921 you will see what might have been!

Very early years are not easy to remember. One of my earliest memories, when I would be five or six, is of my mother being in bed and the doctor coming

Captain Wykeham Clifton, Warton Hall, near Lytham, c. 1905. Dad was his gamekeeper for 14 years.

in a one-horse cab from Lytham, two miles away. He had with him a lady who would be the midwife. After a few hours the doctor went and the midwife took me upstairs to see my new brother, later christened Edward. I can remember the smell of carbolic and the bottle of Parish's food, which was a sort of tonic for invalids. Edward was the seventh son; the second and third sons were twins, and died before I was born.

School days started at five years old and I went to St. John's School (C. of E.) in Lytham, two miles' walk each way. We had to take our own lunch, and ate it with a drink of water in the cloakroom. There were no hot drinks, free school meals or milk, and no motor cars, or bicycles to ride. Five or six of the children living in Lodge Lane went to school together, and we were a happy bunch of kids. There were also four or five lads from Warton Hall Farm and Cottages who went to St. Peter's Catholic School.

On summer evenings we would play cricket with wickets, bats etc. made at home. We had hoops made at the blacksmith's in Warton village, which were circles of ¼-inch-round iron between two and three feet in diameter, with which we used to race up and down Lodge Lane. We had whips and tops and marbles and, depending on the time of the year, there was bird nesting, blackberrying, mushrooming, and helping the farmers in the hay and corn fields. My brothers Charles (the eldest) and Walter and myself had our own jobs to do according to the time of the year: in the cottage garden and orchard; cleaning the ferret hutch out once a week; feeding the hens, dogs and ferrets; gathering kindling wood to light the fire in the kitchen, and wood for the baking oven and wash house boiler.

The days were always full of something to do. In winter we would play draughts, ludo, dominoes and snakes and ladders, or make rugs and mats from scrap cloth and hessian sacks. There was no radio or television. One of our pastimes was to go about half a mile across the fields to watch the trains on the main Preston-Lytham-Blackpool line. Close to the railway was Liggard Brook, a drainage dyke about six or eight yards across and half a mile from the sea. Flukes or dabs used to come up Liggard Brook with the high tides, and we used to fish for them with all sorts of home-made tackle, but I don't remember us ever catching more than two or three any day. We always had to ask permission from Mum or Dad to go fishing and watching trains, which used to pass very frequently, and we were always told not to go on to the railway at any time.

One day, three of us were watching a train and something flew out of a carriage window and floated down inside the hedge. What was it? I dived through a gap in the hedge, ran along the inside of the hedge and recovered a very fancy chocolate box – empty, of course. I dared not take it home, or Dad would guess that I had been on the line, so I left it in the hedge bottom and we eventually made our way home. Dad was in the yard with a man in brown overalls, and looking rather grim. 'Harold, have you been on the railway line?' he asked me. I admitted that I had, and explained why. 'How often have you been told not to go on the line?' I had to answer, 'Every time we go to fish'. Dad said, 'Come on,' and took me and the man in overalls round the back of the outbuilding, and gave me about six strokes on my backside with a thin ash stick. 'So let that be a lesson to you, never go on the line.' I never did, but this was not the end of the story.

In 1928, which would be about twenty years later, in the course of my work as general carrier at Lytham, we did a small furniture removal for some people who had a greengrocer's shop in Park Street, Lytham, and were retiring to live with their parents in Stamford, Lincolnshire. We loaded the lorry on Saturday afternoon and arrived in Stamford at about 7.00am on Sunday. The furniture was unloaded by 9.00am and the owners asked us to have breakfast, which we gladly accepted. We had just about finished when an elderly gentleman came into the room. 'Are you Harry Bridges' lad from Warton?' he asked. 'Yes,' I said, 'that's right.' 'Do you know me?' 'No, I don't.' 'You ought to,' he said, 'I was the foreman platelayer who got you a hiding about twenty years ago!' Evidently he had seen me on the railway line and went and told Dad, who had administered instant justice. Dad was very strict about anything like that, and rightly so. Many times he said, 'Own up if you have been in the wrong, and never tell a lie'.

Keepers Cottage, Lodge Lane was about two hundred yards from the main Preston to Lytham road across Freckleton Marsh. There was a tollgate on this road, and every vehicle and animal had to pay a toll. The alternative road between Preston and Lytham was through Clifton, Kirkham, Wrea Green and Moss Side, all served by the railway, and miles further than the route across Freckleton Marsh. The road to Lytham was of stone and gravel, waterbound, and in dry weather we could see when the occasional motor vehicle went along, marked by the rolling cloud of white dust which followed it. Lytham Shipyard was a hive of industry. We could hear the starting and finishing hooter, and the riveters working on the steel hulls with hammers, in the days before hulls were welded. The shipyard built mainly shallow draught river boats for South Africa, paddle steamers and stern paddle wheelers. I remember once when, on our way home from school, a big steam traction engine was towing a trailer with a very big steam boiler for Lytham Shipyard. The road crossed the Liggard Brook, and the men were laying steel plates along the road to avoid damaging the bridge. To us country lads this was an exciting event, and we were all late home from school that day.

The sea wall and embankment of the River Ribble were about two hundred yards from the road, opposite the end of Lodge Lane, and between the embankment and the sea there was a large area – perhaps forty or fifty acres – of sea-washed turf, covered by the sea at medium and high tides. At the right time of the year we used to go and collect lots of samphire, a sort of sea vegetable which mother used to boil in salt water. It was eaten by holding the stem, putting the piece in your mouth and pulling, and the flesh of the samphire came off quite easily. No sewage was being tipped into the sea in those days. We also used to walk the tide-line after high tides, gathering (if we were lucky) various items of flotsam and jetsam, wreckage, etc.

Around Warton few of the farms had separate barns from the main farm buildings and all the hay and corn was built into stacks, which were usually round. In the winter the corn stacks were a favourite place for sparrows to roost; they were a pest to the farmers, with clouds of them eating the corn in the harvest fields. We used to fix a riddle on a pitch fork and go round the stacks at night catching the sparrows and occasionally we did have sparrow pie, but they were mainly fed to the ferrets.

The autumn called for blackberries to be gathered, and windfall apples, and the making of lovely apple and blackberry pie. Threshing days on the farms did not often fall on Saturdays, or in the holidays. When they did, the attraction of the big steam traction engine, the threshing machine and the machine which bottled the straw drew all the local lads old enough to help on the job. School lessons were all basics: reading, writing, arithmetic, spelling, geography, some history and religious lessons. There was a very strict code of conduct, backed up by the teacher's cane. Once, caught fooling about during the temporary absence of the teacher, I got two strokes of the cane on each hand and had to stay in after school to write out 25 times, 'I must behave in class'. Everyone went home at 3.30pm, leaving me to write my 25 lines during the hour in which the cleaner and caretaker worked. When I had finished I got my cap and coat and found that I was locked in; the cleaner had forgotten me, locked up and gone home. The windows in the school were high, and I could not attract any attention to my plight. Fortunately my brothers, Charles and Walter, had told Mother and Dad that I was being kept in school and, when I did not arrive home later, Dad came to the school with the caretaker and let me out. I arrived home about three hours late.

It would be in about 1908, when I was eight years of age, that I had my first experience of tragedy. We were all at school, Dad was out on the estate and Mother was washing and ironing when she missed Edward, my youngest brother, who was then about two years old and just toddling around. Mother found him, lying face down at the edge of a cattle drinking pond behind the cottage. Little Edward was dead. There was an inquest, and I think the verdict was 'Found drowned'. I recall the funeral and the single one-horse cab, Mother and Dad on one side, Charles, Walter and me on the other side facing them, and the tiny coffin between us. Too late, the fence behind the cottage was repaired and the pond filled in.

On our way home from school we were sometimes able to watch bricks being unloaded from barges which had been towed by a steam tug from Alty's brickworks at Hesketh Bank on the south side of the River Ribble. At high tide they could get to the unloading crane near the road by coming up a creek from the river, past the shipyard. This same creek was used to sail boats, paddle steamers and tugs away from the shipyard slipway after construction.

Another activity nearby was when the sand pumps in the Ribble channel were working, and the sand and sea water were pumped on to an area of low land opposite the Cottage Hospital. During the First World War an aerodrome was built on part of the land, with a slipway down into the sea, and Dick Kerrs of Preston built seaplanes there. The first one was wrecked when it hit the river channel stone training wall which was covered by water at high tide. The aerodrome is now the site of Cookson's Bakery and the Land Registry offices on East Beach, Lytham.

Other events which we looked forward to were Lytham, Warton, Freckleton and Kirkham Club Days, all places to which we had to walk in those days, where there were steam hobby horses, swings and coconut shies. Warton and other nearby villages also had their Sports Days, with all sorts of fun and games. Looking back, it seems to have been a simple, happy life, with no vandalism or graffiti. Keepers Cottage was a semi-detached house built in the late 1800s, opposite the back entrance to Warton Hall, and replaced a pair of whitewashed, thatched-roofed cottages, of which I have a painting done by Capt. Wykeham Clifton. Mother and Dad had lived in one of these, and often used to recall that the stairs were so narrow that they could not get some of their furniture upstairs. The Hall's gardener, whose name was McLellan, lived next door. They had no children, and when Mrs McLellan made a trip to Lytham, a two-mile walk each way, she always brought us a few sweets, or an orange, or some nuts. These were quite a treat for us, as there were six in the family: Charles, Walter, Harold, Reuben, Mother and Dad. We never had any pocket money, and if anyone gave us a sixpence or a penny it went into our own money box. Dad's wages were about 18s. a week, so there was no cash for luxuries. The gardener would bring us surplus vegetables and fruit from the Hall garden, and the cook would also sometimes send a part joint of meat left over when there had been guests at the Hall.

One of Dad's tasks was keeping the rabbit population at a reasonable level, and during the winter months we would have rabbit pies once or twice a week. Dad also used to take the cottagers and farmers on the estate a couple of rabbits, which were always welcome, and we used to catch wood pigeons in traps, which caught them alive. Then we had pigeon pie. I think it was an unwritten law on the estates that the gamekeeper did not take any game birds for his own use. He might have a brace of pheasants given to him after Christmas by the Captain, when usually cocks only were shot. It was perhaps a rather frugal way of life. It did teach us the value of money, to save what we could and not to waste anything, and not to borrow. In spite of living near what would now be called the poverty line, we were quite happy, and the people of the small community round the Hall were very close and helpful to each other in many ways.

The grocer, butcher and ironmonger came round once a week, all with horse-drawn vehicles, which was quite an event for us if we were at home when they called. It was quite amazing what a variety of goods the ironmonger carried around, including a tank of paraffin oil for the oil lamps, as there was no gas or electricity. The oil lamp wicks had to be trimmed, the glass cleaned and the lamps filled every day in winter, and we had candles to go to bed – there was no other light upstairs. One thing we did have, and which is still the same eighty years later, was lovely, clean, fresh tap water. So many villages in those days drew water from wells and hand pumps and, in such a scattered rural area, we were lucky enough to have tap water laid on. There was no bathroom, of course, and we mainly took our baths in a zinc bath in the wash house, heating the water in the washing boiler. The earth closet was outside in the garden and had to be emptied each week, Charles, Walter and I having to take turns at the job.

In about 1909 Dad was offered the position of head gamekeeper at Lytham Hall, the residence of Squire Clifton, and he accepted. The removal was a very exciting event for us lads. I remember the four-wheeled iron-tyred furniture van coming from Lawson's of Lytham, drawn by two horses. It took most of the morning to load, followed by the five or six-mile journey to Keepers Cottage, off Regent Street, Heyhouses (now Islay Road). Though it is all built up now, with the Corporation cemetery adjacent, at that time there were two cottages and two farmhouses in Regent Street. Keepers Cottage is still there, but much altered now.

The job was a big step up for Dad. The estate would be about twenty times the size of the Warton Estate, where he worked single-handed, and at Lytham there were six under keepers on different beats on the estate. A lot of pheasants were hatched in oil-heated incubators, which were not a success in those early days, and Dad preferred the old fashioned method of using sitting hens. This may have been more expensive, but produced better results. The sitting hens were collected from farms which, in those days, all kept free range hens. Dad had a horse and trap, two-wheeled and high up. He also had a milking cow, geese, ducks and a few acres of land with the cottage, a large kitchen garden and, of course, higher wages, which made life a lot easier for Mother and all of us. We still had a two-mile walk to school at St. Cuthbert's, Church Road, Lytham, if we went round by the public road. There was a short cut through the woods, but the paths were often very muddy, and we might arrive at school with mud-covered boots. The headmaster, Mr Hoyle, saw my muddy boots one morning and, as a punishment, I had to stand on the seat behind my desk for the whole of the first lesson – about an hour.

One of my most serious problems during my schooldays was that I had a bad speech impediment. I did not actually stammer or stutter, I just could not get my words out. It was an awful thing to bear, and anyone with similar trouble has my most sincere sympathy. I don't know how or why I had this impediment, as none of my relatives was so afflicted, but Mother thought it was caused by my having had a bad carbuncle on my neck which, she said, had weakened the muscles. Dad used to say, 'You'll never be anything but a navvy unless you learn to talk properly,' and I really thought he was right. In fact, it was this very impediment that, in 1921, changed my whole future prospects, as you will see later.

Squire Clifton had a big white Mercedes car, one of the few cars about then, and a German chauffeur, Karl. There were some miles of private road inside the park and no speed limit, of course. The Squire was very keen on shooting, so there was always plenty of activity in connection with the sport. When the shooting season for pheasants ended on 2nd February, hen and cock pheasants were caught alive in traps and placed in big enclosed pens. They had their flight feathers on, but one wing was cut so that they could not fly out of the pen. One of my jobs was going round the outside of this pen to check the vermin traps set to catch any rats, stoats and weasels which were attracted by the birds and their eggs. The eggs laid in April and May were collected each day and hatched out in incubators or under sitting hens, and when the chicks hatched out they were taken to the rearing field to be reared on before being let loose in the woods.

The Clifton Estate lands reached to the outskirts of South Shore, Blackpool. The Squire was also fond of horse racing and had created a horse race track complete with covered stand and all the usual facilities at Squires Gate, South Shore. The race course was bounded on two sides by public roads, along which was a very high wooden hoarding to stop people watching the races from the roads. In the early 1900s the aeroplane was developing, and in 1910 an aviation week organised at South Shore created immense interest. I am sure that none of us had ever seen an aeroplane, and Mother and Dad decided that we would all go and see if there was any chance of seeing one, so we all climbed into the high two-wheeled horse trap and set off to Blackpool. However, it was too windy for flying and we did not see an aeroplane, although we waited all afternoon. We did hear what we thought might be aeroplane engines, but that was all. Our luck was in a day or two later, when the butler at the Hall told Dad that an aeroplane was to fly from Squires Gate and land near the Hall next day. So it did. The gamekeeper's house was in its direct line of flight and it came right over the house, only about two hundred feet up. It was a single-engine biplane which looked to be a very fragile structure of struts and wires, and was flying quite slowly, piloted by Graham White, one of the earliest aviators.

Walter Bridges, 1908. Lytham Club Day Procession. Walter, my elder brother, died of rheumatic fever in c.1910.

A few days before Christmas each year there was a large Christmas tree at the Hall. All the estate workers, with their wives and families, were invited and received a small present and a tea party for all. I think in our lives that was the most important annual event after Lytham Club Day and the fairground.

We had two or three geese and a big old gander, which Reuben and I used to feed. In the spring, when the geese were laying, the old gander used to chase us away with his neck outstretched, wings beating, and hissing like a steam engine. One day Reuben must have been teasing the gander, and he chased Reuben through the orchard. Reuben fell, and the old gander was on him in a flash, pecking with his beak and flapping his great wings, while Reuben yelled for help. I dashed off to tell Mother, who must have heard the commotion and saw through the kitchen window what was happening. She picked up a heavy yard brush and beat off the gander, who was giving her his mind in goose language! Poor Reuben lost two teeth and his face and head were badly bruised, but he could easily have been blinded. We left the geese alone at nesting time after that.

There used to be big pheasant shooting days, but we were too young to go beating then and had to stay at home, not go wandering in the woods. Dad used to tell us who had been the Squire's guests and one particular one sticks in my mind – the Grand Duke Michael of Russia. The Squire had, over the years, done quite a lot of big game shooting in South Africa, and at the Christmas party we were allowed to see the results in the Trophy Room. There were all sorts of heads and horns, skins and stuffed birds and reptiles.

My only sister, Rose, was born in December 1908. She was one of the second set of twins which mother had, the first twins having been born and died long before I was born; and Rosie's own twin died at birth due to delay in getting the doctor or midwife. There was no prenatal care in those days, and no telephones or taxis, just horse-drawn cabs.

Tragedy struck the family again in 1910. My elder brother, Walter, had been working at Garlick's butchers in Woodlands Road, Ansdell, as an errand boy and to learn the trade. He was taken ill and died at home of rheumatic fever, and we had another sad journey by horse-drawn hearse and cabs to Warton Church. Mother blamed his illness on working in a very damp cellar at the butcher's shop, salting bacon, brining meat, etc. There was no refrigeration then, and salt was used as a preservative. I have mentioned that Dad had a horse and high two-wheeled trap to get around the estate and to visit the under keepers' beats. The Estate got him a new horse, which was quite young and frisky. Dad had to cross a field to get to the road, and Mother used to stand at the garden gate to watch him out of sight. One day he was crossing the field with the horse on a tight rein and very frisky as it had not been out for a few days. Suddenly the left-hand leather rein broke, which caused the horse to whip around to the right very sharply, overturning the trap and throwing Dad out. The loose seat in the trap flew out, hit Dad on the head and knocked him unconscious. With the horse still harnessed to the trap, and kicking wildly as it tried to get up, Dad was in terrible danger. Mother saw all this happen, rushed across the field and, fortunately, knew just what to do; she sat on the horse's

While at Heyhouses I contracted Scarlet Fever and had to go to Moss Side Isolation Hospital near Lytham. The ambulance which came for me was a horse-drawn vehicle, similar to the one shown below.

head, which quietened it down so that it stopped kicking. Luckily the accident had happened not far from the nearest farm, and two men came in response to Mother's shouts for help. They freed the horse's harness so that it could get up, took off a field gate, laid Dad on it and carried him home. There was no telephone nearer than a mile away, so someone dashed off on a bicycle to summon the doctor, but it was hours before he came. Dad had come round, complaining of a headache and a bad pain in his hip; the doctor said that the hip was out of joint and he could not put it back himself, so he would have to get another doctor to help him next day. There was no question of X-rays, or of going to hospital. The doctors came the following day, and were in the room with Dad for two hours or more. Mother nursed Dad, and we all helped with what we could. I know that Dad was in awful pain, and after about two weeks both Mother and Dad became convinced that something was not right. I think it was Mrs Clifton who arranged for Dad to see a specialist surgeon, who examined him and, within minutes, pronounced that the hip had never been put back properly and was still out of joint. They got Dad out of bed to prove it and, of course, he could not stand up. The first two doctors were there, and between the three of them they got the hip back, and Dad was soon on the road to recovery.

Another episode in my life while at Heyhouses was that I contracted scarlet fever and had to go to Moss Side Isolation Hospital, near Lytham. The ambulance which came for me was, of course, a horse-drawn vehicle similar to the one pictured, and more like a big boxed hearse than anything else. On the way to Moss Side Hospital we picked up another patient with scarlet fever, a Miss Lee, who lived in Dock Road, Lytham. Miss Lee attended St. John's School in Lytham when I did, and, ten years later, her uncle Tom Lee taught me to drive. The only thing that I remember about my stay in hospital is the daily bath in hot water with lots of carbolic in it.

On big estates the head gamekeeper would not have very frequent contact with the Squire. All contact, except on shooting days, was with the Estate Agent on the Lytham Estate – Mr James Fair, at that time – who was responsible for the financial running of the estate. From conversations that I heard between Dad and Mother, it was obvious that relations between Dad and Mr Fair were not what they should have been. Dad used to go to the Estate Office in Hastings Place, Lytham, to collect the under keepers' wages and any cash that he had spent on account of his work. The following day – Saturday, as a rule – he would take the under keepers' wages to their homes, and I often went with him in the horse and trap. He had the money in a small brown leather bag; it was all gold and silver coins, and no paper money under five pounds. Similar trips were made with the horse and trap to collect sitting hens from farms in spring. After the hatching season the hens were often taken back to the farms, and I expect that they would start laying again in a few weeks.

It was obvious that relations between Dad and the Estate Agent were not improving, and I was not really surprised when Dad told us in 1910 that we were moving to another part of the Clifton Estate. This was Clifton with Salwick, between Kirkham and Preston, and this estate was let each year to a syndicate of shooting gentry, so Dad was not responsible to the Estate Agent at Lytham, and it was a single keeper's job at Clifton. The move to Clifton involved the usual removal with Lawson's two-horse furniture van, which took a very long time. I never knew whether Dad asked to be moved, or whether he was compelled to, but at Clifton we had a large kitchen garden, a good orchard, and outbuildings, and Dad was a lot happier. A year or two later the same syndicate took the Salwick Estate as well, and the gamekeeper there was Dad's under keeper.

Charles, my eldest brother, had started work at R. Hughes decorators in Station Road, Lytham, and he lived in lodgings. This, I believe, took all his wages in the beginning, but he was learning a trade as painter and decorator. The first big change for me, Reuben and Rose was that the school was just across the road from the gamekeeper's house, and very near Lund Church, and it was much easier to go to church every Sunday morning and Sunday School every Sunday afternoon. Clifton was a country school with about 25 pupils, both boys and girls, and I did very well in all my lessons so long as I did not have to talk, as I still had my speech problem. The teachers were Augustus Lanham, the Head, and a lady teacher for the younger children. The Head was, in my opinion, a tyrant, and we were all scared of him.

The school had a kitchen garden, the boys had two one hour gardening lessons each week, and the girls did needlework and knitting. The schoolroom was one big room divided across the middle by a folder screen, and a large open fireplace at each end. In winter the boys took turns at bringing in buckets full of coal for the fires. One day it was my turn. I brought the buckets in after filling them in the coal house outside. I must have got some coal dust on my jacket sleeve. I went back to my desk and next thing I knew there was a big black smudge of coal dust across my exercise book. When Mr. Lanham saw it, I was marched out in front of all the boys and given three strokes with the cane on each hand, 'to teach you not to get coal dust on your clothes'.

On another occasion a boy called John Cumpsty made a big ink smudge in his exercise book. He was given two strokes on each hand, and also Mr. Lanham said if it happened again he would put him under the floor for an hour. In the centre of one end of the room was a two foot square trap door. Mr. Lanham lifted this up and held John by his feet head first down the hole for several minutes while he lectured us all on book care. What a schoolmaster!

About 100 yards from home was Clifton Windmill. It was a working windmill, the miller was Mr. Crompton. He had a brother and a sister and between them they ran the mill and a small farm, Mill Farm, Clifton. Farmers brought their grain to be ground for cattle food and called for it later, perhaps after a week or so.

Sometimes the grain was not dry enough to grind and was spread out on a tiled floor. The floor was warmed by a fire at one end, the smoke and heat going through flues built in the floor. The miller used to turn the grain with a large wooden shovel-like tool. The sacks of grain to be ground were hoisted to the top floor of the mill by power generated by the mill sails and came down through the grinding stones into chutes with sacks hooked open to receive it.

In summer the miller used to dress the grooves in the mill stoves with special chisels and repair when needed with some special sort of cement which was light brown in colour. The grinding mill stones were about four feet in diameter and about six inches thick. The miller used to let us go up to the top of the mill with him when the wind changed, or if he had work to do on the small windmill which turned the top of the mill so the sails faced the wind. It was a fairly clean operation – no smoke, no smell, power from the wind and lots of creaking and groaning from the cog wheels, although there was lots of dust.

There were similar windmills at Lytham, Kirkham Weeton, Wrea Green and lots more in the Fylde, all or most working at that time, before the first World War, when horses were the local means of transport.

We collected our milk every day from Mill Farm, and took a wheelbarrow to the farm when we wanted any manure for the garden. Dad said as I was being taught about kitchen gardening at school I could look after half our kitchen garden, which I willingly did and enjoyed very much. There were about six big old damson trees in the orchard and they used to fruit very well. It was another job for me to pick the damsons which usually filled two of the old type wicker clothes baskets.

The butcher, Benson from Kirkham, the grocer, Whittaker from Preston, the pork and bacon butcher, and the ironmonger all called once a week with horse-drawn vehicles, and all except the ironmonger took damsons to sell in their shops. In the winter the butchers took any surplus rabbits, all of which helped to balance the books!

My youngest brother, Frank, was born at Clifton but did not go to school there as he was under five when Dad retired when the estate was sold in 1916. I was confirmed at Lund Church 1913, but I never imagined that some 33 years later I would be vicar's warden at Lund Church for 12 years and live at Salwick Hall.

I have told earlier what a tyrant the schoolmaster, Mr. Lanham, was. He seemed to always be picking on my younger brother, Reuben. Mother went to see Mr. Lanham about it but it did not make any difference. Reuben was scared of him and eventually ran away from home. I cannot recall how he managed it but he got to Preston somehow. The police picked him up and Dad went for him on the train and brought him home. It was a great shock to us all and led to Reuben going to Newton Blue Coat School, about one mile away. The headmaster there was Mr. Winchester and he was entirely the opposite to Mr. Lanham. Reuben did very well there, he was quite happy and won a scholarship to Kirkham Grammar School where he went until he was sixteen.

The gamekeeper's house was semi-detached, and the man next door was a shepherd on one of the big farms on the estate. The house was opposite Lund Church, so that although it was half a mile to Clifton village, which was on the main road from Preston to Kirkham, it was only about quarter of a mile to Salwick Station and quite close to the school, church and windmill.

There was a busy little goods yard at the station and a lot of passenger trains stopped on weekdays. The farmers used to bring milk to the station in big milk cans holding about 20 gallons, and take empties away for next day. Some of the farmers made cheeses of all their milk and took them to Preston once a month on horse-drawn flat lorries.

Close to the church was a large country house, 'Oakfield', where a Mr. Dickson lived. He was a solicitor and magistrate's clerk. Each evening about six o'clock I used to collect letters from 'Oakfield' and post them at the pillar box on the station bridge and collect the evening paper from the porter's room on the station and deliver it to 'Oakfield'. This was six evenings each week and every Saturday the cook or butler gave me one shilling for my week's work. This went straight into my money box. If ever Mother was short of any food etc. between the grocer calling once a week I had to run down to Clifton village, half a mile each way, before I went to school, and get whatever was needed from the little grocer's shop in the village, kept by a nice old lady, Mrs. Anderton.

Mother used to cut all the lads' hair until we were 10 years of age, then we went to the hairdresser. From Clifton this was about three miles to Kirkham and three miles back and cost sixpence for a haircut in 1911; sometimes I was lucky and had a lift in a farmer's horse and trap.

Once a year in the school holiday we would all go to Preston on the train for a day out and it was usually the time when I got a new suit, and Mother and Dad would get any items they needed and could not get from the tradesmen who came regularly round the villages.

It would be about 1912 when I had my first ride in a motor car. The members of the syndicate who had the shooting mainly came from Liverpool way and would come in a large Talbot car with a folding back hood. The driver took me to Clifton village shop for something Mother was short of for the lunch. It was quite a thrill. Little did I know that some 55 years later I would be operating over 100 vehicles of my own.

Two of the members of the syndicate were a Dr. Shaw from Kirkham and Mr. Law from St. Annes on Sea. Mr. Law was a very nice elderly man and asked Dad if I would like to carry his cartridge bag and coat. This I gladly did, as it enabled me to see and enjoy all that went on in the fields and woods on a well organised shooting day, and what's more at the end of the day Mr. Law gave me three shillings and sixpence, which went into my money box. There would usually be about eight main shooting days which were, of course, very special days for the gamekeeper and his family. We all seemed to be involved one way or another. Mother always made a great big Lancashire hot pot for the beaters, about ten of them, and usually one or two gamekeepers from adjoining estates would come to give Dad a hand organising the beaters and the guns and picking up game after each drive.

The gentry had their lunch in the front room of the gamekeeper's house, bringing their own food and drinks; mother made tea and coffee. The beaters got their hot pot, bread and cheese and a bottle of beer or soft drinks as they chose, and if rabbits had been shot these were usually divided amongst the beaters and cottagers.

Clifton, Newton, Treales and other villages all had their annual Club Days, often combined with sports, races, etc. and all sorts of fun and games, including the travelling fairground and a feast for all the children of school age. Looking back 75 years they seemed happy carefree days, everyone willing to help anyone in need, no free hand outs of any kind, no graffiti or vandalism There was perhaps one problem – the very low wages, which meant no luxuries. Everyone did get fed and clothed, however, and all were very loyal to their king and country and fully respected law and order without question. What it was like in the towns and cities I do not know, but I was never sorry my young days were spent in the country.

The days, the weeks, months and years rolled on and came the time to leave school, the one problem was what to do about work. Kirkham was the nearest small town three miles away. Preston was eight miles. The only other employment was agriculture, in which the wages were very low. I had done well at school, above average in all main subjects, but, and it was to me a very big but, I had this awful speech impediment, which I felt at the time would stop me getting work anywhere. Lots of people tried to help in different ways, but none of them seemed to work.

I left school on 11th May 1913 when I was 13 years of age, and, though it was hard to believe at the time, I went straight into a job.

Chapter Two

First Jobs. Meeting Alice

IN February 1913 the members of the shooting syndicate changed; four or five left and the new members wanted to rear a lot more ducks and pheasants and have more and bigger shooting days. This meant more work for Dad and the underkeeper at Salwick, so I was taken on as gamekeeper's boy at 10 shillings, now 50p, per week – that is per week of seven days from April–December, six days from 1st January to 1st April. This was a great stroke of luck, as Dad came from a family of gamekeepers on the Royal Estates at Sandringham, Norfolk, and he saw me as carrying on as a gamekeeper. Dad's father was a gamekeeper at Sandringham and his four sons, Ralph, Frederick, Wilfred and Dad were all at one time gamekeepers at Sandringham.

When Dad was 12 years of age he worked as a page boy, whatever that was, in Sandringham House. He said he had often seen the young Prince George, later to be George Fifth, riding on an old sow in the farmyard. Dad had many nephews and nieces, most of whom worked on the Sandringham Estate, on the farm or forestry, or in the estate workshops. His cousin Bert was the House carpenter. May married the kitchen garden foreman, Florrie married the House postmaster, Lily married one of the stud grooms at the stables.

Dad left Norfolk and came to Lancashire as a gamekeeper on the Clifton Estates in the Fylde, after serving under his father at Sandringham. So history was repeating itself, and I was headed for keeping up the Bridges gamekeeper tradition. It seemed to come naturally to me. I had, of course, known little else other than such work, and the great thing was I had got a job and it did not entail much talking. It was May when I left school so I was straight into the busiest part of the gamekeeper year, hand rearing hundreds of ducks and pheasants. We had a large pheasant pen where the pheasants had been kept since March. It would be about 1½ acres. When all the eggs needed for hand rearing had been taken the pheasants were kept in a while to lay eggs and hatch them naturally themselves. About eight weeks after hatching they were let go to the woods and fed daily. Meanwhile the hand rearing carried on, rows of nesting boxes raised off the ground about two feet, each with a sitting hen and a clutch of eggs. The hens were taken off the nest every morning, tethered to stakes, fed and watered and put back into the individual nest boxes.

In a few weeks the hens and chicks were moved to the rearing ground where each hen was in a separate coop with the chicks it had hatched out. After a few weeks the pheasants were taken to the woods and fed grain twice a day for a month or so and then once a day, and the hens were returned to the farmers who had supplied the sitting hens. There were no crumbs, pellets etc. to feed the young chicks as there are today. Each gamekeeper had his own idea and mixtures. Dad used a lot of hard boiled eggs, pressed through a sieve and mixed with meal and meat from butchers, offal boiled and minced. The eggs were mainly Egyptian, packed in large flat wooden crates. These were left at the side of the road in Clifton village by the Preston to Kirkham carrier from his horse drawn carrier's cart or lorry. I had to bring them to the rearing field cabin on a wheelbarrow; they weighed 100 to 120 pounds and it was uphill all the way half a mile, at 14 years of age.

There were no means of keeping the butcher's offal fresh more than a few days, during which it was in buckets under water in a pond in the rearing field. It was boiled in a big wood fired boiler, minced and mixed with the egg and meal, and fed to the chicks several times a day according to age.

Vermin traps were kept set round the rearing field boundary, and Dad always had a gun in the cabin, ready for any flying predators who could play havoc with the chicks. It was a dawn to dusk job with all kinds of hazards to look out for. The coops were all fastened up with a front board at night, which had to be removed at dawn.

When the pheasants were taken to the woods the work did not end; for a month or so they were fed grain twice a day which entailed for Dad and me about a six-mile walk before breakfast with about 60 pounds of grain in a sack over your shoulder, and again in the afternoon. Dad fed the woods on one side of the estate and I did the other. We each had four woods to feed and vermin traps to check. Later as the shooting season approached we fed mornings only, scattering the grain in open places amongst the leaves and debris on the ground. This kept the birds employed looking for the grain otherwise they would fill their crops and roam off anywhere. Pheasants are particularly prone to roam and always seemed to make for the estate boundary. We had to be regularly walking the boundary with a dog and driving birds back towards our own woods.

The nearer the shooting season got the more Dad and keepers from adjoining estates had to look out for poachers, by day and night. Their favourite approach was along the railway line from Preston or Kirkham, or along the canal tow path from Preston. They had of course to travel on foot or perhaps bicycle. Today the poacher problem is far greater due to the motor car and motor cycle.

The shooting days were, of course, the main event of the keeper years, all his twelve months work channelled into about ten main shooting days, and the end result was often critical to his job. There were usually two or three days duck shooting in September, then the pheasant shooting from 2nd October to 31st January. No hen pheasants were shot after Christmas Day; cocks only was the order.

There were smaller days of three or four guns for hares, rabbits, snipe wood pigeon, etc. and the continual round of vermin traps to check, resite and reset. November usually brought rabbiting in earnest, mainly long netting or purse netting. Shot rabbits were often fed to the ferrets or boiled for the dogs, the hens and the pig we always kept in winter.

Dad taught me all the tricks of the trade in all seasons, and I enjoyed this early employment. The only and ever present snag was my speech problem. When I was asked a question by one of the gentry or if Dad asked about my traps or other duties, sometimes Dad would get annoyed with me. Mother seemed more understanding about it.

The shooting year end, as in agriculture and most country employment in those days, was Candlemas day, second of February. I had started work in May 1913 and in January 1914 was looking forward to 2nd February when I thought I might get a rise in my wages of ten shillings per week; for the next twelve months I thought and Dad did say that I might get twelve shillings and sixpence per week for my second year.

However, this was not to be, as several of the syndicates members who had rented the shooting gave up and new members joined. As usual the syndicate appointed a Captain to whom Dad was responsible. He turned out to be very tightfisted. He told Dad they would not require my services in the 1914/1915 season unless I would accept five shillings per week. Dad was raving mad and I was very sad to think I had worked so hard and Dad was so pleased with how I had picked the job up. We just could not believe it at first. However, that was it five shillings a week or nothing. What could one do – there were no dole, job centres, youth training, or other help of any kind, so we had to accept the situation and get on with the job in the hope that perhaps the following year there might be a fresh captain, and more money. So we carried on much as usual, except that Mother had a drop in the family budget from Dad and me of about ten per cent; not much joy in that, with six to keep in the family.

I still took the letters to post for Mr. Dickson at 'Oakfield' and collected papers from the station. On my 14th birthday, 11th May 1914, the housekeeper asked me if it was my birthday. I said, 'Yes, I am fourteen now', not without some difficulty as I still had my speech problem. Next day the housekeeper

My oldest brother, Charles, 1916. Having trained as a painter and decorator, Charles joined the Territorial Army and, later, the regular army. His unit went to India in 1913 and to France in 1914. Letters came at long intervals, censored just to show the sender was still alive.

gave me from Mrs. Dickson two shillings and sixpence for my birthday and I was to have two shillings per week, and do another odd errand or two each week. This was great news for me as mother would not accept it from me so it went into my money box.

The work as gamekeeper's boy carried on normally. I got quite expert on my own with ferrets and purse nets for rabbits and was learning all the time. I had visions of being under keeper on a big estate and perhaps one day be headkeeper. Then came August 1914. I well remember collecting the paper from the station, heavy black type one inch high 'Britain declares war on Germany'. I showed it to Mother and Dad and then dashed off to 'Oakfield' with it. Little did I or anyone else think that four years later I would be in the army and in Germany when I was 18½ years of age.

The first event due to the war was the arrival of enough grain for the coming shooting season. Grain was usually delivered each week through the year. The Captain anticipated difficulty with supplies and stocked up. The housekeeper at 'Oakfield' gave me the newspapers which were a few days old and we did then learn what was going on – of course, we had no radio or television then.

My eldest brother, Charles, who, as I have said earlier was learning the trade of painter and decorator in Lytham, had joined the Territorial Army, the part-time reserve soldiers. He enjoyed the training and going to camp each year. I think it would be in 1912 he joined the regular army in the Royal Field Artillery training, mainly at Aldershot. His unit went to India in 1913 and came from India to France late in 1914 in their tropical kit. Letters came at long intervals, or just field post cards, censored just to show the sender was still alive.

In 1914 shooting season was a much more subdued time than normal, the country was at war and the news was not good. It became obvious early in January 1915 there were going to be problems due to the war and it was fairly certain my continued employment even at five shillings per week would be in jeopardy, so I started watching the newspaper advertisements for 'Labour Wanted'. There is an old saying, 'Better be born lucky than rich' and my word it has applied to me as long as I can remember, and here was one instance. The advert read, 'Strong willing lad wanted for farm work live in' Robert Blacoe, Warton Hall Farm, Lytham.

This was the Hall Farm 200 yards from where I was born and lived for eight years and where Dad had been gamekeeper for 14 years. Mother, Dad and all of us who lived at Warton knew the Blacoe family. They had two sons and two daughters whom we had played with and gone to school with at Lytham. They went to the R. C. School; we went to the C. of E.

Dad wrote to Mr. Blacoe and it was fixed. I was to start on 2nd February 1915 at 14 years of age, live in the farm house with the family, food and laundry provided, with a wage of fifteen pounds for the first year to 2nd February 1916.

This worked out at five shillings, nine pence per week paid at year end in total, or occasionally as subs. What an event to remember! Mother packed all my clothes etc., including a new pair of clog boots in an old tin trunk and Mr. Blacoe came for me in a horse trap next day to start an adventure I had not dreamt of nor thought possible.

Mrs. Blacoe was a very kindly, homely person and was like a second mother to me. The whole family had known us, that is, Mother and Dad, for 14 years and as children we had grown up with the four Blacoe children for about eight years. The two sons, John James, the eldest, and Edward, and two daughters, Mary, the eldest, and Ann, all worked on the farm. Ann was the same age as me, the others all older. My bedroom, shared with the two sons, was over the stables where the three shire horses and one lighter breed were kept.

It took me some time to get used to hearing the horses moving and stamping on the cobbled floor of the stables. They were all tethered in the stalls. In the spring one usually had a foal and the mother and foal were kept separately in a loose box.

John James was the horseman and Edward the cowman. The two girls helped with milking the cows, about sixty in all, and helped Mrs. Blacoe to make the cheese and butter, and with the housework. I was the general go-between, to help anyone for a while. The first thing was to learn to milk by hand as there were no milking machines. Mr. Blacoe took me under his wing for this and I soon had the hang of it. I was, with the girls, allotted those which were quiet and easy to milk, until I got skilled enough, then I milked any. Some cows were never easy to milk, being restless and letting out a good kick occasionally.

We all had a three-legged milking stool and bucket, kept specially in the dairy. As we finished milking each cow the milk was poured into the large milk can kept near the door of the shippon we were milking in, and Mr. Blacoe carried this when it was full (about 10 gallons) to the dairy and cheese making room in the farmhouse.

Apart from milk for own use and nearby cottages it was all made into cheese or butter each day; the process took two or three days, if I remember right, then the cheeses were carried upstairs to the cheese room above the dairy where they were stored on long wooden shelves about two feet from the floor. There would be four or five of these long shelves each with perhaps 25 cheeses on, about six inches apart. Mr. Blacoe used to turn them all over each day, part of the maturing process.

There were, of course, many more cheeses made in summer, when the cows were going out to grass all day every day, than in winter when they were in the shippons. Mr. Blacoe gave us a knock on the bedroom door each morning at 6.30. We had a drink of tea or cocoa and were in the shippon milking at 7.00 a.m. in winter, or in summer bringing the cows in from the fields for milking.

Each cow was individually tethered two to a stall. In front of the rows of cows was a space about five or six feet wide called the range. This was in winter kept full of hay and before we started milking an armful was given to each cow. Each cow also had a container, usually wooden, in those days, about the size of a bucket, usually square with sloping sides with a handle formed on one side. This contained a mixture of sliced or chipped potatoes, turnips, marigold wurzels and various meals or ground grain slightly moistened with water and all mixed together the day before with a wooden shovel in a large wooden trough about six feet long and three feet wide and deep.

Mr. Blacoe decided what amount of each of the various ingredients available had to be mixed. Sometimes there would be chaff or chopped hay or straw, no fancy pellets, pencils and crumbs, and no electric power on the farm to turn the chopper. Roots like turnips and potatoes were sliced or chipped in a machine with a hopper which held about one cwt: one side of the hopper was a big perforated blade with holes and slots turned by a large cranked handle. When the handle was turned the revolving blade sliced and chipped the roots which came out underneath into a wheelbarrow, and taken to the mixing trough. A somewhat similar method was used to chop hay and straw into about one-inch lengths. Each morning as soon as milking was finished and the cows fed and all the milking buckets and cans taken to the dairy to be scalded and washed we all went in for breakfast, usually egg and bacon (own produce), bread and home made butter and jam. Mother used to say in later years 'Harold was the biggest and strongest of my five sons because of his two years on the farm at Warton'.

First job after breakfast was to muck out the shippons with barrow, shovel and brush; usually Edward and I did this while John James was seeing to the horses – cleaning out, feeding, watering, grooming, etc. This took about an hour – no getting on a tractor and pressing a button.

I knew all about cleaning the shippons, but had never before had to wheel a farm barrowful of fresh cow dung and straw up a nine-inch plank onto the top of the manure heap. The farmyard was a large rectangle with buildings on all four sides, the manure heap was in the middle. During early winter the manure heap was low, and spread out. As the winter passed the manure heap got bigger and bigger and as it had to be kept within a given area it had to be piled high. This was achieved by keeping the manure with a lot of straw in it, from the stables and loose boxes on the outside of the heap all the way round. I was responsible for keeping it all straight and tidy. By February the cows had been in five months and the heap was in good shape, with nearly vertical sides, around five feet high, about 20 feet by 30 feet with a long 9" plank to wheel the barrow up at the low end.

In the beginning I did come off the plank odd times but soon got the hang of it. Mr. Blacoe said you could always tell a good farm hand by the shape of the midden. In the spring or in frosty weather the manure was hand forked into the two-wheel horse cart, taken to the meadow, pulled out of the rear of the cart with a long-handled rake fork into heaps about five paces apart in rows five or six paces apart. Later this was spread by hand fork over the whole area. The spacing of the heaps was varied according to the amount of manure available or how heavily Mr. Blacoe decided to manure a particular field.

If the field being manured was for root crops this was done in the spring when the field was ridged with the horse plough; the cart then went along and the manure was thrown off the cart into the ridges a forkful at a time about every four or five feet depending how heavily it was wished to manure the field. The manure was then spread along the rows by hand fork. Potatoes were planted by hand which at first I found a back breaking job, but one got used to it after a few days. Wheat and oats were sown by hand. Mr. Blacoe always did the actual sowing himself. It was a very skilled job to scatter the grains evenly and not too thinly nor too thickly.

John James, as horseman, did all the ploughing, harrowing, ridging, rolling, etc., all with the different horse-drawn machines and equipment. There were always jobs to be done for everyone: cutting hedges, repairing fences, cutting thistles, cleaning cut ditches and drains, haytime and harvest, and the important time when the calves were being born. There were not any sheep on the farm so I never had anything to do with lambing time. Lambs are normally born in a period of perhaps 10 weeks at most in the spring. Cows have their calves anytime in the year and it was normal for one or two to be born almost every week throughout the year.

I had, of course, seen hundreds of duck and pheasant born, breaking their way out of the eggs. Dad did not breed dogs, so I had not seen dog pups born. One day Mr. Blacoe said, 'Keep your eye on that old roan cow in the far shippon today'. It was not long before I could see the old cow heavy in calf was getting restless and eventually she laid down and began straining in the process of giving birth. I got Mr. Blacoe; he said, 'Stay here and watch. You have got to learn sometime'. She was an old cow, had had many calves so I was told; the birth was quite easy and straightforward. It was my first experience of this and quite fascinating to see the two front feet of the calf emerging with its head tucked down close to its two front legs stretched straight out in front. It is not always so easy; odd times one leg or both might be turned back with the head showing first. Then there are problems which in due course I was shown how to deal with. Sometimes if the cow or heifer as they are called, was having its first calf no progress was made after the feet showed, the problem was the calf's head. Once that was free the rest was easy. We always had two strong ropes about five feet long with a loop at the end and big knots in the ropes every foot. If necessary the looped rope was slipped over each of the calf's feet above the first joint and then 'Yo Heave Ho and a bottle of rum', so the old song goes.

The first action to take was to get the calf on its feet, put about a spoonful of salt in its mouth and give it a good rub down with some straw. Then give the cow a good drink of bran mash and warm water and milk her. After a while I did all this on my own if the men were working in the fields. Other jobs I was soon made responsible for were cleaning out and feeding about ten pigs and the bull who was tethered in a pen on his own.

Come haytime all the grass was cut by John James with a two horse mower which had a long blade about four feet long with 12 triangular blades riveted on. This had to be taken out and sharpened by hand with a file. Mr. Blacoe always did the sharpening; usually there were three blades on the go, one in use, one being sharpened and one spare ready to avoid any waiting for a sharpened blade. The worst thing for the blades was if there were many mole hills in the grass being cut, as they took the edge off the blades.

Heavy crops and bad weather caused problems as the grass got flattened down, making it harder to cut clean. When sufficiently dry on one side the swathes were turned over by hand. We each had a long handled wooden rake and worked close behind each-other in echelon, Mr. Blacoe always in front setting the pace. As on most big farms two Irish farm workers came over from

Family photograph, taken in Preston, 1916. Front row from left: Rose, Mother, Frank, Dad. Back row from left: Reuben, Charles (on leave from France), Harold.

Ireland for haytime, harvest and after potato digging, then went back to Ireland. They slept in the farm buildings in a loft set aside, rather crudely furnished. They took their meals from the farmhouse and had them in their own rooms.

I drove the two-horse reaper for cutting the corn. It was all tied by hand with straw bands, amazingly simple and strong; no combine harvesters or baling machines. Handling the corn sheaves to bind them, stack them in stooks of six or eight sheaves and feeding them loose into the threshing machines could be a very prickly job if there were many thistles in the corn sheaves, and there were no industrial or agricultural goves for employees.

With no chemical spraying to keep weeds and thistles down, we did go through the corn in the spring when it was six to twelve inches high, using a long-handled tool with a blade straight out from the handle and about four inches square. This was used to cut off the thistles at ground level. The tool was called a thistle dabber. I spent many days thistle dabbing and also cutting thistles in the meadows and pastures with a scythe and sickle, usually twice a year to stop them from seeding. We had four or five threshing days in the winter; the corn was mostly in round stacks in the stackyard which was about 50 yards from where the actual threshing took place in the farmyard, so the corn to be threshed had to be loaded on a cart or lorry to take it to the thresher; so on this alone there were three men, two horses and carts or lorry kept busy, so that the thresher and crew of three of four men were not waiting for corn. The traction engine was, of course, steam powered. It towed the actual threshing machine and the straw bottling machine between farms and then provided power through a long flat belt to the thresher and bottler. The bottle machine made the threshed straw into straw bottles about five feet long and half as thick tied in the machine. The traction engine had to be kept supplied with water, and my first threshing day job was carrying buckets of water two at a time across the farmyard from the watering trough to the engine about 20 yards, walking across a rough cobbled stone yard – no hose pipes then of course. I also filled my time in carrying the bottles of straw into the barn for storage. It was used for bedding the horses and cattle, some wheat straw for thatching next year's stacks and some of the best oat straw for feeding.

The different skills one had to acquire never seemed to end during this first year. It was hard physical labour, mainly out in the fresh air, and all the good plain farmhouse food anyone could wish for. I enjoyed it all very much and used to think to myself, 'I will be a farmer one day'.

So came 2nd February 1916. I was still 15 years of age. The war was at its worst and I was glad and very thankful when Mr. Blacoe said that if I would stay on another year to February 1917 he would pay me £16 for the year, a £1 rise, about two new pence per week, $4\frac{1}{2}$ pence in the coinage at the time. Well what could one do but accept. I did get a few days' holiday when my eldest brother, Charles, came home on leave from France. All the family went to Preston and we had a family photograph taken, and I got a new grey suit at Hepworths in Friargate.

I was by this time able to carry out a lot of my work on my own without direct supervision, and I was sometimes sent to other nearby farms to give them a hand, particularly when they had their threshing days. It was on one of these days I had my first experience actually on the threshing machine. This was cutting the straw bands for the corn to be fed into the machine, by another of the crew. We were on top of the machine about eight feet above ground level; the sheaves of corn were thrown up to us from the cart, which had brought them from the stackyard. The job was to pick the sheaf of corn up, push the very sharp knife under the band, and in the same operation toss the sheaf into the arms of the feeder who stood facing. We both stood in a lower part of the thresher just above the main drum; the main thing was that every sheaf had to be fed into the machine with the corn heads the same way. The man on the cart could only throw them up with his pitchfork, and I often had to turn them so the heads faced the right way. The feeder just shook them on to the drum. If an odd sheaf was the wrong way and the feeder had to turn it, well I heard about it above the din and hum of the machine, which could be heard a mile away. I had a go at feeding the machine, and it was on these two jobs that I found out what dried thistles were like to handle.

The corn, chaff and weed seeds and rubbish came down separate chutes from the machine. The corn was put into sacks and stored in the granary later to go to Lytham windmill to be ground into meal, fed to the cattle, horses, hens, ducks and geese. Some of the better quality corn would be sold to local corn merchants. The number of different jobs to be learned and carried out by hand in those days was amazing, some easy, some nasty, wet and cold, and all by hand.

One nasty job was spreading lime. It was carted from the rail goods yard at Lytham, loaded by hand shovel into a big two-wheel cart on to the field to be limed. It was in cob form, that is, like a whitish rock about the size of a loaf of bread and smaller. It was shovelled out of the cart into small heaps about two bucketsfull spaced out in rows over the field. Following dampish days or rain, the cob lime 'fell' or turned into powder form like flour now called hydrated lime, and the job was to spread this as evenly as possible over the whole area of the field. If it was not fallen enough or if it was too wet to spread it evenly, the field had to be chain harrowed with a one-horse harrow to spread the lime evenly. Another not very nice job was 'topping and tailing' turnips on a cold frosty morning in October, to be carted to the stackyard and stored in clamps for winter use. Every few days a load of cattle cabbage had to be cut and carted to the farm for the cattle, usually October.

Hay had to be cut from the hay stacks in the stackyard and carted into the farm and barn every few days for the cattle in the winter months. There were compensating days like taking a horse or perhaps two to the blacksmith at Warton, about two miles away, to be shod.

There is no doubt agriculture was a very labour intensive undertaking in those days. In summer there would be the equivalent of six or seven employees for a herd of 60 dairy cows, with no sheep or beef cattle. Today two men would do the job.

So the time passed and I began to wonder what 1917 would bring. Sure enough it did bring another major event for me. In January 1917 Mr. Blacoe said he did not think he would be able to keep me on after 2nd February and it would be wise if I was to seek another job. About the same time, I had word from Mother and Dad that the Clifton and Salwick Estate was being sold and Dad would be out of work early in 1917.

The war was still dragging on with its awful carnage. Charles had been home again on two weeks' leave. Dad felt that, due to the war and his age he would have problems finding another job, so he had decided to retire from gamekeeping and move to Lytham. He had contacts with two of the shooting syndicate who lived in or near Lytham who thought he would find work as a freelance jobbing gardener.

A friend of Charles was leaving Lytham and Dad bought this friend's house and moved to Lytham, 34 Warton Street. I think Dad paid £360 for it. It was leasehold on a 99 years lease, with about 20 years to go. This left me with little time or I would be be out of work and living at home. I think perhaps Mr. Blacoe's decision was influenced by the fact that conscription was now in; he had two sons of military age on the farm and a strong lad coming up to 17. It was likely one of the sons might be exempt from call up but not two while I was there, so Mother and I started watching the papers to see if anyone was seeking labour, and my luck was in again.

There was an advert in the Lytham Times – 'Strong youth wanted as horse van driver used to horses, honest and willing and able to start soon, 30s. 0d. per week. Blackpool Princess and Ribble Laundries, Dock Road, Lytham'. By now I had left Warton Hall Farm and was living at home with Mother and Dad. I applied, got the job and started next morning. It appeared Bill Candlish, a horse van driver who was 18 had received his enlistment papers and had to join the forces in two weeks' time.

His father was in charge of the three-horse van fleet and his brother, Joe, was the other driver. The laundry had one 3-ton motor van driven by a Tom Lee, whose brother was the laundry engineer. It was the laundry engineer's daughter who went with me to Moss Side Hospital with Scarlet Fever long ago in a one-horse ambulance.

My duties were briefly outlined to me as start 7.30 a.m., help clean out the stables, which we did jointly, then each groom our own horse, and make sure the harness was clean and polished. We had sometimes to wash the van which we were to take out that day. Three vans were four wheel iron tyred box type vans with a drivers seat outside at the front of the van, and doors on the left side for loading and unloading. There was also a two-wheel open front van like a hansom cab. They were all painted bright yellow with black lettering.

The area covered by the three vans was the whole of Lytham, and St. Annes on Sea, before they were amalgamated into Lytham St. Annes, and also the immediate rural areas of Ballam, Weeton, Westby, Singleton, Warton, Moss Side, Wrea Green, Ribby.

The whole area was divided up into rounds for each van, each round had a list of all the regular calls made to collect laundry, with columns to be marked each day to show if the laundry had been collected and, if not, why. The laundry was collected Monday, Tuesday and Wednesday and delivered after washing and ironing Thursday, Friday and Saturday.

Collections were made from private houses, shops, hotels, cafes, boarding houses etc., mainly in parcels, laundry bags or wicker baskets, the clean laundry was delivered in brown paper parcels tied with string and the laundry book for each customer was put with the parcel under the string or inside the hamper. Some customers had to pay cash when the delivery was made so the drivers all had a cash receipt book. Others paid weekly or at various intervals up to four weeks. We had to give a receipt for every payment and pay all cash collected into the office each day. We would make on average about 40 collections or deliveries per van per day. I had never been to St. Annes and only knew the main streets through Lytham solely through going to school at St. John's and St. Cuthbert's. So I had only one week to learn most of the streets and that meant I went to each of the customers on my rounds once collecting and once delivering, before I was on my own. Bill Candlish went off to war and I was in a job which apart from looking after the horse was completely new and strange to me, and I still had the speech impediment, which in my new job was a very great disadvantage. However, I battled on and after a few weeks got the hang of it all, and had not

Myself, at 17 years of age.

to ask so many questions for directions and advice. Once I got used to the rounds it was a rather routine or repetitive job each week, nothing like the variety or the skills required on the farm. I seemed to get on very well with everyone in spite of my impediment. There was, of course, no radio or television, the war was in its third year, and casualty lists appeared regularly in the papers; the news was heart breaking for everyone. Not a week passed without some bad news.

The Lytham Shipyard was next to the laundry in Dock Road, Lytham, and they were working day and night, on shipping and munitions work, and were now employing women in the engineering department (a huge new engineering shop had been built opposite the laundry and was working day and night).

The power for the laundry was provided by a big horizontal steam engine and in the laundry there seemed to be miles of shafting and scores of pulleys and leather belts to each machine, no individual electric motors. The washing machines were huge drums about six feet long and four feet diameter, and all the other machinery in proportion, all driven by belts and pulleys from the one steam engine. The ironing of most flat laundry sheets, pillow cases, table linen and so forth was done by passing it through a series of huge steam-heated rollers; any fancy and personal laundry was ironed by hand by about 20 girls using gas fired irons, all in all a hive of activity.

During the summer of 1917 I became acquainted and made friends with other youngsters of my own age whom I met during my work, and who lived close by.

One such was Colin Dronfield who lived quite close with his sister and

Ribble Laundry motor van, 1918, which I learned to drive in late 1917.

1917

widowed mother who kept a small grocers shop. Colin was apprenticed to a boot and shoe repairer and when he was working late I used to go and watch Colin and his employer repairing all sorts of leather shoes and clogs. On a Saturday afternoon he used to run errands, deliver bread and cakes for the baker, Lucas', Church Road, Lytham, which was a very good high class bakers and confectioners. Some Saturday afternoons, when I had nothing else to do, I would go with Colin and help to carry the huge baskets of bread and cakes he had to deliver. It was when returning to the shop with Colin from one of his rounds we met a short, dark haired plump young lady passing the County Hotel. Colin said, 'Hello Alice. Have you a minute?'. The young lady said, 'No, I haven't. I'm going to Nottingham's the butchers for some meat for Bob Lucas in the bakehouse'.

Colin said, 'I just want to introduce you to a friend of mine, Harold Bridges'. Colin then turned to me and said, ' This is Alice the 'Ice Bun Queen' from

September 1917. Myself on left wearing Dad's old gamekeeper jacket and waistcoat. Seated: Tommy Lee who taught me to drive. Note solid tyres, oil sidelamps, no headlamps, two-piece flat windscreen and no side doors.

1916: Tommy Lee (right) with his mate. Note solid tyres, oil sidelamps and one half windscreen.

Lucas' the Confectioners'. We just said 'Hello' to each other and our eyes seemed to meet and hold for a few seconds, then we went our ways. Little did I think that seven years later I would marry Alice, we would have six children and be happily married for fifty three years, that's life.

I mentioned the encounter to Mother who said, 'Oh I know little Alice, she serves me with bread and cakes when I go to the shop. She is a very shy quiet lass'. It appeared in the course of her work Alice used to spread the icing on the large quantity of buns baked each day and Colin had given Alice the title to tease her. Fate or luck or whatever it is (if anything) which controls our destiny is stranger than fiction. A few weeks later, due to an increase in the laundry collections to be made, the Lytham rounds were re-organised and lo and behold in my rounds of collections Mondays and Fridays was Lucas Bakers, 2 Church Road, Lytham, to collect linen tablecloths, serviettes, towels and bakery white coats, hats, aprons, etc in hamper. This entailed my collecting Monday and delivering and collecting Friday and then delivering and collecting Monday.

On my first call I met Alice, and it transpired she was responsible for assembling and listing the soiled laundry from the bakery, the shop and the tea room and checking it when it was returned. It followed from this that I saw Alice at least twice a week in the course of my work. I could not hide my impediment in my speech and it was Alice's most sympathetic approach to my problem that I found attracted me beyond belief. From this a very close friendship developed and Mother was very pleased. She had a fondness for Alice, whose home was in Willenhall, Staffordshire. I was now 17 and Alice was 19 and it did not appear likely the war would be over before May 1918. I would be 18 then and due for call up. Dad was fully employed in his jobbing gardening and passed a few jobs to me which I could do on Saturday afternoons; the rate was 1s. 0d. (5p now) per hour and it all went in my money box. Alice's time off when she could go out was two or three hours Thursday and Sunday evenings, and one Sunday afternoon each month.

We eventually met regularly, walked and talked, sat under the Lifeboat house shelter and very occasionally went to the cinema in Henry Street.

The laundry motor van was a solid tyred 3-ton Maudesley box van, petrol engine with overhead valves, there were no side doors or windows to the cab and it was engaged collecting and delivering laundry in Blackpool, mainly from hotels, cafes, restaurants, boarding houses and the military camp at Squires Gate, Blackpool, previously the racecourse. The driver, Tommy Lee, was over military age and due to the weight of laundry handled always had an assistant.

The assistant was about eight months older than me so in September 1917 he received his call up papers and I was asked to take on his job, which I gladly did. It was an extra 5s. 0d. (or 25p per week now) and I would be taught to drive.

The journeys were to Blackpool every day and the work was much heavier as the laundry was normally packed in hampers weighing up to 100 pounds. Most of the linen rooms at the hotels were up two or three flights of stairs and there could be six or eight hampers for the big hotels, which were always full up with military personnel billeted on them.

Tommy Lee and I got on very well together. He taught me to drive which I picked up very quickly, so I had my licence to drive at around $17\frac{1}{2}$, with no L-plates or tests. Tommy and I did most of the routine maintenance; greasing was done by screwing off a brass cap, filling it with grease and screwing it on to force the grease in the spring shackles and other bearings, steering joints and pins.

Oil level in the engine was checked by taking off a round plate about six inches diameter from the side of the crankcase, rocking the flywheel to move the crankshaft and see that the oil was high enough in the crankcase for the big end bearings to dip into the oil when the engine was running. We used to decarbonise the engine and grind the valves about every six weeks. I found the maintenance work very interesting and a welcome change from the routine of collecting and delivering.

This change of job meant I did not see Alice in the course of my work; once again fate and the war intervened. Colin Dronfield was nearly six months older than me, he received his enlistment papers and went to war. Miss Lucas said if I would give a hand Alice and I could do the Saturday afternoon and evening deliveries that Colin used to do, which we did and Miss Lucas rewarded me with a bag of 'goodies' from the bakehouse. My brother Charles came home on 14 days' leave again, having been in France since 1914. He had had three slight wounds and a whiff or two of gas, nothing serious enough to send him back to England. He was originally in the Royal Field Artillery with a six inch gun battery attached to the 5th Canadian Division and was transferred to the Royal Engineers Signals.

My younger brother, Reuben, had left school and found employment for a start as a tram conductor on the trams then running between Lytham and Blackpool.

My only sister, Rose, and my youngest brother, Frank, were attending St. John's School, Warton Street, Lytham, where Mr. Collinson was the Headmaster as he had been when I was at school there 10 years before.

The war still dragged on. Every few weeks some local men would be reported 'missing', 'killed in action', 'believed taken prisoner', 'lost at sea' or would arrive on leave wounded or disabled. Lytham was, like most towns on the Fylde Coast and elsewhere in the North West, full of soldiers billeted in hotels, boarding houses and private houses, and young men were all being called up for military service when they reached 18 years of age, unless employed in some special exempt categories. Came the spring of 1918 my friendship with Alice continued. We now spent a lot of our off work time together, and I had learned that Alice's home was 39 Spring Vale Street, Willenhall, Staffordshire and that her full name was Alice Lewis Vale, two years older than me, she had two sisters. Edith, the eldest, and Freda, the youngest of the three, and John her brother was in the forces in France. Alice's father had been a miner, and key maker and her mother had when younger been in charge of a local brickworks. We found we had a lot in common from our lowly beginnings of which neither of us had anything to be ashamed of, far from it. It's what you make of life and what you do that matters.

Chapter Three

Into the Army but not in the Black and Tans

MAY 11th 1918 duly arrived, along with my calling up papers to report to Fulwood Barracks, Preston, June 10th 1918, with my railway warrant ticket. Dad came to the station to see me off and Alice was there to wave goodbye, and wonder what lay in store for our friendship. The war was still raging and now was going in the allies' favour, or appeared to be from what the papers said. I arrived at Preston station and was met by my NCO. There were five or six other young chaps my age from the Fylde coast on the same errand.

We were taken to Fulwood Barracks on the tram. The trams in Preston covered all the main routes from the town centre to the outskirts of the town.

The first day was taken up by medical inspection, a real one too, then recording all details including any identification marks; the only one they could find on me was a tiny scar on my left hand forefinger and it is still there today – I got it while splitting kindling wood for the fire. I nearly chopped my finger off. It was cut halfway through to the bone and bled like a tap. No going to hospital or sending for the doctor then; Mother held it under the cold tap for a minute and wrapped it up with a piece of clean white cloth – we had no proper bandages or first aid kit in the house. Mother washed it morning and evening and put clean cloths on it. It started to heal on the outside first and after a week it began to fester, so I had hot linseed poultices on it morning and evening for a week. It cleared up, healed eventually and I still have the scar to remind me.

Next we were fitted out with 'off the peg' khaki uniform, boots, underwear etc. and all the lot in a kit bag stencilled with name and number 418449. We stayed one night at the Fulwood Barracks. Next morning it was down to the station on the tram and off to Kinmel Camp in Wales by train. This was a wooden hut army camp, where for a few weeks we received very basic training in drill and instructions of all kinds: how to salute, to address NCOs and officers and how to roll our puttees on, and no end of other matters. We slept about forty in a hut; sanitary and toilet facilities and arrangements were, of course, a big change from home. It all seemed very crude; meals were taken in a larger hut, six to a table, with the very minimum of necessities, no tablecloths, salt and pepper, just what was brought and put on the end of the table. I suppose it was all part of the breaking in process, and it was on the whole accepted as what to expect. Like most of the larger army camps and depots there was a good YMCA hut which was a godsend to us everyone agreed. There was also a good NAAFI hut – Navy, Army and Air Force Institute, we called it the 'Naffy' – where, as with the YMCA, we could buy tea and cocoa, biscuits, cigarettes, etc. and this was where we spent most evenings.

After about another week of basic drill, lectures and physical exercises we were issued with our full equipment – rifle, bayonet, pack and haversack, etc. and our full kit – and shown how to put it all together, clean it and what it was all for. We were also shown how to lay out on our bed all the army kit which had been issued to us, every item in its correct place, clean and tidy, ready for the weekly kit inspection. Every item that could be was marked with your own regimental number for identification; mine was 418449.

We could not go out of the camp without a pass. We seemed to be miles from any town, and spent a lot of evenings in the YMCA and NAAFI.

We could now write letters from the camp as in the 53rd Y.S. Battalion Kings Liverpool Regiment and our cap badges etc. were issued to us, all brass to be polished daily. The training now went on to basic arms drill, lots of physical training and some short route marches, which were longer each week. About early July, we were informed at the morning parade, there would be a Battalion inspection the following morning by the Brigade C.O. and we were given the afternoon off to make sure the whole camp, huts, kit, ourselves and our equipment were in tip top order, and if anyone failed the inspection, or a hut failed inspection, we knew what to expect, so everyone was busy. The N.C.O. informed us that an inspection by the Brigade C.O. usually meant a move to a real army training camp in a few days as Kinmell Park Camp was really just a fitting out camp. This proved to be correct; two days later we were ordered to parade in full kit and kit bags, everything we had, as we were to be moved; no one seemed to know where. It would be about mid-July, we only had a few weeks basic training, so it would not be overseas. After a whole day's slow train journey we arrived in Suffolk, our kit bags piled in the road to go by R.A.S.C. Transport from the station and we marched to Henham Park, which was a large army training camp.

Sleeping accommodation was in army bell tents supposed to be eight men to a tent, but we had to sleep and make do 12 men to a tent. There was just room to lie down nearly touching each other, 12 kitbags, 12 rifles and all our equipment, and in mid-July.

The sanitary arrangements were very basic indeed, more so than Kinmell Park, only salty water to wash and all drinking water came in by road tanker and was very strictly rationed, so the YMCA and NAAFI did a roaring trade in drinks of all sorts. We now began our training in earnest with rifle drill, and practice with blank ammunition and bayonet fighting, throwing dummy Mills bombs and grenades, trench digging, and now longer route marches, mostly in what was known as fighting order, occasionally we did a march in full marching order, carrying everything except our kitbags. The NCOs and officers were all men who had been on active service and who for various reasons were no longer fit for active service. They were on the whole, I thought, not the type usually portrayed as shouting and bullying all the time, they were, of course, very strict on discipline, cleanliness, and general behaviour, but would during rest periods chat quite normally about home life and things in general.

We had not been at Henham Park very long when I had what I thought was a sore throat, and so following the procedure laid down I reported sick. It did not take the medical officer many minutes of examination, and he said, 'Mumps - isolation hospital today'. Right away I had to leave my tent. I was taken to a small clump of trees a few hundred yards from the main camp. There were two empty bell tents, each with one bed, and I was told to stay there till an ambulance came for me to take me to hospital. There was apparently a slip up somehow and no one came near me till next day, so there I was, 24 hours in a bed of army blankets raised 12" off the ground, no food or drink for 24 hours. The orderly who brought my breakfast said someone would be 'up for the jump and a big drop' about it. I never heard what happened.

An ambulance arrived and took me to the isolation hospital in Norwich. This was a large house on the outskirts of the town, requisitioned for the purpose of isolation hospital. I was in a room at the front of the house, looking into a big garden mostly shrubbery, in a proper bed with sheets and all the usual facilities in that type of house at the time. After a few days I felt alright but the R.A.M.C. doctor who came to see me each day with a sergeant said I would have to stay 14 days at least. During all this time I had been writing to Alice and to Mother and Dad every week and receiving letters back which we always looked forward to at both ends. It was not always the same R.A.M.C. doctor and orderly sergeant who visited me each day. I was always asked a few questions and in consequence my speech impediment was revealed. On two occasions the R.A.M.C. doctor and the orderly sergeant had a chat with me about it, and raised the query whether I should be in the army at all, due to my speech impediment, or that my medical category was A1.

My 14 days isolation came to an end and I was returned to my unit at Henham

Park Camp with orders to report sick for light duty next day. This I duly did and was excused all drills and training for 14 days, but to report to the sergeants' mess for duties. This involved helping in the cookhouse, waiting on the sergeants at meal times, washing up and so forth. It was quite a change and 14 days soon passed. Then it was back on parade, lessons in bayonet fighting, close combat conflict, fire arms training with live ammunition, throwing live Mills bombs and firing, rifle grenades (these were like a Mills bomb with a rod about a foot long, which was slid down the rifle bore and a blank cartridge used to propel it about 100 yards). All very exciting stuff, this.

I was in B Company and in due course we went to Bedford for the day to fire our proficiency test course, which was a test of our marksmanship, firing at fixed targets at 200, 400 and 600 yards range, five rounds at each distance in our own time, then ten rounds rapid fire in a limited time at 400 yards. We also had a session firing at targets the shape and size of a man which were exposed to view a limited time.

Each platoon of the company took a turn in the butts where the targets were situated and operated. We were behind a huge timber and earth embankment and the targets were raised above this to be fired at. When the firing was taking place bullets were passing just above our heads and splinters of targets and wood flying all over the place. There was a pre-arranged method of signals to the firing line, to give the results of each target score for each type of test, and points. I passed with over 125 points which entitled me to wear the marksman's badge, two crossed rifles badge on my sleeve.

We had been at Henham Park through the summer of 1918 and beginning to wonder where we would spend the winter, when another Brigade inspection meant we would likely be on the move again. So it was, though it was not far this time, just to Woodbridge in Suffolk.

We were billeted in permanent brick buildings. I think they were malthouses, dry and warm, the only drawback being that the ceilings were only about six feet from the floor and there was a round steel supporting column about every 10 ft. each way. Woodbridge was a small town, with shops and some amusements. We were allowed out in the town till 9.00 p.m. so had some choice of entertainment from the YMCA and NAAFI.

The accommodation was far superior to either Kinmel Park or Henham Park. We had almost finished our six months infantry training and we began to speculate whether or when we would go overseas and where to. The war was by now moving towards Germany, and there was much speculation whether we would go overseas before the war was over.

About this time I was detailed to duty in the Sergeants' Mess for duty as before. The Mess and facilities were in what had been a large hotel; it was also used as company offices and everything was of a much higher standard in every way. I was waiting on at table three times a day which meant amongst all the other NCOs I was serving my own platoon Sergeant Donkin of Grenadier Guards and my Sergeant Bracegirdle, so I looked after them!

This was only temporary and I was back with the lads on parade and down to earth. I shall never forget the next noteworthy event. The Company was having midday meal when as usual the orderly officers and sergeant came in to walk round the room and ask if there were any complaints. That done the sergeant called us to attention, but to remain seated. We knew then something big was coming and it was, the date was 11th November 1918.

The officer announced the Armistice had been signed at 11.00 a.m. We were to have 14 days embarkation leave and then we would be going overseas, probably to Germany. Well, pandemonium broke loose for quite a few minutes. The sergeant could not make himself heard, but he could not put all the Company on charge for not behaving, and after all, such good news was enough to make anyone wish to cheer and sing.

So it was a few weeks later the whole of B Company went on 14 days embarkation leave. We received our return railway warrants and 14 days leave pay in advance, and were on our way home next day.

I visited Blacoe's Farm, Warton, Ribble Laundry and met many of my friends. The family were delighted to see me and Miss Lucas gave Alice extra time off while I was on leave. Quite naturally, everyone was very happy the war was over, and Alice and I were looking forward to my demobilisation, which would not be likely for perhaps another two years.

Fourteen days passed very quickly and my return to Woodbridge followed without incident.

Another Brigadiers Inspection soon followed and in due course we entrained for Dover, with all our full gear and equipment. The trip from Dover to Calais was quite an experience for me. I had only seen the sea at Lytham and Blackpool and never been out in any sort of boat, not even a rowing boat on Fairhaven Lake, Ansdell, Lytham. We had to wear very clumsy cork life jackets. Quite a few of the lads were sea sick and others looked very groggy and fed up. I quite enjoyed the trip and did not feel any ill effects.

At Calais we had a meal at the staging post on the docks where all embarking and disembarking troops were checked and fed and watered, and spent the night in wooden army huts close by.

Next morning we marched to the station and saw our first bit of France and Calais. One of the sights very strange to us was the open urinals on the edge of the pavement, which consisted of a sheet of corrugated iron bent in the shape of a J fixed to two posts about six feet apart. The high side of the sheet was to the road, and men just stood on the footpath facing the lower upturned edge of the sheet to urinate and the urine ran out of the end of the sheet into a gully drain. Quite a change from the men's underground toilets in Lytham Square where there was a prominent notice: 'Please adjust your dress BEFORE leaving'.

When we arrived at the station we were surprised to see the train was a long one made up entirely of box van goods waggons, used on the railway for general mixed, packed traffic.

Each van had about a foot of straw over the floor area, and nothing else. We were all checked in twenty in each van with all our equipment and kit bags, and after about two hours we left Calais for Bonn on the Rhine Germany. The journey took two days and two nights with frequent stops up to half an hour; very often the train was so slow some of the lads got down on the track and ran or walked alongside. We also stopped about every four or five hours in the day at Staging posts for meals, washing, etc., and at night got down in the straw after a sing song session.

I expect as hostilities had only ceased about four weeks the whole railway system was be in chaos and we had no personnel carriers in 1918. I suppose we were lucky we had not to march from Calais to Bonn, or part of the way. We duly arrived in Bonn and after a meal and what seemed a long wait the train took us on to Obercassell a few miles along the Rhine Valley, a smallish town.

The first night my platoon were billeted in a small hotel commandeered for the night. Most of us slept on the floor, where there was just about room to turn over, and we were all glad to get outside early in the morning to a breakfast of 'Iron Rations' – bully beef and army hard tack biscuits – and have a shave and wash in cold water out in the yard at the back.

After morning roll call we were marched to the other side of the town, where the army had commandeered a large college where B Company were to be billeted. We were given the rest of the day off to get cleaned up after our journey and settle in our rooms, which I suppose had been student dormitories and studies. I was lucky to get a study or students' room with three others. On each floor there were bathrooms and toilets, so it was almost home from home, and best of all there was a large indoor swimming pool, which we were to sample later.

Next morning we had breakfast from Army Mobile Field Kitchens set up in the grounds. The first parade was in the form of a lecture on the 'dos and don'ts' of our behaviour and attitude to the local populations – some parts of the town were out of bounds to troops and we were warned not to fraternize too freely. I suppose after all we were on the winning side of the war, and in these early days of the occupation no one really knew what the reaction would be to the occupying forces. As it turned out there were very few problems. I suppose, like us, the Germans were glad it was all over. At the end of this lecture, it was explained that the Battalion and Company cooks and mess room staff had been left in England as they were partially disabled men not fit for overseas service; in consequence each company had to organise its cooking and feeding arrangements and volunteers were wanted to take up duties in the kitchen and messrooms. We had been allocated one cook, but he was due for discharge soon, so any volunteers who had experience in civilian life of such duties were asked to step forward; not one man stepped out.

We still had Sergeant Donkin and Sergeant Pollard who, I found out later, had been a window cleaner in St. Annes. They had a bit of a 'conflab' and Sergeant Donkin came along the line having a good look at each man. When he came to me he said 'Ah, Bridges, you had two spells in the Sergeants' Mess in England; you will do for one. Fall out'. Two more were picked out and off we went with Sergeant Pollard to the College kitchens, very well fitted with coal fired stoves and ovens, and pans, crockery and cutlery, etc. which had been used for the College. The orderly officer for the day later explained my duties. I would be excused all parades and training and would be in complete charge on a day to day basis of feeding B Company, around 300 men.

I would have to put requisitions in for all the food etc. required, see it was cooked and served, and keep all clean and tidy. I was to ask the Company Sergeant if I wanted extra help and told 'Now get on with it', the quarter master will help you with any difficulty. I thought, 'Well, 18 years and six months, you never know what life has in store for you'.

After about a week supplies became organised and more varied and on the whole we did not do too badly. There were problems occasionally when the rations asked for did not arrive, and the alternatives we had to improvise did not suit everyone. If we had eggs for all the men and bacon for half of them, who got the bacon? Each man got one slice instead of two. The kitchen and messroom staff had to start early before reveille, and did not finish till long after the evening meal so we had most afternoons off. There were lovely walks along the Rhine banks and the hills around, we could ride on the electric trains free and would to into Bonn not many miles away or into Cologne on a day off once a week.

In time sports were organised between various units, football, cricket, swimming, boxing and the like. The kitchen and mess staff made good use of the indoor swimming pool, and so the first half of 1919 passed with all its varied memories. One parade held every two weeks, the kitchen and messroom staff had to attend; there was a very strict roll call for it and woe betide anyone who missed. It was a medical inspection for V.D. and I am sure for a lot of the lads it was at first, to say the least, somewhat embarrassing. Two platoons of men were lined up facing each other, two officers from the R.A.M.C. and two of our own sergeants carried out the inspection. On the command 'Trousers down' one section on each line facing each dropped their trousers and lifted their shirts for the officer to look at each man's private parts for any sign of V.D. The inspection normally passed off quite smoothly and only took a few minutes for each section. There was only one occasion when I was on the parade that anything out of the ordinary happened; the inspecting officer of the

*Myself (left) in Bonn,
Germany, July 1919.*

line facing mine stopped about four men to my right, and was heard quite distinctly to say 'Where the hell have you been? You have had that thing where I would not put my stick. Fall him out Sergeant, to the Guardroom. Put him on a charge'. So the youth of 1918/19 had the corners of any shyness or other private feelings disposed of.

We had now been overseas six months and were due for 14 days leave, which everyone was looking forward to with eager anticipation.

Our journey from Bonn to Calais was a very different journey than when we came out, the army, of course, requisitioned anything needed and were fortunate to find a German ambulance train that had been used for carrying casualties from the western front to hospitals in Bonn and Cologne and as a German leave train.

Six months had passed since the war ended, the rail tracks and whole transport system had been greatly improved and we had a fairly comfortable and quick journey on the leave train to Calais, where we stayed a night, then over to England and home; the journey time each way was not included in the 14 days leave until we arrived in England or left England.

Everyone was naturally delighted to see me, the war was over, and thoughts were already turning to discharge and home.

I went to see the Blacoe's at Warton Hall Farm, and the Ribble Laundry. There did not appear to have been much change in the twelve months since I joined up. I was soon in touch with Alice Vale. We had been writing regularly all the time I was away. Miss Lucas, Alice's employer, gave Alice extra time off while I was on leave so we spent a lot of time together. Mother and Dad made her welcome at home, and Rose, my sister, and brothers Reuben and Frank, we all got on well together. Brother Charles was still in France; he had been on leave while I was in Germany. It was while I was on leave I learned more of Alice's early days in Willenhall. On leaving school she had worked packing locks at Josiah Parkes the lockmakers and at H. & T. Vaughan. She had come to work at Lucas the confectioners in Lytham when she was seventeen years of age and in 1919 was being paid ten shillings per week, live in and all found.

In Lytham, Ansdell and St. Annes there would be hundreds of young girls in domestic service from the Midlands, Cumberland and the North East. All the business and professional people's homes had at least one and many two or three domestic staff. Fourteen days soon passed, goodbyes were said and it was off back to Germany.

By now I had my staff and duties running quite smoothly; the orderly officer of the day and a sergeant came round every midday meal for 'any complaints' and walked down the rows of tables, about 50 in all, six men to a table. The NCOs had two tables to themselves on one side and we always served their tables first. Various matters of interest, instructions and information were

Loading the famous Apollinaris mineral waters at Remagen, Germany.

displayed on notice boards at each end of the messroom, showing who was on leave, who was due to go during the next week, streets, places, pubs, etc. which were out of bounds. One notice appeared asking for anyone who could drive a motor vehicle to report to Company office. I went along to see what it was about. It appeared that early in the war before conscription there was a shortage of motor drivers and any driver fit enough could join up voluntarily and get six shillings per day above the usual pay. These men the army wished to discharge or in some cases could claim to be discharged which would save the six shillings per day. I could drive having learned at the laundry and had my driving licence with me and so gave all the details required, having in mind when I was discharged I would want a job.

In three days I had been transferred from the Kings Liverpool Regiment Infantry to the Royal Army Service Corps. Motor Transport and I was attached to R. E. Signals 32nd Division Headquarters in Bonn, the Divisional Headquarters were in Poppledorfer Allee, Bonn, where the premises had been a fairly large hotel requisitioned by the army. I was billeted not far away in another requisitioned building, where I had a room of my own and a very comfortable billet; other members of the Divisional Headquarters staff were also billeted there and a NAAFI in the building was always busy in the evenings and off days.

There were several motor vehicles based at the Headquarters on a permanent basis and extras when needed came from the R.A.S.C.M.T. Co. – Royal Army Service Corps Motor Transport Company. I was allocated to a Talbot tender based on a 25 h.p. Talbot car. It had a tilt cover over the driver and passengers or goods, it had twin tyres on the rear wheels, was very sturdily built and easy to drive, and had a crash gearbox and right hand drive, but no self starter or windscreen wipers.

My duties varied from delivering and collecting documents and the like from battalion and brigade headquarters, to collecting rations from the quartermaster's stores for the officers and men's messrooms and cookhouses. On occasions I went to the Apollinaris Works near Koblenz which was in the American section of the Rhine Armies of Occupation to collect a load of crates of bottles of the famous mineral waters, for the officers' mess.

The Headquarters cricket team also used the Talbot and me and other vehicles when they went to play other units in the B.A.O.R. ie. British Army on Rhine.

We occasionally took parties of officers to various functions, dances and the like which were organised between the various units, in the evening. At the bigger events there would be up to forty vehicles of one sort and another and these events sometimes went on till midnight, much to the disgust of the waiting drivers. It was when returning from one of these late dances about 1.00 a.m. that I had my first driving accident. It was a moonless night, the Talbot car had good sidelights, no headlamps, the road was dead straight. I had been along it many times in day and night. On each side of the road was a long row of tall poplar trees which seem to be a feature of the roads and although there was no moon the faint light of the sky and the stars showed the way ahead, and enabled a steady speed of about 25 miles per hour to be maintained comfortably, which I was doing. The first thing I saw was the back end, or perhaps I should say backside, of a big cart horse which I saw in my side lights. The Talbot radiator guard hit the horse at about 20 miles an hour and the horse disappeared into the night; next second the car hit the rear left wheel of a large four wheel cart, bang in the middle of the radiator guard which was a pretty hefty one, and it saved the radiator and fan from damage.

The six officers in the back of the Talbot ended up in a heap, and I felt sure I would be up for the high jump in the morning. However, lucky me again – it turned out that this particular journey had not had the official permit required for journeys after dark so I did not hear any more of the incident. It appeared there were two Germans with the team of two horses and this large four wheel cart. They had delivered a large load of soft brown coal briquettes used in closed stoves. The loaded cart required two horses and as the cart was empty one horse was loosely tethered walking behind the empty cart. What happened to the poor horse, I did not hear; it had acted as a good shock absorber and as the cart was moving away from the car this also reduced the impact. The cart had no lights at all. Quite likely under the military rules in force they should not have been on the road after dark, they did not speak English, and none of my party spoke German, so after quite a lot of gesticulating and sign language in the light of the car side-lamp, we parted and went our separate ways at 2.00 o'clock in the morning under a German star lit sky on the banks of the Rhine.

The damaged radiator guard and one wing were repaired on the double next day, and that was the end of the matter. If the cart had been loaded with five or six tons and been stopped when we hit it, there would have been a different end – no seat belts, and perhaps no one to tell the story.

In the early days of the Rhine Army there were occasions when supplies failed to arrive so make do and mend had to apply. One such was when our motor engine oil ran out, and none was available for over a week. We had gear oil and we had paraffin, so we thinned the gear oil with paraffin and used it as engine oil, and it worked. I expect the slow running engines with heavy cast iron pistons would not be so particular about oil as today's high speed engines with light aluminium or alloy pistons. We did get lots of oiled up plugs, and the exhaust smoke came out in clouds, but we were able to keep on the road. Once regular supplies got organised we had no problems, and the supplies position improved each week.

Another incident I shall never forget might have blinded me for life. One of the vehicles in 594 M. T. Company attached to 32nd Division Headquarters was a 4- or 5-ton A.E.C. lorry (Associated Equipment Co.). This company originally manufactured buses and heavy lorries; lots of A.E.C. buses were operated in London after the war ended in 1918.

However, this particular vehicle had an electric generator and ancillary equipment as its load, used to charge batteries and provide electricity direct if required. Every week it used to go round all the Brigade Headquarters and charge or recharge or exchange batteries which were used by Royal Engineers Signals for communication by field telephone services.

A number of the Brigade Headquarters were right on top of the hills on the banks of the Rhine usually in a large hotel, country mansion or castle.

This particular vehicle was normally driven by one of the volunteer drivers on six shillings per day above normal privates' pay and in due course, as I have mentioned earlier, his time came for discharge, and I was put in charge of the A.E.C. vehicle and generator. This was in mid-summer 1919. The duties were quite interesting, a different journey each day, change of meals and work to do which did not entail a lot of talking to people, as I still had my speech impediment.

One of the Brigade Headquarters was almost at the top of a hill or mountain which entailed a long winding journey of about three miles, in very low gear and it was a blistering hot day. When we arrived at the top of the hill I parked the vehicle where it had to be for the job we had to do. I was sure the engine must have lost cooling water, and it would need topping up.

The top of the A.E.C. radiator was about 5 feet from the ground, cast aluminium and the radiator cap would be three inches diameter. The radiator cap was unusual as it was not screwed on, but had a hinge at the back and a strong spring arrangement that held the cap firmly closed or if lifted slightly it sprang fully open itself, full open at once. So I went to the front of the vehicle and just touched the radiator cap. It flew fully open at once and boiling water and steam gushed out right in my face. I was 5ft.11in. in boots so my face was just above the radiator cap.

The engine cooling water must have been boiling hard and the release of the spring cap let all the pressure out at once. I yelled out, of course, I could not see and it was very fortunate there was a Royal Army Medical Corp. Officer in the Headquarters, and in a few minutes he had my face, eyes and neck all smothered in vaseline like thickly buttered bread. This I feel saved my sight and my face from scald scars, and I learned a lesson about AEC radiator caps at that time. I had a few days off and was quickly back to normal.

It was about four weeks before I was taken off the Talbot tender that I had my first ever bottle of beer. I had been with a corporal from the officers' mess to collect ten crates of bottled beer from the quarter master's stores. When we were unloading word came that Alcock & Brown had made the first flight across the Atlantic Ocean and had landed in Ireland. The corporal said this called for a drink so we had a bottle of beer between us, courtesy of the officers' mess. I was not at all impressed with the beer and never have been since; in the seventy-odd years since that first beer I have not had more than seven.

The summer of 1919 had long spells of very hot weather and towards autumn the 32nd Division Headquarters to which I was attached was preparing to leave the Rhine Army. In due course this took place and I was returned to 594 M.T. Company R.A.S.C. We had a variety of vehicles, a lot of them American manufacture, including a number of four-wheel drive three and four tonners; there were also Peerless and Packhard, the former having wooden wheels. Among the English made vehicles were Crossley, made at Stockport, Lancashire; Albion, made in Scotland; and Commer, made in the south of England. The Commers had chain drive to the rear wheels and a type of semi automatic gear box. The gear quadrant was lateral and mounted under the steering wheel; to change gear the gear lever was moved into the gear required and the driver simply pressed the clutch pedal and let it back and the gear change took place automatically, this in 1919. All other vehicles were the usual crash gearbox, which required a fair degree of skill to change gear quietly.

The vehicles of 594 M.T. Company were parked along one side of a long straight main road and we were billeted in a factory building close by. Our duties were moving men, equipment, stores and the like about and between the many units which made up the B.A.O.R. sector.

Our thoughts were now on when are we likely to get demobilised. It was realised that older men, married men and those with years of service since 1914 were likely to have preference. As always there were lots of rumours and false alarms around. However, lucky me again, it was late October 1919 when I was ordered to report to Company office next morning for details to be taken of my

Alice Vale, 1920.

date of call up and other matters. I was still suffering from my speech impediment and so had some foreboding of embarrassment. However, what it was all about was my speech, which was, it seemed, on my records and also they had in the records that I had joined the forces under age, by one or two days, and as such could claim discharge at once. Where or how they got the date wrong I did not know, not for me to dispute it.

It took a few weeks for the paper work to be sorted out, and lo and behold I was for discharge at least twelve months sooner than expected, and perhaps two years sooner than expected. During all my time in Germany I had been writing to home and to Alice every week so I really had something to write about that week.

There were four of us for discharge the morning I left. We were taken to the station with all our gear, equipment, kit bags, etc. That night there had been

A good character reference from my former employer, the 'Blackpool Princess and Ribble Laundry Ltd.'

about 12 inches of snow, and we said goodbye to Germany and 594 M.T. Company, on our way to Calais. We stayed the night in Dover then on to London next morning, then on to Prees Heath, Shropshire to No.1 Dispersal Unit on the 15th December 1919, where we handed in all our equipment, and received £2. 0s. 0d. for one week's advance pay, and 28 days paid furlough, during the remaining three weeks the £2 per week was to be collected from Lytham Employment Exchange on Army Form Z11.

We were allowed to keep our uniform, underwear, towels, boots, etc., not to be worn as a uniform after the four weeks' furlough.

Everyone was, of course, delighted I was home so soon and I was more than pleased to renew my friendship with Alice Vale. We had written to each other every week during the whole of the 1½ years I had been away and we were now able to meet regularly on Thursday and Sunday evenings, and on Alice's Sunday afternoons off. Once a month Alice came and had tea with us all at home, 34 Warton Street, Lytham. Alice had a full head of dark hair. Dad teased her by calling her golliwog, and she was made very welcome by all the family.

When the four weeks' demobilisation furlough at £2. 0s. 0d per week was over, if unemployed I could sign on each day at the unemployment exchange over the Midland Bank in Lytham Square and receive 29 shillings per week for six weeks, after which you could sign on each day and see if any jobs were on offer, but there was no unemployment pay after six weeks; this was to be the 'Land fit for heroes'. I cannot remember who quoted this or where and when.

However, so far as I was concerned, the main and most important thing was to get a job. Men were coming home from the forces who had joined up as volunteers in the early days of the war. Naturally my first application was to my old employer, The Blackpool Princess and Ribble Laundry Ltd., Dock, Road, Lytham. The same manager, Mr. Herbert Willacy, was still there, and I went to see him just after Christmas, 1919, to see if I could have my old job back, or employment of any kind as soon as my four week furlough ended on 15th January 1920. He said he was sorry but he could not do so as the job was being done by a former employee who had joined the forces before me, and had been discharged disabled from military service. However, at my request, he did write me out in his own handwriting a good character reference dated 31st December 1919 which I still have. The next thing was to call in at the public library in Clifton Street, Lytham, and look through the *Lancashire Evening Post* every day and on Fridays the local papers, *The Lytham Times* and *The Lytham Standard*, to see if any vacancies appeared, but without success. There were very few large employers in the area. Now the war was over work at Lytham Shipyard was slowing down, and while I spent a lot of time each week calling at any likely employer, without any luck, my efforts were not made any easier as I still had my speech impediment. I did receive lots of kindly advice from very sympathetic people on how I might overcome it, but to no avail; it was there; I was stuck with it. Nobody was to blame, and thank God, my dear friend Alice seemed to understand, and it did not affect our now becoming very close. Our relationship had now reached the stage where I was considering if I dare ask Alice if we might become engaged. I hesitated in this, as being unemployed I did not feel it would be the right thing to do. When my six weeks' unemployment benefit ceased I did find occasional jobs for a day or two each week, gardening at a house in Seafield Road, Lytham, where the owner was an elderly man in a wheelchair. He used to sit in the garden and watch my work and occasionally talk about my speech impediment in a helpful way.

I also had the odd day washing and driving a large Talbot car for a family in St. Annes Road East, St. Annes; strange it should be the same make of car I drove in Germany. I think it was an ex-army car. These were coming on the market from ex-army vehicle sales of surplus vehicles. I even had a few days spreading farm yard manure at Hardman's Farm, Lytham, a job I knew from my Warton Hall Farm employment. During all this time Alice and I often talked about our future, getting engaged and married. We always ended up quite amicably with the decision that it should wait till I had a regular job. No job, no dole, no training schemes. What did the future hold for us?

I had, of course, learned to drive in late October or November, 1917, and would gladly have taken any kind of job, especially driving, but who wanted a young chap with so little experience? In 1920 the only motor vehicles in Lytham were one Napier 3-ton tipper (operated by hand) which was run by Lytham Shipbuilding and Engineering Co. Ltd. in Dock Road, Lytham, one Vulcan 3-ton flat lorry owned by Foster & Whyatts Corn Merchants delivering cattle and poultry food and one Vulcan 3-ton vehicle used by the Council Cleansing Department, and two Vulcan taxis, one run by William Bros., Garage in Henry Street, Lytham and one run by a man who had previously driven the William Bros. taxi.

The Vulcans were built at Vulcan Engineering Co., Crossens, Southport. Every day you could sign on as unemployed at the Labour Exchange and hope something would turn up.

At this time William Eaves & Co. Ltd. from Blackpool were building Victory Parish Hall near St. Cuthbert's Church in Church Road, Lytham and one day when I signed on I was told they wanted two builders' labourers, preferably experienced, so off I went to the site. The foreman said he would give me a trial for two days, provided I could wheel concrete in a barrow up a 9 inch plank. I said OK, just what I was doing when I was 16 but it was cow muck in a farm barrow up a 9 inch plank. So I had a job 8.00 a.m. to 5.00 p.m. and four hours on Saturday mornings.

The concrete wheeling job only lasted a few days and I was then shown how to use the mortar mill, which had been erected on site to grind clinker, ashes, lime and sand and water into black or white mortar as required. The mortar mill was a very heavy iron piece of machinery driven by electric motor. The base part was like a huge iron saucer about 5 feet across and 15" deep which when working revolved round and round. Resting in the base were two rollers about 18" across the flat and 4 feet diameter. The saucer-shaped base revolved and this turned the two rollers. A series of guide vanes kept the material passing under the rollers. The base held about three barrows full of materials, put in and taken out by hand, and while it appeared a big heavy machine it did a good job, and for me was experience in new semi skills. I was also shown how to erect and fix the scaffolding round the building, all wooden poles held together with wire, multiply ropes which had to be fixed a certain way to be safe. This was all new experience and knowledge for me. I was always very willing to learn. After about two weeks two more bricklayers were taken on; each had a labourer or perhaps shared one with another bricklayer depending on the height from the ground of the actual bricklaying operation. All the bricks and mortar were carried up ladders on to the scaffolding in a hod which was a sort of open top box on a four foot pole or handle; this was to be quite a tricky job to get the knack of and some labourers never did. However, I picked it up very quickly and, therefore, got another one penny (four farthings) per hour.

The normal load of bricks was 8 per hod, packed in such a way that when the hod was emptied the bricks were in a neat square pile. I could and did carry 16 common bricks up to a first floor scaffolding, just for a show-off, I expect. 16 bricks in 1920 weighed 112 lbs.

The bricks were loaded in the hod, holding it standing upright with one hand and packing the bricks in a square; mortar went up the same way, loaded in the hod by shovel, then up the ladder on to the scaffold. I was also shown how to mix and lay concrete for foundations, excavate for and lay drain pipes and a lot of other jobs incidental to a building site. One of the new bricklayers taken on was a man I had known when we lived in Lytham Hall Park when Dad was Head Gamekeeper, Jonathan 'Jonty' Allanson. He was very tall, about 6' 6" and in 1910/12 was a bellringer at St. Cuthbert's Church, Lytham. My eldest

St. Annes-on-Sea, 1920. Myself on right, leaning on a home-made hod. 4th from right is tall 'Jonty' Allanson.

brother, Charles, was at that time also a bellringer at St. Cuthberts, so we knew each other from 8 or 10 years before. This was very fortunate for me as we were now working together. Just after the 1914/18 war, bricklayers were in great demand to such an extent that when they went on a job they could insist on their own labourer being employed with them. It did in effect work to everyone's benefit; the employer had a good bricklayer, the bricklayer had a labourer he knew and could work with amicably, and, most important to me anyway, the labourer (that's me in this case) had a job. It was the practice in the building trade as a particular job was drawing to a close for employees to be warned a few days beforehand, and then get their insurance cards and last pay on a Friday night – no real seven days' notice redundancy pay, etc. A lot of building trade employees were really casual workers all the time liable to be more or less employed on a day to day basis and in consequence, liable to be paid off anytime of the day or week.

The larger firms had a small core of regular fully experienced tradesmen and labourers, who had usually been with their employers many years.

It was, of course, possible to tell by the progress and state of the work on the site how much longer a particular job would last, and for a bricklayer to have another job lined up ready to start. For a builder's labourer in the normal way, when he finished on a job it was just a case of 'signing on' at the Labour Exchange each day in the hope something would turn up as it had done for me, and at the same time calling at any building site or civil engineering job which was starting up in the district to seek employment.

It became obvious after about four months that the full number of bricklayers and labourers would not be required much longer, and there was the distinct possibility that I would be out of work possibly by mid June 1920.

Jonty, my bricklayer friend, and I got on very well together and I was greatly relieved when he told me he would be taking another job as employee bricklayer and that if I was willing he would take me on the job as his labourer. This was great news for me, as I was aware his father was in business in Lytham on his own account as a jobbing builder, doing small repair and maintenance jobs. I knew also that Jonty's father was nearing retirement age; he had just one employee as labourer, who had been with Jonty's father most of his working life and I knew if Jonty's father did retire Jonty would go into the family business and I would be out of work.

The building trade is not like a factory or production line; each job or site starts and finishes in maybe weeks, months or on big jobs, years, and so apart from a firm's core of regular staff in the larger firms, there is no certainty of continuous employment.

So came the day early June 1920 about 4.30 p.m. The site foreman handed me my wages for the week with my insurance cards and said, 'Thanks, Harold. You have done a good job. Sorry you don't need to come in Monday. Hope you get fixed up soon'.

Jonty finished as well the same day and told me he was having a week off and to get in touch with him in a week or ten days, so I signed on at the Labour Exchange. This I did and was delighted when Jonty told me he was to build a bungalow at South Shore for an elderly lady, and he would like me to go with him as his labourer on the job.

This was to entail travel from Lytham to South Shore on the train. Luckily we could get off at a small unmanned train stop called Gillets Crossing. This was about half a mile from the bungalow site.

The arrangements were: we could work as many hours as we wished at normal hourly rate of pay, no overtime rate. This we did. Jonty and I left Lytham each morning around 6.00 a.m., were on the job by 7.00 a.m. and worked till about 7.00 pm. including Saturday, so we had a very nice pay packet each week. The old lady used to come occasionally to check progress and the architect in charge came once a week.

It was a virgin site so Jonty and I were on our own right from the foundations up to being ready for the joiner to fix the roof timbers. Jonty showed me how to lay bricks, build a semi-circular arched doorway, and complete circular windows and lots of other building tips and 'know how' which I could not have acquired on an ordinary building site with gangs of men, foremen and chargehands.

Luckily 1920 was a lovely, dry summer and we made good progress by our long hours and hard work. The old lady for whom we worked was very pleased and expressed her appreciation financially when the work was finished.

We only built the main building from foundation to roof; the incidental brickwork to completion after or with joiners, etc. was to be carried out by a local firm. So again, around September 1920 insurance cards and last pay and what next?

Jonty again was to have a break of a week or ten days and let me know what turned up, so once again it was a case of sign on at the Labour Exchange and wait. I could not forget Jonty's father might retire at any time, and knew what the consequences could be for me.

Two weeks passed and mother came in from shopping one day and said, 'I met Jonty's mother on Clifton Street today and Jonty wants to see you. He has another job lined up for you both'.

Off I went to see Jonty right sharp. The job was in St. Patrick's Road North, St. Annes, a large house was about half built and we could start the following week. Good news indeed. Winter was approaching with the inevitable slow-down in the building trade. The job was likely to last about five months and that should see us through the winter. Also there would be a fair amount of inside work for us after the roof was on and would ensure employment even in bad weather. Normally in bad weather building trade employees could be, and were, sent off the job anytime, which resulted in short pay that week.

It was a fairly big house being built and eight or ten men were working on outbuildings, garden walls and the like, and were engaged on different parts of the job: joiners, electricians, plasterers, etc.

We were fortunate as in the autumn of 1920 a 48 hour guaranteed week came into operation for the building trade, so whatever the weather we were assured of a full week's pay.

I well remember several days when the weather was so bad nothing could be done outside and four of us were sitting in the cabin waiting for the weather to clear when the man who was having the house built came in. I think we all felt self-conscious about sitting there doing nothing and he was paying us. He gathered how we felt as the guaranteed 48 hour week had not been in force long. However, he soon put us at ease. He said, 'Not to worry; I am in the raincoat manufacturing business. This rain is good for trade. So it's an ill wind that blows no one any good!'

Jonty and I still got along very well together and all the time I was picking up very useful tips of all sorts. Jonty was very good; he seemed to appreciate my interest and desire to know all the ins and outs of all sorts of jobs.

I continued my very close friendship with Alice Vale. We saw each other and went out together or she came to my home, 34 Warton Street, Lytham on every possible occasion. Dad, mother, my sister Rose and three brothers, Charles, Reuben and Frank, all now accepted Alice as almost one of the family.

I was at this time, that is most of 1920, giving Mother thirty shillings per week as my contribution to the household budget, so each week I was putting a few pounds into a post office savings account and Alice was saving all her tips from the tea room customers where she worked, all to be put together when we married; while we had decided to get engaged and eventually marry we both agreed we should wait awhile and continue to make whatever savings we could.

Jonty and I travelled to work on the electric trams which ran from Lytham through St. Annes to Blackpool. Early in 1921 it was obvious there would not be work for all the men much longer on this job at St. Annes. So again the question arose as to whether Jonty's father would retire and Jonty take over, and I would be left to find a job as a builder's labourer without a bricklayer. I knew very well there was not much chance of that succeeding.

Once again, however, our luck, or my luck anyway, was in, and here's why and how. In Church Road, Lytham not far from where Alice worked and within walking distance of where Jonty and I lived was a large school for girls, Lowther College, almost opposite Lowther Gardens. It had been there many years. When I worked at the Ribble Laundry in 1916 I used to collect and deliver laundry there twice a week. I think it would be late 1919 or early 1920. It took fire and was very badly damaged, so badly that the governors decided not to rebuild it and the college moved into Wales.

Whoever owned it then decided to rebuild it as three fairly large residences. The first Jonty and I knew about the rebuilding was on the way home from work together one evening. We saw a large sign had just been erected in the grounds facing onto Church Road. The sign read, 'Mullen & Durkin Builders, Burnley. Rebuilding to commence shortly, bricklayers and labourers required. Apply on Site'.

What a lucky do – if we could get in at the start there would likely be a few months work and then it would be summer again, with usually more work available.

Jonty saw the foreman, told him he had his own jolly good labourer, skilled, willing, strong and a good worker and timekeeper. We were to start the following Monday morning. What a friend to have, I always felt very grateful to Jonty for all he had done to keep me in employment and to in effect train me to be a skilled builder's labourer. So off we were again, together on the same job within easy walking distance of home, so we could both go home for lunch if we wished. It was about 15 minutes' sharp walk each way. Once again this job was to teach me through Jonty lots of know how. It was really a different type of work than new building. There was a great deal of pulling down, piecing up and so forth, to divide the college into three houses, each with its own front and rear doors, etc. Mullen & Durkin were a lively go ahead firm. They soon had a lot of men on the job, among them were a number of their own regular employees from Burnley, who lodged in Lytham for the week.

Twice a week a big Leyland lorry came from Burnley with a load of various sundry materials. When these were unloaded three labourers went with the lorry and driver to Lytham Goods Station and spent most of the day loading bricks from railway waggons then to the site in Church Road and then unloaded. The journey time was only about ten minutes. The lorry was not a tipper so every brick was loaded and unloaded by hand, and bricks were 7 lbs each then, so quite a lot of sweat was generated. The brick carting was usually complete by 3.00 p.m. then the lorry and labourers went to near Queen Mary's School, St. Annes, and loaded about 7 tons of sand from the sandhills to take back to Burnley on the return journey.

This all had to be shovelled on by hand, the top of the lorry sides were five feet from the ground, so it was quite a job after heaving bricks all day. Usually the foreman sent four labourers to load the sand, two loading at each side and the driver at the back, and we had to be back at the site for 5.00 p.m. This was usually achieved by some hard graft on the part of all the gang.

The lorry had to reverse about 25 yards along a railway sleeper track to get to the sand and when loaded draw out slowly to the main road, Clifton Drive. One day we loaded the lorry with a good load and as the driver was drawing out along the sleeper track, the two nearside wheels slipped off the edge of the sleeper track into the soft sand and down they went up to the axle hubs. 'Oh hell', it was impossible to get the lorry back on the track with the load of sand on and we had to shovel it all off, every bit of it, then get the lorry back on the track, reload it and back to the site about three hours late, so the four labourers had three hours overtime each which the foreman, charge hand on the site did not like at all. I expect he was on some sort of bonus, but it was not our fault; how the driver fared we never heard, he did not come to Lytham again while I was working on the site. It expect he got his cards. How different today – mechanical diggers, fork lift trucks, mechanical, single, two or three way tippers, etc.

So 1920 slipped away, Christmas gone, New Year 1921 came and what a year this was to be for Alice and me, to affect the whole of my life and hundreds of others for the next 50 years. It is a great blessing we cannot foretell what the future holds for us. Here I was, 20 years of age, fit, strong, healthy and so willing to learn, to work, to get on, and help my fellow men not so lucky, to marry and have a family. Oh, if only I could talk like most of my friends, I am sure the prospect for the future would be brighter.

On the other hand I was lucky in so far as I was working, although each job only lasted about average four months, and for this I had to thank Jonty Allanson. By early spring 1921 it was obvious the work at Lowther College was nearing completion and in early April 1921 came the day when the foreman warned us that next week would be the last we would be required and our pay would be made up to Friday the following week and our insurance cards handed to us then, so here we go again. What next?

Sign on at the Labour Exchange and hope something would turn up. There did not appear to be any major building projects starting and as I had feared and expected might happen Jonty's father now around 70 decided to retire and Jonty was to go into the family jobbing builders business full time. Jonty's father had a full- time fully skilled builder's labourer who had worked for the family business for many years so there was no place for me. So I was on my own now and set about looking for work of any kind within cycling distance of Lytham, but no joy, none at all.

I did apply for several driving jobs, but in each case, I am sure my speech impediment failed me. Then, out of the blue or black came the occasion and chain of events which shaped my life, my future, and was to lead from me being out of work to being an employer of over 300 employees. The 1916 Irish troubles, Home Rule and so on, led to the reformation in 1921 of volunteer units in the armed forces to serve specifically in Southern Ireland to help keep law and order; they were known at the time as 'The Black and Tans' as they wore black berets and brown uniforms.

The main requirement at this time was for volunteer ex-army motor drivers who had been demobilised from the regular army. My attention was drawn to this advertisement by a friend in Lytham, Jack Winrow, who like me was a demobilised army driver, and we both sent off for application forms and further details. This was really something for Alice and me and my family to talk about and we did. The details we received pointed out that due to the state of affairs in Ireland and the condition under which we would be employed, we would be subject to military rules and discipline and in consequence there was a certain element of risk attached as we would, if accepted, be mainly employed driving vehicles carrying stores, ammunition and personnel, sometimes in very high risk territory.

Many talks with Alice and my parents all expressed serious doubt as to the wisdom of such a step. Dad put it very bluntly in saying, 'If you are accepted, as the details say, you will be in Ireland in a week, and in another week you might be dead'. What a cheerful thought! From my point of view it was a job, the pay was very good, and the initial period of service was for one year only.

After much talk around all aspects of the matter I decided to have a go, on the basis it would be experience. It would be a job for at least a year (if I lived) and it might lead to something better and more permanent, so I sent in my application form. My friend Jack Winrow also applied.

In due course we both received railway warrants to Preston and notice of time and date to report for tests, etc. at Fulwood Barracks.

The first test was a very rigorous medical which I passed, but my friend Jack failed so he was out at the start. I then went through driving and physical tests, all ok; luckily I had little or no talking to do so my speech impediment did not arise unduly.

I was then taken to a large office with a long table at one end at which were sitting four army officers, one a R.A.M.C. (Royal Army Medical Corps) Captain. He had a pointed beard and moustache very like King Edward VII used to wear.

The officer in charge said, 'Now Bridges, you have passed all the tests so far. We now are each to ask you three simple intelligence questions we want you to answer at once; do not pause to think what the answer should be, just say the first thing which enters your head after the question is asked. The questions are quite simple general knowledge questions, and should be quite easy. This was just what I dreaded, the questions were asked and, of course, I knew the answers but I could not give the answers due to my speech impediment. I was asked to leave the room for a few minutes. On my return the officer in charge said, 'We are sorry, Bridges, we cannot accept your application due to your speech problems. You are just the type of applicant we are looking for, but we cannot accept you, as in case you had to give evidence on any incident or enquiry in Ireland problems could arise'. So my instant thought, 'Hells Bells, I can't even get a job where I might be dead in a week!' As I was leaving the room the R.A.M.C. officer said, 'Wait outside, Bridges. I want a word with you'. I thought, 'Hello, here we go – another lecture on how to overcome my problem of speech'. Not so, however. The next ten minutes were to shape my whole life and future, and the lives of scores of families and employees to be.

In a few minutes the R.A.M.C. officer came out. He put his hand on my shoulder and said, 'I want to tell you something you should think about seriously. I have a nephew in London like you. He has a speech problem; like you he came home from the army and was out of work as you are. Six months ago he bought a secondhand car and started on his own, hiring the car and himself out. Last week I had a letter from him. He is doing very well and has just bought another car and has a man working for him'.

'Now you go home, buy a car, van or lorry, and get in to road transport. You cannot go wrong. Get in at the start, do something no one else is doing, but get in to road transport; that's the job for the next 50 years.'

Well, it just took my breath away and all the time he was talking to me he kept tapping me on the shoulder with his right hand as if to emphasise the importance of what he was saying. I thanked him as best as I could and that was the end of the Black & Tans episode.

Chapter Four

First Vehicle and Marriage

NATURALLY I told Jack what had happened and strange as it may seem, he had worked for a few months in 1920 driving a van for a garage in Park Street, Lytham who ran for a brief period a parcel service to Preston and Blackburn so he started giving me all sorts of tips and much information on his short experience in transport. All very exciting stuff, but at what cost, and where is the money to come from?

I was out of work, no unemployment pay, I was giving Mother twenty four shillings per week towards my keep, some of which came out of my post office savings account.

However, long talks resulted at home and the first time I met Alice we talked of nothing else; there was lots to find out about, what sort of vehicle, passenger or goods, what would it cost, how much would I need to earn to break even. I decided to go for goods transport by providing a parcel collections and delivery service between Blackburn, Preston and the Fylde coast.

I was influenced in this decision as there was no regular goods service by road direct to or from Blackburn and the Fylde coast. The only carrier between Preston and Lytham was based in Lytham with a 3-ton Austin lorry. His father had operated the service originally with a horse-drawn vehicle before the war, so I would have old established opposition. My enquiries showed that this carrier was very unreliable. He had a drink problem and with three public houses along the twelve miles from Preston to Lytham, there were all the opportunities for delay. I had not the faintest idea what it might cost to run a goods vehicle, what to charge, or what the prospects of finding enough regular work might be.

I first called at Lytham passenger station parcels office and obtained their printed sheets of charges for consignments from 7 lbs to 1 cwt. I also made enquiries at Lytham Goods Station for charges up to 5 cwt for up to 50 miles.

By now the whole family and Alice were talking of nothing else than Harold may be starting his own carrier's business, and it was surprising the amount of information we were able to put together.

From enquiries made it appeared the only vehicle I would possibly be able to afford would be a secondhand 1-ton Model T Ford which would cost around £150. I was by now fully convinced I could and would make a go of it, but I did not like the idea of a 12-month-old Ford at £150.

Naturally Alice and I talked often and long about the whole project and its possibilities and problems, the major one of which was finance to start. I had £140 in the Post Office Savings Bank saved up for many years and intended to help start a home maybe someday when I had a regular job and Alice and I got married. Alice had £130 in the Post Office and during one of our frequent talks on the project she said, 'Look, we have both agreed and decided we should not get married until you have a regular job. If you are sure you can make yourself a job so we can get married you can have my £130 until you can pay me back, to enable you perhaps to buy a new 1-ton Ford'.

What a gesture, we were not even engaged, but very much genuinely in love with each other, and Alice's confidence and trust in me was all any man could wish for. So I could now make enquiries about the cost of a new vehicle and the attendant cost of getting started in business on my own.

Enquiries showed the agents for the Model T 1-ton Ford were W. & T. Aked Ltd., St. George's Road, St. Annes on Sea. The only Model T Ford I had seen was a Cash Bakery bread van from Blackpool. I had several talks with the driver about the machine and from this I felt with the right type of bodywork it would do the job I had in mind for a start anyway, so, along I went to Akeds, speech impediment and all, to find out the price, delivery date and likely cost of the type of body I had in mind for the vehicle, painted and lettered and ready for work. I was informed delivery time was about two weeks and one week would be needed to fit a sheet rail and tailboard and paint the vehicle which would come from the works with a flat platform body all in works grey.

So far so good. How about price? I held my breath and heard what I thought would be the end of my dream – £280 delivered ex-works, plus an estimated £20 for bodywork painting and lettering etc., £300 all told and payment within seven days of delivery. I informed Akeds I would think about it and let them know inside seven days. While I was there I got all the literature and details for the Model T. Ford, and was quite happy about it; how I was to find the shortfall in the cash required was another matter.

However, the outcome of long talks with Alice, Mother and Dad was that I should ask Akeds for £50 credit for three months.

I had rather hesitantly asked Dad if he would lend me £50 to see me over the first few months if Akeds would not agree to give me £50 credit. Dad said he was sorry, but, as I knew, he had been a gamekeeper all his life with a large family to bring up and really could not see his way to give me a loan from the few hundred pounds he had saved.

I fully understood, we had no rich relation or anyone I could turn to for help in what I suppose looked a very hazardous venture, but I was convinced myself that the R.A.M.C. Captain was right and if only I could get started I would succeed. Dad was not so convinced as I was, and he said sometimes he was afraid I might not succeed and I would lose all my savings and Alice's as well, but he wished me well and naturally did hope I would succeed, and said he would help me in any way he could apart from cash, and he did later in one way, by delivering advertising leaflets for me to all shops and businesses in Lytham and Ansdell.

I could not help reminding Dad in a joking way that if I had been christened Harold MAFEKING Bridges in 1900 I would have had a nice little sum to draw from the Fylde Water Board in 1921: £25 capital and all the interest for 21 years at 5% compound would have been a total of around £60 and would have solved my problem. Apart from my talks with Mother and Dad on how the finance shortfall might be met I quite naturally talked the problem over with Alice many times and we always ended up with the hope Akeds would give me £50 credit.

In due course I went along to see Akeds with my proposal for credit, and had to wait for half an hour as the man I had to see was out. However, when he arrived I was bracing myself for what I feared might be a hopeless request, for occasions like this did nothing to help my speech. His first words were 'Oh you lucky man, you may know that the model T Ford is built in the U.S.A. What you may not know is that there is a £30 import duty payable on each vehicle and that from 30th June 1921 this import duty is to be abolished'. So if I ordered the vehicle and took delivery after 30th June 1921, the basic price would be £250 and also as an unemployed ex-service man they would charge the bodywork and painting at cost only.

It did not take me many minutes to decide to go ahead. I ordered the vehicle, to be collected Saturday 2nd July 1921, using Monday 4th July as a test run. Akeds accepted this arrangement. This was great news for all concerned and Alice and I in particular. I had now to get busy with lots of details to settle. I had first to find where I could garage the vehicle at night as hopefully there would be goods on it to be delivered next day. I have mentioned earlier the aerodrome built during the 1914/18 war, where Dick Kerrs of Preston built seaplanes. When the war ended the whole site was for sale and a large part including the huge west hangar was bought by the Parkstone Film Co., a new venture making mostly advertising films for cinemas to show. It was such a huge building they let parts off to various people, amongst whom were Lytham Badminton Club, and a firm of three ex-Royal Flying Corps pilots. They had two planes which they hired out for advertising and for flights from Blackpool

The Lytham Aerodrome, built during the 1914/18 War, where Dick Kerrs of Preston built seaplanes. In 1921 a small area was let to myself and used as a garage for my Model T. Ford until 1927.

round the Tower, 5s. 0d a trip. Parkstone Film Co. agreed to let me a small area for my vehicle, next to the flying men's area; this was very convenient as it was only about five minutes' walk from home.

Next I had 250 small handbills printed at the Lytham Standard Printing Co. in Pleasant Street, explaining the services I would operate from 4th July 1921. I went to Preston on my cycle to arrange for a lorry sheet to be made at Mayor & Son, Wharf Street. This was late June 1921 and Bridges Transport Ltd. were still using Mayors sheets in 1968 when I retired, a 47 year unbroken business relationship.

I also arranged with Mayors to pay for the sheet in 30 days, £4 15s. 0d.; in 1968 similar sheets were costing £50. I arranged for a supply of petrol in cans, enough to last the first week at 2s. 7d per gallon (14p today) and three shillings deposit on each can. I still have Akeds bill for the vehicle, Mayors bill for the sheet, and Shell Mex ticket for the first petrol, all in one picture frame.

It was usual for all the carriers operating parcel collection and delivery services to have a point of contact for customers to bring consignments or to leave requests to collect.

This was a follow on from the old horse drawn country carriers days when the contact point was usually a public house with yard room and stables for the horses and carriers' carts. John Eccles, the Lytham, Preston, Blackpool carrier used Allsups Yard near the Public Hall for his contact point in Preston, along with Lund and Parkinson, the Preston Southport Carrier. The Waterloo Hotel in Friargate and Farmers Arms in Market Street were each used by carriers for the country districts, villages and towns all within 20 miles of Preston.

Facing page, clockwise: A Shell Mex ticket for the first petrol, Akeds bill for my first vehicle and Mayors bill for the lorry sheet.

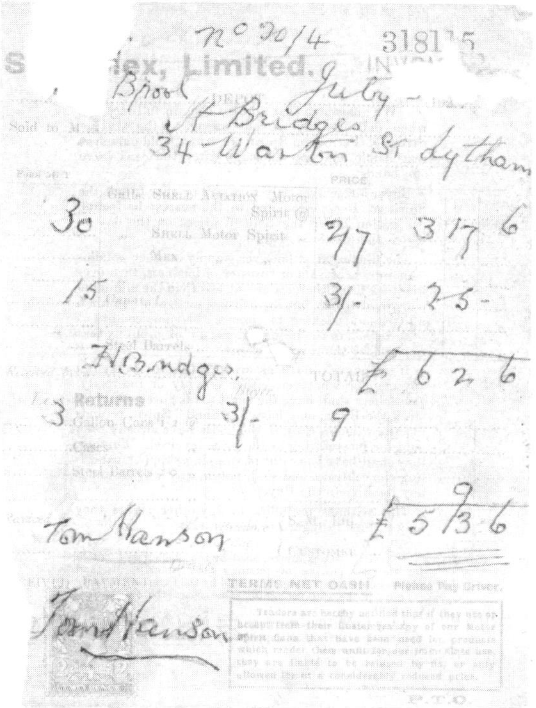

No 90/4   3181 5

Shell ...ex, Limited.

B/ool   July

Sold to M...
H Bridges
34 Warton St Lytham

	PRICE	
Shell Aviation Motor Spirit @		
30	27	3 17 6
Shell Motor Spirit		
15	3/-	2 5 -
H B ridges	TOTAL £	6 2 6
Returns		
3 Gallon Cans @	3/-	9

Tom Hanson   £ 5 13 6

FIXED PAYMENT   TERMS NET CASH   Please Pay Driver

Tom Hanson

P.T.O.

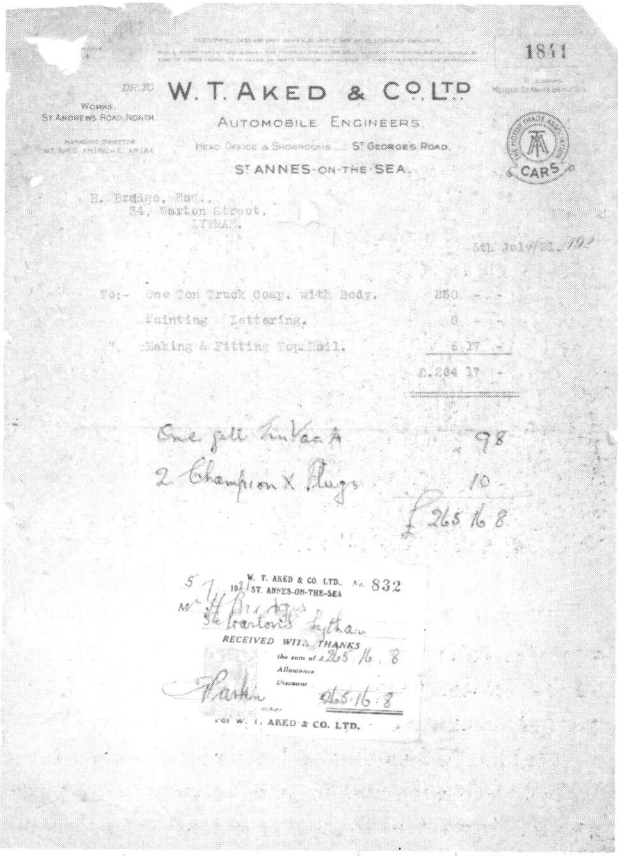

1841

DR. TO

W. T. AKED & CO. LTD

AUTOMOBILE ENGINEERS

WORKS
ST ANDREWS ROAD NORTH

HEAD OFFICE & SHOWROOMS   ST GEORGES ROAD

St ANNES-ON-THE-SEA.

H. Bridge, Esq.
34. Warton Street,
LYTHAM.

5th July/21. 19...

To:-	One Ton Truck Comp. with Body.	250	- -
"	Painting Lettering.	8	- -
"	Making & Fitting Top Rail.	6 17	-
		£ 264 17	-

One gall. hi Vac A   98
2 Champion X Plugs   10

£ 265 16 8

W. T. AKED & CO. LTD.   No. 832
19 ST. ANNES-ON-THE-SEA

Mr H Bridges
34 Warton St Lytham

RECEIVED WITH THANKS
the sum of £ 265 16 8
Allowance
Discount   £265 16 8

Hanson

for W. T. AKED & CO. LTD.

INVOICE

Mr. Harold Bridges 34. Wharfe St
Lytham.

Bought of **MAYOR & SON, Ltd.**

8 WHARF STREET PRESTON.

Manufacturers of Waterproof Wagon, Stack and Cart Covers,
Saddlery, Ropes and Twines, Horse Clothing, &c.

July 2. 1921

18.0 Two green colour of
canvas 12'8 long 13' ... to ...
Harold Bridges
Carrier
34. Wharfe St
Lytham   4-12-0

18... 1¾" Oc. Manila cart rose   -5-6

Call   Nett. £ 4 17 6
                    £ 4. 15. 0

1921

Myself and my Model T, 1-ton Ford in 1921. A 'general carrier's load'.

My enquiries led me to the Derby Arms in Lord Street, Preston, where Harrison Bros. the Preston Leyland carriers, and Swann the Preston Kirkham carrier used the yard at the rear.

I fixed up with Mrs. Knowles, the landlady, to accept any messages or goods for me and I would call each Monday, Wednesday and Friday in the morning on my way to Blackburn and in the afternoon on my return journey to Lytham. The charge was to be five shillings per week paid monthly in arrears.

I asked Jack Winrow about Blackburn and he told me that the Blackburn carriers operated from three public houses near the market place, and that I should try Harry Garstang's Garage, Mincing Lane, Blackburn, which he knew had been used by carriers in the past. So never having been to Blackburn in my life, out came my bicycle and off I went to Blackburn. I found Harry Garstang and his son Robin and their staff very helpful and fixed up ideal arrangements for ten shillings per week paid every Friday.

While in Blackburn I delivered a lot of my leaflets to business houses and Harry Garstang put them up in the showroom windows. They were agents for Dodge Cars which had larger than normal road wheels and steering wheels; in fact, they were nicknamed Big Wheel Dodge. Little did I think or dream that between 1934 and 1960 I would buy scores of Dodge commercial vehicles, the first order for ten in one delivery from Kings Road Garage, St. Annes in 1934.

Due to the carrying capacity of the Ford being one ton with not much leeway for overload it was obvious I would not be able to accept any heavy traffic, and would have to concentrate on parcels traffic or at most consignments up to 5 cwt. To this end I obtained the Royal Mail parcel rates; these with the rail charges passenger and goods which I had, would enable me to formulate some kind of rate or charges scale.

While all this activity was under way Alice decided to leave Lucas' the confectioners and take a situation as housemaid, cook and nurse for a Mr. and Mrs. Almond, Eddington Road, Ansdell. Alice took the chance of a few weeks' holiday in between the two jobs, so was at home in Willenhall, Staffordshire when I actually started on 4th July 1921, American Independence Day.

Before leaving for her holiday Alice gave me the £130 she had saved towards our sometime marriage and I was to draw my £140 from my post office account to pay Akeds for the vehicle on 5th July 1921. Mayors had sent the lorry sheet on to Lytham by passenger train, so on Monday morning 4th July 1921 Harold Bridges, General Carrier, Lytham, set off for Preston and Blackburn with one parcel to deliver in Preston for which I had charged nine pence and £1 for working capital in my pocket. Little did I think or imagine in my wildest dreams and fancies what was to follow from this humble beginning. I delivered this one parcel near the covered market in Preston, called at the Derby Arms, Lord Street, Preston, my call depot, where I found four large parcels of Barrets Directories which were printed by Mathers, Lune Street, Preston, for delivery in Blackburn; so on to Blackburn. To my pleasant surprise there were several requests at Garstangs Garage for me to collect, one a paper bag merchant and another a tea and coffee merchant. In each case I was asked to call Monday, Wednesday, Friday; charges were agreed. The tea was 2s. 6d. per chest weighing around 100 lbs., and the parcels of paper bags 1s. 0d. per cwt to Preston.

I used my spare time in Blackburn to deliver my leaflets to any likely looking business premises. I was fortunate in that there was no other road service from Blackburn to the Fylde coast. My only competitor was the railway. I could easily beat the railway for delivery by goods train, and my charges were well below passenger train parcels.

I used to leave Blackburn about 3.00 p.m., make any deliveries I had to do in Preston of goods from Blackburn, then call at the Derby Arms in Lord Street, Preston, for any goods or messages which may have been left for me to call.

On this my first day I had a pleasant surprise as several packages had been left at the Derby Arms for me to deliver to St. Annes and Blackpool. Also there were several rolls of felt and parcels to deliver to Ashtons Nurseries, Mythop Road, Lytham; when I delivered these Mr. Ashton, who had several sons, was there and asked me a few questions about my intentions.

The outcome was that during the tomato season July/August they would hire me and my vehicle to deliver baskets of tomatoes to shops in Blackpool several mornings a week. The goods were loaded late evening and we were usually in Blackpool by 7.30 a.m. and the job finished by 10.00 a.m. This was a good start on my first day and what surprised me was the knock-on effect; two weeks after I started Ashtons tomato job, a local greengrocer hired me to go to Preston

The Model T. Ford fitted with replacement rear wheels. These were steel discs with solid rubber tyres.

wholesale market for his week's supply of apples, oranges, onions, etc. In Blackburn this knock-on effect was very noticeable; within two weeks of my collecting at Milton Hindles tea merchants, Water Street, two other tea merchants asked me to call every Monday, Wednesday and Friday. The same applied to paper merchants, paint and wallpaper merchants, wholesale drapers and many other merchants, wholesalers, small works and manufacturers.

The carrying capacity of my Ford 1-ton truck was officially 1 ton, and as always, generally speaking, you get what you pay for. There was no margin for overload but due to the early success of my efforts, in order to cope there had to be occasions when I had to overload 25% to 50%. The machine was not designed or built for this and naturally the overloading created problems, the first being the rear wheels, which had wooden spoke wheels and pneumatic tyres, not intended for overloading. I had recurring tyre trouble and the wooden spoke wheels soon showed signs of early collapse. This was a problem apparently fairly widespread with many Model T Ford 1-ton trucks now in the country and led to the Mackintosh Rubber Co., an associate or subsidiary of the Dunlop Rubber Co., to bring out replacement rear wheels; these were steel disc wheels with a solid rubber tyre which had a pyramid-shaped-hollow centre to give a cushion effect. I had these fitted in Preston and they were a good job.

Another problem was the ignition system on the Ford engine, of trembler coils which had to be very finely adjusted to produce a good spark. There were four of them and the contacts gave trouble, which in response to demand led to a firm in London buying ex-army or airforce six-cylinder engine magnetos converting them to four-cylinder operation and supplying them with bicycle chain drive and sprocket on the front of the crankshaft of the Ford engine.

All a bit 'Heath Robinson', but my word, it worked; no starting problem, no running on three cylinders instead of four, no trembler to adjust frequently and better fuel consumption. It naturally followed that due to the success of my activities I did not see very much of Alice except at weekends. On her evenings off in the week she came to Mother's to await me finishing work, and we often only had an hour or two together during the week.

The amount of traffic I was being asked to carry was steadily increasing and often entailed me having to go back to Preston in the evenings for goods which I could not bring on my way back from Blackburn.

Dad sometimes went with me on this evening journey and it was on one of these extra journeys Dad said, 'You should be getting a bigger machine. You want one to carry two tons'. I said, 'Yes, I know but where is the cash to come from? I am doing well. I am now on a sound profit-making basis, but I have only been in business four months, and not making money that fast I can afford to or be able to pay £500 for a larger lorry, which is the minimum I could expect to have to pay for a 35/40 cwt carrying capacity Vulcan lorry'.

However, something had to be done, new business was coming along all the time and it appeared certain that by January 1922 or before I would be unable to handle all the traffic being offered to me.

I talked this over with Alice and she was all for going ahead if it could possibly be done. So making enquiries from Williams Bros., Henry Street, Lytham, who were agents for Vulcan Motors, Crossens, Southport, I found that a Vulcan 30 cwt chassis and cab would be £500 delivered in Lytham. The bodywork, rear wings, painting and lettering and a new sheet would be around £150, total £650.

I had so far not had an account at a bank; any surplus cash after paying outgoings in cash I put into my post office savings account. Any cheques I received Dad cashed for me at his bank. After lots of talk with Alice and Dad, I decided to order the Vulcan lorry from Williams Bros. to be delivered to Richard Hall, body building and coach painter, North Clifton Street, Lytham.

Dad said he would lend me £250 for 12 months. I had about £250 in the post office. I expected to sell my Ford lorry at 6 months old for at least £150, so I should just about be able to get by. However, when Williams Bros. examined the Ford they said it would need such repairs, repainting, etc. that they could only allow me £130 for it, but if I could sell it for more that was O.K.

This led to further talks with Alice and Dad as my sponsors. I still, of course, owed Alice the £130 and would owe Dad £250. I knew I was operating at a profit, and provided I continued with my so far very good health and had no major repairs or unforeseen expense, I would just about be able to make it.

Then once again, my dear sweetheart Alice came to the rescue for my peace of mind. She was so convinced I could and would make it and had such faith and love for me she had written to her mother in Willenhall, Staffordshire, explained all the circumstances and her mother had sent her £50 to help out. Once again, what a gesture from ordinary, simple hard working folk; this is now 68 years ago (as I write) and it still brings a tear to my eyes.

Alice was very keen and interested in the whole project, as was I; it was our whole life and future together which we were planning. Quite rightly she expressed her own views and thoughts and one incident, at this stage, still recreates happy memories.

When Akeds were painting the Ford they suggested a very bright startling red and yellow lettering on the cab and tailboard. This was something I had not asked Alice's opinion on and when she saw the Ford the first time she said, 'What a HORRIBLE colour!'. I explained Akeds thought it would attract attention and it certainly did. From an advertising point of view it was right. Alice suggested darkish royal blue with white lettering. It was quite effective and little did we know that during the next 45 years hundreds of 'Bridges' vehicles would be in Alice Vale's royal blue and white lettering. I ordered the Vulcan chassis and cab, arranged for the body building and painting to be ready for the road first January 1922.

The Vulcan was a very solidly built vehicle, very heavy unladen for its weight carrying capacity. It had solid rubber tyres, twins at rear, oil side and tail lamps, no headlights, no side windows to cab, and a four cylinder side valve engine. It turned out to be a very reliable vehicle, and as it would carry two tons, it increased my load carrying capacity by one hundred per cent, at little extra running cost. Also the depreciation charge spread over a useful economical life of five years would be just about half the depreciation charge of the Model T Ford.

So in 1922, I withdrew £280 from my account at the post office and closed the account. Dad gave me a cheque for £250, Alice gave me the extra £50 in cash, I paid Williams Bros. for the Vulcan chassis and cab, less the £130 allowance for the Model T Ford. R. Halls account for the body building and painting, and Mayors account for the new lorry sheet would be payable by 15th February 1922, so I had made it.

I opened my first bank account at Midland Bank, Clifton Square, Lytham, in January 1922 and now felt I was in business. My new vehicle in its smart blue and white attracted quite a lot of favourable comment and new business; some were regular calls, some one or two days a week and others just occasional requests by post, or by messages left at home, 34 Warton Street, Lytham, or at my call points, the Derby Arms, Preston or Harry Garstang's Garage, Blackburn.

Many perhaps rather crude ways to get me to call at farms, poultry keepers, etc. on the main road between Lytham and Preston were used. Some would put a sack, or bucket on a gate post on the road side, others a board or slate marked

H.B. or BRIDGES TO CALL. In the towns I passed along the main streets at fairly regular times and the various works and warehouses where I did not call regularly had a board or card they would put at the front or in a prominent place marked 'Bridges to Call' or 'Blackpool Carrier to call'.

I did consider having a 'phone, but decided as I was out all day everyday and Mum and Dad had never used the 'phone it would not be worth the cost. Dad had a small board fixed at the front door. 'H. Bridges Carrier', which proved very effective.

It was really surprising how and where new business came from, and the somewhat strange jobs I was asked to do, one of which was collection of one or two new born or two or three day old calves from farms on the main road through Warton and Freckleton. The calf or calves were put one in a hessian sack, the sack tied round the calves' necks at the top of the sacks, with the calves' heads out at the top. These I took to the cattle market, Preston, on Wednesdays only, gave the farmer's name and address at the cattle market auctioneer's office and received a large adhesive label with a number on. I stuck the label on the calves' rumps and turned them loose in the calf pen to be sold by auction later in the day. On my return journey I gave the farmer each calf's number. I received 2s. 6d. per calf. This led to my being asked to take Lancashire farm made cheeses from the several farms between Lytham and Preston to the wholesale cheese merchants in Preston. The first of these was Robert Blacoe, of Warton Hall Farm where I had worked for two years in 1914-1916, and two other farms soon followed when they heard of my service. I charged sixpence per cheese, so if I took forty cheeses, as I often did, I had received a pound before I got to Preston. The alternative was that the farmer loaded the cheese on a flat horse drawn lorry the night before and set off to Preston early next day. It was roughly twelve miles each way so with unloading, feeding and watering the horse, perhaps one or two calls shopping it was a full day's work.

This also had a useful knock-on effect. The cheese warehouse often used to give me a few cheeses to deliver to grocers in Blackburn, Lytham or Blackpool, or the farmer might ask me to bring two cwt cob lime, or bags of cement, wire netting or barb wire on my return, all revenue producing, and cash business.

The Vulcan lorry proved a good advert in its royal blue and white livery, was easy to drive, economical to run and carried around twice as much as the Model T Ford.

Apart from the traffic received from warehouses, manufacturers, wholesalers, etc. I now began to have an increasing number of requests to collect and deliver odd pieces of furniture from private houses. These odd jobs paid well and were part of the service I was offering to the public, but did sometimes create problems, when I had no knowledge at all about furniture removing. I had I think lots of common sense and soon got the hang of it.

Dad would have a day with me on occasions, and quite enjoyed it and at the same time came in very handy as help. My brother Reuben was three years younger than me and worked as a tram conductor on the electric trams which ran between Lytham and Blackpool. On his days off he very often came with me and during 1922 I taught him to drive the Vulcan lorry, which was to prove useful sooner than I thought. The business was now going so well that by June I had repaid Dad's £250 loan and had money in the bank, so that with the future now looking more secure Alice and I became engaged to be married hopefully within two years. Mother and Dad and all the family were very pleased.

In the latter part of 1922 it became obvious that I would soon not be able to handle all the traffic being offered to me with one vehicle, and that the acquisition of another vehicle would have to be seriously considered.

I talked this over with Mother and Dad and Alice, of course, and all agreed it was the right step to take, as it would increase my capacity by over 100 per cent, and I ordered a 40/50 cwt Vulcan lorry from Williams Bros., Henry Street, Lytham, to be delivered 1st January 1923, cost £650. The bodywork and painting to be done by R. Hall, North Clifton Street, Lytham, in Alice's royal blue and white. Towards the end of 1922 my younger brother Reuben, whom I had taught to drive, gave up his job as tram conductor and became my first employee, and for the remainder of 1922 came with me every day, as his training period.

I was to drive the new larger vehicle and Reuben the smaller one, now approaching one year old; he had to get to know the 'ropes', his way round Blackburn, Preston, and Blackpool, how much to charge for cash jobs, etc. Reuben was very quick to learn and we got on well together. Dad thought it was ironic that I left school when I was thirteen to earn ten shillings a week so that Reuben who had won a scholarship could go to Kirkham Grammar School till he was sixteen and now he was working for me, as my first employee.

So the remainder of 1922 soon passed, and 1923 looked very promising. We arranged the journeys and work so that we had one vehicle in Blackburn and Preston every day instead of just Monday, Wednesday and Friday, and one vehicle in St. Annes and Blackpool every day, instead of just Tuesday, Thursday and Saturday. My only competitor in Lytham, whom I have mentioned earlier as having a drink problem, was so neglecting his work that it fell into my hands, more or less automatically. As I have mentioned earlier the knock-on effect in many ways was remarkable. He had one job collecting fairly regularly from Preston cattle market abattoirs several sides of fresh killed beef, for delivery in Lytham which would normally be about an hour or at most two hours after collection.

His calling at two of the public houses on his journey made the delivery so late he lost the job to me, and right away I was asked by the butchers concerned if I would bring their block ice from Blackpool Cold Store three days a week, for their cold rooms. There were no electric refrigerators in butchers, fishmongers and ice-cream makers in those days, they all depended on block ice and freezing salt to provide some degree of cold room facility.

In a very short time we were delivering ice and freezing salt to all the butchers, fishmongers, ice cream makers and the big hotels in Lytham three days a week in winter and six days a week in summer. In the height of the summer we ran a special vehicle every morning on the ice run from Blackpool to Lytham, and often delivered two tons of block ice before 9.00 a.m.

Again this led to taking scales to be repaired at Blackpool or Preston from butchers and fishmongers which led to the scale repairers asking us to collect coal merchants scales for repair and testing and return to the coal merchants. The coal merchants in turn sent coal bags to be repaired at Preston or Blackburn and when they bought new coal bags we were asked to collect them from the makers, which put us in touch with the makers to deliver new sacks to other coal merchants, corn and provender merchants, etc. These were all hessian sacks as there were no paper sacks or bags, even cement was in 2 cwt hessian bags; 2s. 6d. charge on the returnable bag. Another rather unusual job was to collect from St. Annes Gas Works 10 or 12 gas meters each week to deliver to Blackburn Gas Works for repairs and testing, and take back the meters from the week before. They were very awkward to pack safely in the load and easily damaged, so I had two crates made about six feet long and one and a half feet square. The two crates each held six meters safely and we could load any other goods on them.

The most awkward items were bicycles, perambulators, invalid chairs, etc., which were so bulky and easily damaged and nothing could be packed on them; however they were not very frequent and often created an opening or a recommendation for normal traffic.

On the other hand we had traffic which did not go on the lorry flat at all. This consisted of flat or round iron for blacksmiths; the bars or bundles were usually about 15/18 feet long and, of course, quite heavy for their bulk. The Vulcan lorry's chassis frame was quite flat and the bodies fitted I had made so there was a space about three feet wide and nine inches deep. This with the length of the body enabled us to carry up to 20 cwt of iron bars underneath the body. This space could also be used for bundles of electrical conduit which was in wide use, and also for the odd ladder or timber.

The Vulcan body cabs were built with a box on the top of the cab about 12 inches deep, and four sides open top, the front of the box acted as the name board and the box was used to hold large bulky items, like rolls of netting, chestnut paling, bundles of buckets, etc. which did not need protection from the weather.

The constant endeavour was to provide a reliable service to accept and

deliver within 24 hours, any traffic which was offered and which we were capable of handling ourselves. My main problem during all this time was my speech impediment, which was still as bad as ever and was an awful handicap. However, I always hoped somehow or someone would find a solution or a cure, and I was all the time very much aware of the patience and sympathy I received from the people I had to talk to. During 1923 the steady increase in the amount of traffic we were handling continued. One new development was that the local carriers who came into Blackburn daily from nearby towns began to bring traffic from their home towns for delivery to the Fylde coast. These carriers were mainly old established family businesses which had operated for many years with horse-drawn vehicles, in fact, in 1923 Coleman, the Darwen to Blackburn carrier, still used a horse-drawn lorry, as did also the carrier from Hurst Green, Langho.

Others who had changed to small motor vehicles, mainly Fords, came from Accrington, Burnley, Nelson, Colne, Whalley, Clitheroe, Great Harwood; from these places to the Fylde coast the only alternative was rail, and the joint service could deliver within 24 hours of collection at a joint charge below rail. It was during the latter part of 1923 many of my own regular customers began enquiring and offering support for my services to be extended to include

Bert Bradley, or 'Old Bert', 1925. Bert worked for me for over forty years and was one of the best employees I ever had.

Bispham, Cleveleys, Fleetwood, Poulton-le-Fylde and districts adjacent in the Fylde, and, in fact, some customers did give me traffic for Fleetwood, which I passed to a carrier who operated between Blackpool and Fleetwood daily with a small 10 cwt Ford van, at such time that we could by our joint Service deliver within 24 hours of collection. All this activity meant that we were now fully employed six days a week and that again the purchase of another vehicle had to be considered to keep up with the demand. Once again I talked the matter over with Alice, Dad and Reuben, and it was decided that a 35 cwt vehicle would be ideal for the extended service to the Fylde coast, and to help out generally. The vehicle decided on was a 35 cwt Bean lorry built by Harper Bean Dudley; this was a more modern machine than the Vulcan with pneumatic tyres, later converted to Macintosh N.A.P. tyres all round, all round electric lighting and cost £700.

It came into service early in 1924, was paid for in cash; late in 1923 when I had decided to acquire another vehicle I engaged a driver a little older than me. I had known him since before we both went into H.M. Forces in 1918. He had been driving for a local furniture removal firm, T. Towler, Bath Street, Lytham, so knew quite a bit about furniture packing and very soon learned how to handle and deal with our type of traffic.

Apart from one short break of about one year, which I will explain later, he worked for me over forty years; in the later years everyone called him Old Bert. His name was Bert Bradley, and was one of the best employees I ever had.

So on to 1924. The normal working week was 7.30 a.m. to 6.30 p.m. Monday to Friday, and on Saturdays we mostly had finished by 4.30 p.m. Sunday mornings and sometimes all day Sunday, was maintenance time, greasing, cleaning, changing oil, now and then a broken spring to change, and at least every 10 weeks valves to grind in on the four-cylinder side valve engines, which meant that one Sunday each month was spent all day on engine maintenance.

Any book-keeping I had to do at night, many times in the small hours. This was another side of being in business I did not know anything about; with no training schemes, free state hand outs and the like, it all had to be done the hard way. The periodicals *Motor Transport* and the *Commercial Motor* did at times carry articles on book-keeping, costing and so forth, so I got by and either by luck or good management had no bad debts or bad payers.

The first week in July Alice and I decided we would have our wedding in September at St. Annes Church, Willenhall. It was to be a quiet family ceremony; Alice hated fuss of any kind and so did I. I began to wonder how with my speech impediment I would make the marriage responses in church, not that there was much time to worry, as the business continued to grow at a steady rate, and for me it was mostly a 12 to 14 hour day, six days a week. This did not worry me at all. I was fit, strong and willing and was on my way to building up a business which I was now certain, given a normal state of affairs, would continue to develop and prosper. Towards mid 1924 for about eight weeks I had frequently to hire a vehicle to help out on very busy days, usually from Towlers, Bath Street, Lytham or Alan Whittle, Freckleton, both of whom had Model T Fords similar to my first vehicle. One new line of seasonal traffic in 1924 was the collection and delivery of holiday luggage sent in advance to the Fylde coast holiday resorts. All the Lancashire towns had their holiday weeks in the summer and usually a shorter one in the autumn.

The luggage was normally one average size suitcase per person and the charge was 2s. 6d. The follow on from this was the collection of luggage from boarding schools and Lark Hill Convent, Preston at the end of term, for delivery to the students' homes, and return to school after holidays.

Having decided on our wedding date Alice and I were looking out for a place to live, not with much success – we could not afford to buy a house even on a mortgage and very rarely was there vacant property to rent. It was a problem. Alice and I were fully aware of this when we decided on a September 1924 wedding, so we did not make definite fixed arrangements.

There was no room at 34 Warton Street where I lived with Mother and Dad, Reuben, Frank my youngest brother and Rose my only sister. However, our luck was in – next door at number 36 Warton Street lived an elderly spinster lady, Miss Mottram, who had been our neighbour for many years and, of course, knew Alice and me very well, and in fact, all the family. Miss Mottram used to be away weeks and sometimes months at a time and when she heard of our problem from Mother she said right away, 'They can have two rooms at 36 and look after the house when I am away.' This was fine; Alice was delighted. There was a telephone installed which we could use and just pay for the calls we made.

The house was not fully furnished so Miss Mottram re-arranged her furniture and left some main items in our rooms. We had a nice bedroom, sitting room, use of the kitchen and wash house, etc. There was an old greenhouse in the small back garden and in 1925 I grew my first tomatoes, the first of 64 years of growing tomatoes.

Alice gave her notice to leave Almonds in August to have her holiday before the wedding and Mrs. Almond very kindly told Alice that after the wedding if she had any spare days she would be glad to have Alice to help as before. Alice was very pleased about this, as she was very fond of the Almonds and their little daughter, Doreen, and also it would enable her to contribute to the housekeeping costs. Alice had taken out a driving licence in June 1923 and had the occasional driving lesson from me on one of the Vulcan lorries, when she had a day off and had the day with me. She was keen to learn to drive and also in the business as a whole, rightly so, as she had a half share in it from the start and without her help I do not see how I could have started.

Came 16th September 1924, we had an early morning wedding, 10.00 a.m. It was a very quiet ceremony, just Alice's two sisters and brother and a few personal friends. We had three days' holiday after the wedding and then it was back to Lytham and work.

One notable account opened in the latter part of 1924 was with Lytham Shipbuilding & Engineering Co. Ltd., Dock Road, Lytham, who were engaged in the building of side paddle and stern paddle steamers for use on rivers in South Africa. After partial assembly, quite a lot of the steelwork was taken apart and went to Liverpool to be galvanized, then brought back and rebuilt, painted and when fitted with boilers, engines, etc. went out to Africa where they operated on the big rivers. The reason for the galvanizing was that there were not any dry docks on the African rivers, so I suppose once in the water they were there for life. The work we did for the Shipyard was taking wooden patterns from the pattern shop to Dewhurst Iron Foundry in Preston and bringing back iron castings and returning the patterns. It was a steady regular job, varying from 2 cwt to 1 ton and three times a week.

We also took patterns and returned brass and phosphor bronze castings from Friedenthals in Preston, who also made ships' propellers. I have little doubt we got this work because my brother Reuben, who drove the 1922 Vulcan, was keeping company with a young lady who was a daughter of the main store-keeper and, of course, for the Shipyard it was much more economical than sending their own 4-ton Napier motor lorry to Preston most days in the week. The shipyard also had a Foden steam waggon and trailer used mainly for carting coal from Lytham Goods Station to the Shipyard and also for taking the steelwork to and from Liverpool.

1925 was a year of slow steady progress; the possibilities of road transport were now becoming apparent and two new operators each with one vehicle started services between Preston and Blackpool. Naturally they took some traffic from us from Preston to Blackpool, one of their advantages being that they were based in Blackpool, so if they collected in Preston, say, from 11.00 a.m. to 2.00 p.m. they could if required deliver the same day. One of them gave up after six months. Alice and I were very comfortable and happy, and we settled down to a very busy married life. We saw very little of our landlady, Miss Mottram, who was away frequently for long periods.

I was busy on the job six days a week and vehicle maintenance on Sunday mornings. Alice usually came with me on the lorry two days, went to Mrs. Almond's two days and spent two looking after No. 36 and also did a good job with the book-keeping and accounts which as the business grew demanded more time.

We were still using the part of the Parkstone Films Co.'s section of the wartime seaplane hangars as a garage for the three vehicles, and one problem we felt might arise was that as the business looked set for steady expansion, with the likely, almost certain, addition of extra vehicles in 1927 and 1928, the need for more garage or depot room would become urgent. There certainly were not any premises in Lytham available, or likely to be so far as we could see, and this did cause Alice and me some concern.

It was by no means certain that our use of Parkstone Film Co. space would continue indefinitely. The flying men had taken extra space, and a badminton club had been formed, again taking quite a large area for playing area, toilets, changing rooms, etc. We had no written agreement, lease or tenancy, so could quite easily get notice at any time. We also had to be planning for the next vehicles, so had plenty to think and talk about. We were in complete agreement that come what may we must make every effort to cope with the expansion in the business. Another more personal matter on which we agreed before we were married was that we would not start a family of our own for at least two years, and when numbers were mentioned Alice said, 'Two to fight, one to separate them, and then we shall see how many drivers we want!'

So it came about that on 11th May 1926, my 26th birthday, Alice informed me she had been to see Dr. Wagner, whose practice and home were quite near where Alice worked when at Lucas' the confectioners in Church Road. The Wagner family were often served by Alice in the shop, they were quite friendly. The doctor's opinion was that Alice would be expecting a baby towards the end of October. We were both very happy with the news. Mother and Dad were delighted in anticipation of their first grandchild. Mother said right away it will be a boy, why she was so certain I don't know; Mother had ten children and only four were left in 1926, such is life.

The summer of 1926 kept us very busy and Alice gradually reduced the number of days with me on the lorry and the days she went to Mrs. Almond's, as October approached. Mother and Alice arranged for Nurse Wolfe, an experienced midwife, to attend Alice and, of course, Dr. Charles Wagner, whose father was a German. Nurse Wolfe had been mother's midwife with most of her children, and had actually brought me into the world 26 years before. Mother had not been to hospital or nursing home with any of her childbirths and Alice said she did not intend to if she could help it and so it was to be with the six children she bore between 1926 and 1938. They were all born at home, no pre-natal or post-natal examinations other than the family doctor, Dr. Wagner.

So it came 2nd November 1926, our first son was born about 9.00 a.m., a fine boy. Alice had the name ready – Charles Harold, born at 36 Warton Street, Lytham, and everything O.K. and perfectly normal in every way. All concerned were very pleased and Miss Mottram in particular. Mother being next door at No. 34 was able to help Alice, if any problems arose, so we were very fortunate, and fully appreciated our good fortune.

Chapter Five

Business Expansion

Early in 1927 it was indicated to me by Parkstone Film Co. that by the summer it was expected changes might take place in the ownership of the aerodrome site and it would be advisable to be seeking alternative accommodation. But where? There was certainly no vacant premises which would suit our purpose, particularly in view of the anticipated expansion.

Then, once again out of nowhere our luck was in. There was in Victoria Street, Lytham, a very old established furniture removal and storage business named Lawsons. They had been in the furniture removal business longer than I could remember. I know they moved Mother and Dad when they moved from Warton Hall Keepers Cottage to Lytham Hall gamekeeper's house in Lytham Hall Park, now Islay Road. They also moved them from Lytham Hall Park to Clifton with Salwick; these movements would be about 1908 and 1912 and again in 1916 they moved them from Clifton with Salwick to 34 Warton Street, Lytham, when the Clifton Estate at Clifton and Salwick was sold and Dad retired as gamekeeper. These movements were all done by horse-drawn vehicles which were proper vans for furniture removal with two horses. It appeared Lawsons had sold out or merged with Shaws Depositories who were in exactly the same business. Shaws had large storage premises in St. Annes and Blackpool, and the Lytham property was for sale, as surplus to the joint requirements. The property for sale consisted of two separate buildings in Victoria Street; one was a very well-built brick building large enough to accommodate five vehicles like ours with private open air parking for two more. This building was ideal for our purpose. We could not have wished at the time for anything better. It was very high inside as Lawsons used demount-able van bodies at times and could hoist these off and on inside the building. The doors were in one end very high and wide, just the job, so how much and how was it to be paid for?

The other building was a three-storey storage warehouse, centrally heated all through by a coke fired boiler. One section of the ground floor was similar in size and height to the other building and there was an ancient hand operated lift to the two upper floors. The two buildings were in a short side street cul-de-sac off Victoria Street with room for three vehicles to park alongside the storage building. The only other properties in the side street were a very small engineering workshop run by a retired engineer from Lytham Shipyard named Swift and a large little used open builders yard.

It did not take Alice and I very long to decide we must try to buy or better still rent the garage building, as ideal for our purpose. When I made enquiries to this end I was informed that lots of people had shown great interest in the garage building, but no one was the least bit interested in the big three-storey building which while soundly built was very much older.

Several offers had, in fact, been made for the garage building, and I rather gathered that all the interested possible purchasers and, in fact, Lawsons themselves thought a three-storey building like that, the only one in Lytham, would be a white elephant. As there was so much interest in the garage and none in the white elephant, they had decided not to sell the properties separately. They did not want to be left with an empty three-storey building, and from their point of view this made sense. For Alice and I this created a problem, the like of which we had never anticipated. It was, therefore, after very much debate we decided to go ahead and negotiate for the two properties. Perhaps the Bridges' luck would hold. We could have a go anyway. Faint heart never won fair lady! Nothing ventured nothing win! To this end we eventually agreed a price for the two properties. If I remember rightly it was in the £35,000 region. We appeared to be the only possible purchasers for the two properties so Lawsons were prepared to wait while we tried to raise finances.

While this was going on we were, of course, on the look out for a house to rent or buy. We obviously did not want to stay in rooms with Miss Mottram longer than was necessary. Again our luck was in when 137 Warton Street, Lytham came on the market for sale with vacant possession. It was a soundly built house with four bedrooms, front and back sitting rooms, kitchen, etc., just the job. It was the end house in a row of three and next door was Lytham Cottage Hospital, at the other end of the row was a corner confectioners and bakers shop. The position was ideal on the main street and only five minutes walk to the premises in Victoria Street which we hoped to buy. Making enquiries of my friends and customers in Lytham I was advised to see J. Robson Byers who practised as a solicitor in Lytham from after the war ended.

It was on such occasions as this when my speech impediment was troublesome, but I always found a lot of sympathy and understanding, patience and some, what was intended to be, helpful advice.

In due course Mr. Byers informed us he could arrange all the finances for the house and Lawsons's properties on a long mortgage with the Skipton Building Society. The terms appeared quite reasonable and within our capacity to meet and we told him to go ahead with all the legal requirements – buy the house and the properties and arrange for completion as soon as possible. We moved into 137 Warton Street in April 1927 and took possession of the Lawson's properties in May 1927. We named the garage Victoria Garage and the warehouse building Victoria Buildings. We found out later that agents for the Skipton Building Society were J. Entwistle & Co., Auctioneers and Estate Agents, Kings Road, Ansdell, and that, in fact, Alice had met Mr. Entwistle very often as he had married Mr. Almond's sister, and with his wife often visited the Almonds in Eddington Road when Alice worked for Mrs. Almond.

J. Entwistle & Co. had not long before built a new Auction Room and Estate Offices in Kings Road, Ansdell, where we sometimes delivered and collected odd pieces of furniture so I too had actually met Mr. Entwistle in the course of business. Perhaps these personal contacts smoothed the way a little for Mr. Byers in his negotiations on our behalf for the mortgages.

We soon settled into 137 Warton Street, had the telephone fixed and a sign on the front of the house near the front door. Alice now gave up coming with me, no longer next door to Mother's, a growing son to care for and more book-keeping to do.

The amount of traffic and new customers were still steadily increasing and to cope we had to have extra vehicles. Also the first Vulcan was now five years old and the second was four years. Both had been very reliable, economical and done really good service, with in recent years a considerable amount of overloading. We realised that we would have to consider replacing them, or having major repairs and overhauls to maintain their reliability. As a temporary measure we bought a second hand Ford 30 cwt van from Loxhams, Preston for £150, and a big second-hand Talbot car for £80 from Garstang's Garage, Blackburn. We cut the back of the car body off just behind the front seats and bought a small flat lorry body for £2 from a bakery at St. Annes and we had a somewhat Heath Robinson looking vehicle which would carry one ton.

We then ordered three 35 cwt Bean lorries from Williams Bros. Lytham, and they took the two Vulcans in part exchange.

We were now operating six vehicles, young local drivers had been employed, and my time was now less employed in actual day to day driving. Alice did a lot of the book-keeping and accounts, and all seemed to be going very well, and so we passed into 1928.

The type of operation in which we were mainly engaged was the collection and delivery of small consignments mainly under 4 cwt, the average weight of each consignment was just over 1 cwt. The operation was that each vehicle delivered every day on a particular route covering one or more towns and villages *en route*; deliveries were usually completed around 2.00 p.m. and the vehicle then collected goods on the return journey for delivery to any place in the whole of the area we covered, which was gradually being extended.

Some collections were regular every day, some on certain arranged days and others on request by 'phone or mail. This entailed every vehicle being unloaded on its return to depot and the goods being sorted out into loads for each separate vehicle and the particular area it covered. This became increasingly difficult as all the goods collected had to be unloaded and sorted on the garage floor and then loaded on to the delivery vehicle ready for next day. The only solution was a loading deck or platform, about lorry floor height. The garage was about 40 feet wide and if we built a loading deck across the far end we could load, sort and reload the vehicles in one quarter the time and effort, and deal with three vehicles at the loading deck at one time. This would reduce the inside garage room to two vehicles, the others would have to park outside in the side street even if loaded. This was debated at great length by Alice and I and the longest serving drivers, my brother Reuben and 'Old Bert'.

The question arose what about the future if the business continued to expand as it had so far; more loading deck room would be required.

The garage building was about 60 feet long; along one side was a very little used builders yard, the tenant of which was due to retire. He had been in business on his own account for many years, and both Dad and I knew him well. His name was Johnson, and I thought if I could rent the yard, we could make three openings in the side of the garage, two for two vehicles and one for one vehicle with sliding doors; five vehicles could unload and load at the same time and we could also unload and load two vehicles at the front door of the garage, seven vehicles in all at one go, so at a pinch fourteen vehicles could be dealt with on two shifts. All this, of course, only if the loading deck covered the whole of the garage floor.

After much debate we decided this was the right thing to do. I arranged an annual tenancy of the builders yard, had the yard cleared and tidied up, and some hardcore put down where needed. We had the builders open up the three doorways for five vehicles in the side of the building and build the brickwork walls to support the wooden loading deck, which was built by Eli Berry, a local joiner and undertaker.

When completed this was a very big improvement on the past arrangements. So far when each vehicle returned to the depot the driver unloaded his own vehicle and sorted the goods into the delivery areas, and each driver loaded his own vehicle next morning. During the evening I made out the delivery sheets for each vehicle for next day ready for the drivers to load the goods in the right order for delivery. This usually took me till towards 10.00 p.m. On many nights Alice helped. As time passed and the traffic handled steadily increased it became obvious some relief would be required for the depot work. One of our drivers whom we thought was suitable was approached and willingly took on the job of unloading the vehicles each night, sorting the goods into the delivery areas, and making out all the delivery sheets, so the depot was now operating 24 hours a day, Monday to Saturday.

Soon after we had got organised on a 24 hour basis new developments arose which made further demands on our services. We began to receive goods brought into the depot in the daytime for delivery next day. An instance would be a firm from Manchester, Liverpool or East Lancashire delivering to the Fylde Coast would perhaps have several deliveries for Lancaster or Morecambe which entailed over fifty miles journey. It was far more economical for them to pay our charges for delivery next day and save their time and mileage, on a few deliveries. Another development was we began to receive traffic at the depot in the same way from other operators, on a regular daily basis.

Blackburn Parcels Express Ltd., based in Blackburn, operated services to Manchester, Bolton, Wigan and the whole of East Lancashire, and parts of the Rossendale Valley. They did not operate any service nearer the Fylde Coast than Preston, so were not really serious competitors, at the time.

They were apparently having numerous requests, particularly from Manchester for delivery to the Fylde Coast and Lancaster and Morecambe. They did not wish to deliver direct and suggested they would send a van each day Tuesday to Saturday about 7.00 a.m. so that we could deliver the same day the goods they had received the day before. Rates were agreed and before the arrangements had been operating very long they were delivering to us Monday to Saturday between two and three tons of traffic each day. I have mentioned earlier the knock-on effect when a new customer or type of business started to use our services; their competitors sought to join in on the use of what was evidently better service by us. Blackburn Parcels Express had only one real competitor between Manchester, Blackburn and East Lancashire. This was a firm called Same Day Delivery Ltd. Based in Burnley they were an associate company of W. V. Greenwood Ltd., based in Burnley who operated also in West Yorkshire. They in turn were a subsidiary of Bouts-Tillotson Transport who operated services from London to Burnley and many other Northern towns.

We were approached by Greenwoods to accept traffic for Lancaster and Morecambe and occasionally Fleetwood, Cleveleys and Poulton. They operated a service to the Fylde Coast almost wholly traffic brought to them by Bouts-Tillotson from London so all got fixed up. Greenwood's van came in every day in the course of his journey to the Fylde Coast, usually about noon and left us goods collected in London the day before. We delivered next day, so it was a 48 hours service. It was all very profitable traffic to us, no collection costs, monthly settlement and the offer if we wished to collect traffic to hand to them.

81

Alice and I did have some doubts about the likely long term effect of accepting this traffic on a big scale from other operators. The doubt was, what if they were just using us to build up a connection for the extension of their own services? However, we decided to risk it to maintain our requirement for an increasing cash flow, in view of current commitments.

While all this activity was taking place on the business side, on the private side of life changes were taking place. Alice's younger sister, Freda, now 18, came to work as housemaid for Dr. Wagner and Mrs. Wagner in Church Road, Lytham. Alice's Mother and Dad were on their own in Willenhall and not in such very good health so they came to live with us at 137 Warton Street. Since moving into 137 we had electricity installed throughout, refurbished the bathroom and decorated all inside and out.

I had plans in mind for a greenhouse and coalhouse in the back yard and to rent a rather derelict area of land immediately behind the house for a kitchen garden as a hobby. Kitchen gardening is one of the hobbies with an end product. My only other hobby at this time was motor cycling. I bought my first motor cycle (cost £27 10s. 0d.) at Cunningham's Garage, Lea Gate, Nr. Preston. It was a brand new 250 cc New Imperial and on the petrol tank in gold letters was printed, 'This machine is capable of a speed of 60 m.p.h.' Alice and I had a lot of fun on the bike. Alice rode pillion. We went to Scarborough and back one Sunday with two other motor cyclist friends and pillion riders.

The amount of traffic being brought to us to deliver continued to grow, and it did at times cause bottle necks in our normal operations. While the goods we had to deliver were brought in by our own vehicles, the same vehicles could handle that same traffic next day, but when goods brought in to us exceeded our spare capacity we had to have the means to deliver traffic we had not collected.

We had to have extra vehicles. We could not afford new and by again a stroke of good luck, we were able to buy back from Williams Bros. the two Vulcans they had taken in part exchange for the three Beans. The Vulcans had been completely overhauled by Williams Bros. and we had been the only previous owner, so we had our two faithful old workers back, and 1929 to look forward to.

The first worry in early 1929 was a letter from the Inland Revenue asking for an income return. While I was employed before July 1921 I or my various employers had to send an income return in each year, no PAYE then. Due to my periods of unemployment in 1920/21 I had little or no tax to pay on my wages. From 1921 I had not been asked for or sent in an income return, and had, in fact, not had any audited or other accountant-prepared accounts.

I asked J. R. Byers, the solicitor, what I should do. He advised me to see a William Latham who had started a practice as Chartered Accountant in Park Street, Lytham. He was the son of a coal merchant, had been in H.M. Forces during the war and was about my age. I explained the position to him and he said when we bought 137 Warton Street and the garage and warehouse the papers would go to the Tax Office for stamp duty to be assessed and that would be how they got track of my business. I explained I had not kept any proper formal books which could be audited, but Alice and I knew and could account for the starting capital. All the money we had received had been paid into the bank and all expenses including petty cash drawn from the bank. We had, of course, kept all receipts for payments and had copies of all accounts sent out. Mr. Latham saw the Inland Revenue, explained the whole position and it was agreed that accounts for the whole seven year period should be prepared and submitted to bring us up-to-date. In the event, we had some tax to pay, and we appointed W. Latham & Co. as our accountants, following which they acted for us for the next 45 years.

Lathams also set up a simple book-keeping system for us to follow in the future and we arranged to have an audit at six month intervals with the year ending 5th April. While all this was going on we were expecting an addition to the family and on 25th May 1929 Alice gave birth to a lovely baby girl. Alice chose the name Alwyn Joyce for our daughter. Dr. Wagner and Nurse Wolfe attended and everything was O.K. Mother and Dad were very pleased, and me. Having Alice's parents living with us was a great help; with the children, the telephone, people calling at the house, etc. Alice was kept very busy. Even so she managed and would insist on helping any way she could, mainly now with the book-keeping. It became obvious that before long we would have to engage someone permanently to do the office work and the obvious place for this to be would be at the garage or depot as we now preferred to call it.

Obviously they would need an office to work in and keep all the paperwork etc. But where? I have mentioned earlier that the garage building was very high inside and this caused me to put my thinking cap on! And I had the idea of putting in another floor on which we could build an office and also have some storage space. This is where my work in the building trade came in. I found that by fixing two heavy girders across the garage we would have just enough convenient headroom for both floors. We fixed the girders ourselves one Sunday morning. I had previously made preparation to receive the two girder ends in the side walls and Hey Presto, we were ready for the floor.

We engaged Eli Berry, the local joiner to lay the new floor and build the office, which was in one corner with separate stairs. While the floor was being laid Mr. Berry asked what we were going to use the floor for, as he was looking for a workshop and would rent all or part of the new floor. We agreed to rent him two thirds of the new floor and we kept a third for storage and our office. This had not been completed very long when a customer, Crosfields of Warrington, asked if we would collect cooking fat from them in two ton lots, bring it into our store and deliver to their customers, mainly fish and chip shops, when they sent us orders. The idea was to speed up the delivery time and in some cases to enable the customers to collect from us.

Rates for storage and handling were agreed and with the collection charge from Warrington, storage and delivery charges to customers from our store it was good business, and the new floor with Mr. Berry's rent was already paying its way. This was followed by other similar collection storage and delivery arrangements. As 1930 came in we were again requiring extra vehicles, which had to be carefully chosen second hand of various makes. We did buy one Chevrolet converted to a six wheeler new from the agents in South Shore. It was a 4 tonner and did very well.

By now we had to make arrangements for regular maintenance of what was becoming a very mixed fleet of makes and sizes which was far from ideal. A young motor mechanic I knew had started a motor repair and maintenance business in Pleasant Street, Lytham, behind the Ship Hotel, Ernest Tomlinson, and we made arrangements with him for greasing and general maintenance of the vehicles at regular intervals.

My brother, Reuben, who came to work for me in 1923 was now married, and I am sure his wife was jealous of the progress Alice and I were making and persuaded Reuben to start on his own operating a service from Blackburn to Preston and Southport. We did not cover Southport in our area, and I told Reuben I did not think he could generate enough traffic in Blackburn to sustain a service to Southport. They went to live in Blackburn. After a few months he came to see me. He was not making any progress, was considering giving up, and wondered if I would find him a job. I suggested he should have another go but from Liverpool to the Fylde Coast. I was sure there was plenty of scope for a service similar to ours. He had one vehicle, a 2 tonner. He moved to Liverpool and it was an instant success. By 1934/5 he was operating three vehicles and my youngest brother, Frank, was working for him. The vehicles had all been acquired on hire purchase from Williams Bros., Lytham. The largest was a five ton Luton body Vulcan, a 4 ton W.D. type Thornycroft and a Morris Commercial 3 ton van.

Unfortunately, the marital side of Reuben's affairs did not go so well. Reuben got into extreme financial difficulties and came to me for help and advice. Williams Bros. were threatening to re-possess the vehicles at the end of the week, and there was nothing Reuben could do to stop them. I talked the whole matter over with Alice and Reuben and the outcome was we took the whole business over, accepted liability for all Reuben's debts and found him a job as driver on the big Vulcan van. The cost to us just about covered the value of the business as it stood then as there were money lender loans, trade debts etc., as well as the arrears of hire purchase payments.

While Reuben was in Liverpool, Bert Bradley, our second employee, decided he would have a go on his own, gave me a week's notice and started doing local work and occasional journeys with a 30 cwt lorry. Bert was one of the best employees anyone could wish to have working for an employer. He was happy and quite satisfied. I feel again, it was jealousy on the part of his wife which pushed Bert into it. I felt certain Bert would never make it and when he was leaving I said to him, 'No ill feelings, Bert. You have a go. I'll give you six months to try and don't be afraid to come and ask for your job back'. In five months he was back and worked for me for the following 31 years.

March 29th, 1931 another birthday, another daughter, Nancy this time. Dr. Wagner and Nurse Wolfe in attendance and everything O.K. at 137 Warton Street. Three in the family now, so quite a houseful, with Alice's mother and dad, seven in all. We had by now been fortunate to secure the services of a retired Regimental Sergeant Major Noble as book-keeper full-time which was a great relief to Alice and me, and he did a great job well. During all this time the three-storey warehouse bought in 1927 was empty except for part of the ground floor which we used for storage and garage for four vehicles.

We had a customer in St. Annes, Fylde Printers Ltd., and about once a month I called to collect bales of waste paper from the printing works which went to Blackburn for recycling at Blackburn Corrugated Paper Ltd. Next door was a small shoe and slipper works, H. Worswick Ltd. I was loading the bales of waste paper one day when Mr. Worswick asked me if we had a small vehicle which could take a big electric motor to Manchester, wait for it to be repaired and bring it back the same day. I said, 'Yes, certainly'. I took the motor next day, brought it back and after unloading Mr. Worswick said, 'Come in the office and have a cup of tea and I will pay you'.

It was a pouring wet day and while we were having the cup of tea the works foreman came in and said, 'Sorry, Mr. Worswick, I thought I had better let you know, we are flooded out again and have had to stop production'. Mr. Worswick said a few swear words then turned to me and said, 'Do you know anywhere in the district where we can find suitable and larger premises than this place? I am sick and tired of the trouble we have with the roof and drains'.

My heart nearly stopped beating, but I managed to stammer out, 'Yes, Victoria Works, Lytham'. Mr. Worswick came next day with his co-director, Mr. Rothwell, liked what they saw and inside a week a seven year lease was fixed up at a rent which more than covered the monthly mortgage repayments on the works, garage and 137 Warton Street. Is it chance, fate, luck, or what that brings about such opportunities? 'Better be born lucky than rich?'

Road transport throughout the whole country was now expanding quite rapidly, and in consequence the railways were losing a lot of traffic to road general hauliers, and to operators of regular services for what were termed 'smalls', that is, consignments mainly under 4 cwt, the average usually being around 1 cwt. We were in this latter class of operator. This led to calls for legislation to control and regulate the growth of road transport, to fix wages, hours of work, holidays with pay and guaranteed working week, etc. This was viewed with some concern by operators; so far it had been a free for all situation, and restrictions of any kind were not going to be welcome.

The industry was represented on the goods side by the C.M.U.A., Commercial Motor Users Association, which had membership of operators for hire or reward and of firms operating vehicles for transporting their own goods.

We had been members of the C.M.U.A. since 1926. Many meetings were held about the proposed legislation, and it eventually came to be felt by the responsible operators anyway, that legislation of some kind was bound to come. It would affect all and sundry and would in the long term be for the benefit of the industry. One problem which now arose was the number of different makes and sizes of vehicles we were operating, nine in all; the Beans were all one size and model, the three Vulcans were all different sizes and models, 2 Fords were again not alike and the Thorneycroft another odd one. It was obvious some form of standardisation would have immense benefits in

An Indenture Apprenticeship form, dated 20th June 1879, given to me by Alice's father, Edward Vale. His employer, to whom he was indentured for eight years to learn the trade of key maker, evidently could not write: he has signed the document with a cross, witnessed by a solicitor's clerk.

operating flexibility and efficiency, but as always how about finance, and where was it to come from? We had to give long and very serious thought to this problem created by our own success and so we did. This in its turn gave rise to another problem which was bound to arise if the business continued to grow as it had in the past. That was the depot and garage. Due to our type of operation, which entailed unloading, sorting and reloading 95% of the traffic we handled every 24 hours, the depot would be the limiting factor in our expansion which I was now certain could and would continue, provided we continued to handle the traffic on offer as efficiently as we had done in the past.

The annual accounts now produced by our accountants William Latham & Co. were very satisfactory, and showed we were operating on a very profitable basis, and there did not appear to be any reason to doubt that this would continue, provided the depot problem was solved. Apart from the regular daily services we operated we were asked to do all sorts of odd jobs which somehow we managed to fit in, and were always very profitable.

One such job was the recovery of an aeroplane. Our flying friends at Parkstone Film Co. had a small three-seater plane make a forced landing on the sands out from Granny's Bay, Ansdell. Fortunately, the tide was out and it was evening. Bill Williams, the aero mechanic asked me to provide a vehicle to recover the aircraft before dark and the tide came in so off I went to Ansdell not knowing how we were to carry an aeroplane through Lytham.

When I arrived Bill was there and a big crowd of sightseers. The plane was about 250 yards out on the sands. Bill called for volunteers and about ten chaps went out to the plane, took the wings off in about two hours and carried them up to the beach where there was a rough stone slipway from the beach road to the sands. I had reversed down this slipway to the edge of the sands. Bill and his gang then dragged the plane, tail first across the sands. It had a fixed two-wheel undercarriage. The tail of the plane was put on the middle of the lorry flat, the wings and loose gear packed on each side and away we went to the aerodrome at Lytham.

It was the first time I had ever seen a plane going backwards and the crowd cheered as we moved off. Bill was happy. So was I and we got a useful free write up in the local weekly paper.

We were also employed by Holts, billiard table builders, Poulton le Fylde to deliver full size billiard tables to their customers. These weighed about two tons, and were loaded and packed on the vehicles by Holt's staff; at the customer Holts unloaded them and assembled them; on occasion we brought an old table back taken in part-exchange, sometimes to be reconditioned.

We also from early days did small household removals locally. This was a rather specialised job and we gradually phased it out as problems arose in always being able to have available staff who knew how to handle and pack household furniture. After several years quiet retirement with us Alice's father passed away peacefully and was laid to rest in St. John's Churchyard, Lytham. He was a very small quiet, homely man. He gave me an Indenture Apprentice-ship form dated 20th June 1879. It is signed by Alice's father, Edward Vale; his employer, to whom he was indentured for eight years to learn the trade of key maker, evidently could not write. He has made his mark X and it is witnessed by a solicitor's clerk, William Sansome. It is a most amazing document, far removed from Contracts of Employment in the 1980s.

The traffic being brought to us by Blackburn Parcels Express, developed on a new line which I did not care for. They had for some time brought us parcels from Lewis' Store in Manchester. The deliveries were all for private houses which were amongst the least popular to us, as very often no one was in at the delivery address, particularly if it was afternoon. That meant the parcel coming back to the depot and going out again next day. The new problem was Lewis' were offering their mail order customers C.O.D. facilities which meant that we had to collect cash on delivery. This gave rise to a lot more recording, and delays in delivery time, having change and also if no one was in, a parcel could not be left next door without the cash. Sometimes customers had changed their minds and did not want to accept the goods and pay cash, or wanted to examine them before they would pay. For all this we received 2% of the amount we were asked to collect, so that all in all the Blackburn Parcels Express traffic was not so attractive.

We had in the meantime made a most noticeable addition to our fleet of vehicles. Mr. Rothwell at the Victoria slipper works was changing his car and I bought his old one, a 12 h.p. Austin Saloon for £25. It was a bargain which eventually was for about six years used as a workshop hack. After I bought my second car, an American Dodge; I used the Austin 12 for business and Alice and I had our first holiday since we married. We took Charles with us, went down to Lands End in Cornwall via the Wye Valley, back along the South Coast to Plymouth an up through the Midlands.

Alice sometimes came with me if I was going to Preston or Blackburn in the car, it enabled her to do some shopping and get a change of scenery. Alice's mother looked after the children. Charles and Alwyn Joyce were at school; some friends brought them home from school if we were away. If not, Alice used to go for them. It was on such a journey Alice and I had gone to Blackburn. I had to see several customers. We left Lytham about 2.00 p.m. and got back about 6.00 p.m. to be greeted by Alice's mother and Freda with the terrible tragic news that Alwyn Joyce had been knocked down by a car opposite 137 Warton Street and was in the Cottage Hospital next door very badly injured. Alice and I went to the Hospital at once. We knew Matron and the Sisters very well. Matron told us Joyce was very badly injured, still unconscious, but if they could keep her going for 24 hours there was a chance she might pull through. Sister also explained that due to her head injuries, they had not been able to examine her properly, to hope for the best and be prepared for the worst.

Alice naturally was in a terrible state. I sent for Dr. Wagner and he gave Alice sedation and said he would call again in the morning. He also arranged for Alice's sister, Freda, to come and stay with us for a few days.

Early next morning Alice and I went to the hospital. Joyce was just as we had seen her last night, swathed in bandages so pale and so still. We stayed until the little darling died two hours later, 18th April 1934.

The gardener said, 'Who plucked this flower'

I said, 'The Master'

'The gardener bowed in silence'

Alice's mother saw the event in all its horror and tragedy from the bay window facing the street, and later explained what she saw.

Charles and Joyce often went to play with a boy who lived opposite to 137 Warton Street, with his mother and grandparents. His grandfather was our book-keeper at the depot, R.S.M. Noble. On this day they had as usual crossed over about 4.30 to play with their friend for an hour, and their grandma would be looking out for them about 5.30.

We had always told Charles to keep hold of Joyce's hand when they were crossing the road and also to be sure to close the garden gate. Grandma saw them come out of the front door opposite. Charles was holding Joyce's hand. Joyce was pulling to hurry, when Charles pulled the iron garden gate to. It banged back open, Charles reached back to shut the gate, their clasped hands parted, Joyce stepped off the pavement into the road, just at the very instant the car was passing, and that was it. At the inquest the coroner gave a verdict of misadventure and little Joyce was laid to rest at St. John's Church quite close to the school she had just started to attend. It was an awful shock for all the family and our many friends. Alice could not be consoled, which was only what one could expect. We had, of course, been greatly blessed with all the children being no problem at birth or subsequently and were indeed fortunate that we had another son, David Henry, born 16th February 1933, in addition to Joyce, Nancy and Charles.

I thought when the funeral was over that in a week or two I would get Alice away for a week or two holiday. Alice's mother and Freda could manage the three children. Dr. and Mrs. Wagner were very good in that they let Freda have time off whenever Alice needed her help. However, Alice would not hear of going away and it became a regular daily event for her to go to the Church where Joyce was laid to rest, just to make sure the small side gate into the churchyard was closed. Alice never missed this every evening without fail. She called at the church whenever she went shopping and passed that way.

I made Dr. Wagner aware of this. He said it would take time for Alice to become reconciled to the facts, that no amount of worry and sadness would bring Joyce back, and she would no doubt in time come to realise that the rest of the family needed her, and that life must go on for those left to mourn.

Meanwhile the family business continued to progress and as we approached 1935 I had come to the conclusion we really must take an early decision on vehicle replacement and standardisation of the fleet of now ten vehicles. Enquiries were made of all the most suitable makes and sizes of vehicles, prices, delivery dates, unladen weight, with the type of body we needed, and trade in price we might obtain for the old vehicles. We would also be looking for the maximum discount off the new vehicles, as if we replaced the whole fleet at one go it would be an order for 10 or 12 vehicles, and most important of all how the deal would be financed.

All our enquiries, quotations, negotiations etc. ended in our making a deal with Kings Road Garage, St. Annes-on-Sea for twelve new Dodge vehicles, built in England, to be delivered all at the same time. All the old vehicles were to be taken in part exchange, the deposit would be paid in cash from our own resources and we would sign a hire purchase agreement to pay the balance at £124 0s. 0d per month for two years. The bodywork would be to our specification and would be carried out at Altrincham, where Dodge had arrangements with a vehicle body builder who could handle the order quickly. When all was agreed the order was placed. I signed the agreement, and only then went and told the company's accountant, William Latham of Park Street, Lytham. To say the least I am sure Mr. Latham, was so amazed he thought I was joking, till I showed him my copy of the agreement and explained how I was sure the deal was right. Repair costs for two years would be negligible, the operating side of the business would benefit from much increased flexibility, reliability, economy, etc. I was sure also we would get a good deal of publicity and advertising value from the new fleet all in the Bridges' royal blue and white with white lorry sheets. The new vehicles were delivered on time all one day, ten two ton, one three ton and one fifteen cwt van.

It was a very proud day for Alice and me; fourteen years had passed since my first venture with the Model T one-ton Ford, and from being unemployed in 1921 I now had 18 employees and the future seemed assured.

Chapter Six

Move to Preston and War Work

THERE was still the problem of Alice's continued grief, and now becoming urgent the depot, which was quite inadequate for the traffic being handled and offered to us.

The only solution appeared to be to consider a move from Lytham. I happened to mention this problem to Dr. Wagner on one of his visits to see Alice, and right away he said, 'That would be one of the best things that could happen to help Alice. Get her away from Lytham. You live too near the churchyard'. This set me thinking very seriously about a move, and I soon realised the very great advantages there would be if we were based in or near Preston.

Preston was the hub of the road system in the North West, on the main A6 road from London, the South, the West, the Midlands, Wales to the whole North West England and Scotland. What a centre this would make, I was certain this was the solution to our two problems when it was realised that our operations involved two vehicles going along the Fylde Coast each day from Lytham, eight vehicles were going from Lytham to Preston each day just to go through Preston to the destination or route they were operating on. The change would right away show a nett saving of six journeys each day to Preston and back, say, 150 miles and about one hour's time for each of six drivers and three drivers' mates.

It was also reasonable to assume that Preston would be a far better centre for the business to develop. Alice and I talked this all over at great length on many occasions and finally decided to seek suitable premises in or near Preston, and to seek the views of our employees about their willingness to move. We realised there might be problems in so far as employees who recently married might not be prepared to move, with the possible almost certain loss of purely local work in Lytham, which would not be economically possible to operate from Preston. There was also the question of moving the operating base from

Lytham to Preston. This would require an application to the Licensing Authority, which under legislation introduced in the 1933 Road & Rail Traffic Act had to be published in a booklet called Application and Decisions. Anyone interested in road or rail transport could object and this could cause our application to be heard at Public Enquiry. Luckily for us there was, surprisingly, no road operator in our type of business based in Preston, so lucky again, there were not any objections, and our application to move our base to Preston was granted.

This was the most important of our problems and it was a great relief when our application to move our base to Preston within one year was granted. We could now redouble our efforts to find suitable premises with room for expansion.

Alice and I had for some time, together with our accountants, been trying to sort out some form of profit sharing for our regular employees. It was my firm conviction that some form of profit sharing was bound to have a very important impact on our progress and expansion. Alice and I both felt it was only right that those who, by their efforts in our employment, played such an important part in our progress and expansion should share in our success. After much thought and joint discussion with the senior long serving employees, the outlines of a scheme were agreed and that it should be introduced when we moved to Preston.

We had now had assurance from almost all the employees that they would be happy and willing to move to Preston, or travel to Preston to continue in our employment. This was good news, we had a very good team of drivers, experienced in handling the multiple delivery traffic we handled and the various routes and districts in which we operated.

Alice and I were not unaware that we too would require suitable accommodation, within reasonable distance of the new depot which we had yet to find.

I have mentioned earlier the rapidly changing transport market of the 1920s and early 1930s, and the likelihood that legislation to regulate road transport was bound to follow. The 1928 Royal Commission on Transport recommended heavier road taxes, road haulage licensing, vehicle fitness, wages and conditions of employees, etc. Nothing was done until 1932 when the Minister of Transport convened a conference of representatives of railway and road haulage interests under Sir Arthur (later Lord) Salter, which made widespread recommendations for the control and regulation of road transport. This resulted in those on excise tax being put into effect in the 1933 Finance Act and the remainder in the 1933 Road & Rail Traffic Act:

1(i)

    Subject to the provisions of this Part of this Act, no person shall use a goods vehicle on a road for the carriage of goods –

(a)   for hire or reward; or

(b)   for or in connection with any trade or business carried on by him, except under a licence.

The effect of this was to be very dramatic indeed, particularly on 'A' licensed operators who were those working for hire or reward, like ourselves.

There was widespread concern in the industry about the possible consequences. I for one did not worry, I had realised for a long time the free for all situation would not continue, and that in our rather specialised type of operation we had nothing to fear and much to gain if the industry was under some form of control. At the time we were planning our move to Preston. We had nearly three years experience under the 1933 Act and found it no great inconvenience. It did benefit us many ways; the 'A' licensed operators were now what amounted to a closed shop as every extra vehicle required had to be applied for addition to the 'A' Licence. The need had to be proved, the applications were published in A & D and any other operator and the railway could and did object. When a vehicle was replaced by one more than 10 cwt unladen heavier than the old one, it had to be applied for, might be objected to or refused. When objections were received, the applicant could if he so wished appear before a Road/Rail Committee to explain the application and perhaps be successful in having the objections withdrawn, when the application would normally be granted particularly if it was for a single extra vehicle or increase in unladen weight over 10 cwt.

While all this was going on the traffic we were being called upon to handle continued to grow, and our accountants felt that it would be wise and make good sense to form a Limited Liability Company to take over the family concern. So in due course Harold Bridges Ltd. was registered in early 1936 and took over the whole of the operating side of the business. Alice and I were directors and 1,000 shares issued.

The New Year 1936 was a few days old when on 5th January Alice gave birth to another son, John. Dr. Wagner again attended, John like our previous four children was born at home. Nurse Wolfe had retired, so Alice had a Nurse Cartmell, a very capable homely person. Alice's mother was a great help and Freda spent most of her time off with the family.

During all this time I still had my old, what seemed lifelong, pal in daily attendance, yes my speech impediment. It did not get any worse, but certainly no better, and I suppose I got so used to it, I had given over worrying about it, due, I feel to the great sympathy and understanding of the many people I had to talk to. Alice in particular was most understanding, never criticised, found fault or in any way was other than helpful.

Our search for premises in the Preston area continued, with advertisements, enquiries to Estate Agents and the like, and once again out of nowhere came the answer. We had a driver, Jack Ashby, who lived at St. Annes, his normal daily journey being from Lytham to Preston. Then he started his deliveries in Walton-le-Dale on to Chorley, Wigan, Warrington and return, deliveries were made of goods collected the previous day from all over Lancashire and on his return goods were collected for delivery anywhere in Lancashire next day.

Like all drivers on various routes he had a number of regular daily collections, others on specific days and others were requests to collect which we had received by post or 'phone. One such special call was to collect at Record Manufacturing Co., Flatts Mill, Walton-le-Dale. This was on the main road A6. Jack had his instructions to make clear on collection; we must have a consignment note, etc. and most important that payment was expected and must be made before or during the month following delivery of the goods. We were most emphatic about payment. My slogan was, 'Pay and be paid'.

When Jack collected a few cwts of soap and candles which they were making in a small way and supplying mainly to market traders, all the conditions were agreed, and Jack found in the course of casual conversation that Flatts Mill, like many more in Lancashire between 1925 and 1935, had been closed down in the cotton recession.

Flatts Mill had been bought by a Mr. Outhwaite who lived at Starr Hills, Fairhaven. He was using part and wished to let or lease the remainder to industrial and commercial tenants. Jack had the good sense and interest to obtain some brief details of the ground floor parts still to be let, and reported to me on his return to Lytham in the evening.

This seemed very promising. An appointment was made to see Mr. Outhwaite at the Mill. Alice and I went along in great hopes and my word, our luck was in; Bridges' luck again. One of the sections of the mill available was the cotton warehouse. It was about 200 feet long and 70 feet wide, large sliding doors and ceiling 13 feet high with large windows all along one side. There were two rows of steel columns about 15 feet apart and a very good wood block floor, water and electricity close by and toilet facilities.

Mr. Outhwaite was anxious to let, we were anxious to rent (I hoped without showing it) and it did not take long for us to agree the broad terms and conditions for a ten year lease with option to renew subject to rent review at five years. During general conversation which followed, Alice mentioned the housing problem we anticipated, for us and our employees when the move came about. Alice and I could hardly believe our ears when Mr. Outhwaite said, 'Oh, that's no problem. The mill manager's house next to the mill on the main road has been empty for years. It is badly in need of internal decorating. If you will do it up and keep it in repair and insured I will put it on the lease and you can have it for ten shillings per week'.

The house, called Walton House, 84 Victoria Road, Walton-le-Dale had a large hall and curved open staircase, large kitchen, pantry, scullery and three large rooms on the ground floor, which we used as lounge, dining room and billiard room for a full size table, five good bedrooms, bathroom upstairs, toilet, etc. There were also large dry cellars under all the house, a large floral and kitchen garden and a large fruit orchard at the rear, no front garden, just a few bushes between the house and the footpath. The whole area was in an unkempt state. Alice and I had no hesitation in agreeing to lease the depot and the house, which was only about 100 yards from the depot.

I could visualise the depot with a loading deck 200 feet long, 20 feet wide which would enable us to unload or load over 20 vehicles at the same time and any vehicle to back in or draw out without any trouble and a 20 feet clear road in front of the row of parked vehicles, just what we had dreamed about. Bridges' luck? I asked Mr. Outhwaite if he knew a local builder who would build a loading dock and offices. 'Yes', he said, 'J. C. B. Hardman, Cinnamon Hill, Walton-le-Dale, he is building houses for sale or rent in Windsor Road, Walton-le-Dale, he will I am sure do it for you and I know he has some finished houses on sale now'. Alice and I went along to Hardman's office, got details of the properties for sale or to let and returned to Lytham very pleased with our day's work.

Everything now seemed to be falling into place. As soon as the lease was signed I saw J. C. B. Hardman about building the loading deck and offices, and some building repairs at Walton House, arranged with Stewart Porter, Electrical Contractor, Chorley for work at the house and complete lighting and power wiring in the depot. Alice arranged with Hudson's decorators, Lytham for completely decorating Walton House inside and out, and with Rakestraw's, Blackburn for linoleum, carpets, etc. It was a very hectic time – insurances to arrange, new stationery of all sorts, watching the work done by contractors, and at the same time operating vehicles and depot at Lytham. All the employees who needed houses got fixed up. Jack Ashby rented a small shop next to the mill on Victoria Road, another driver rented a house next door to Walton House and several rented or agreed to buy houses in Windsor Road.

Everything went very smoothly and on 1st April 1936 Harold Bridges Ltd., vehicles, stock, goods in storage, and everything connected with our operation moved to Walton-le-Dale. At the same time Alice and all the family furniture and all we possessed at 137 Warton Street was moved to Walton-le-Dale.

Freda left her employment with Dr. Wagner and came to live with us. Alice's mother was now semi-invalid, and with the family and a big house to run this kept Freda and Alice busy.

It very soon became obvious the move was right. For Alice it was a complete change in fresh surroundings, her sister for company and little John a few months old to care for. On the business side, goods were brought into the depot by new customers before we actually moved on 1st April.

The depot lay out was ideal, we had our own underground storage tank for petrol and the office accommodation and workshop facilities we had organised were ideal. We were now organised for expansion. We had the 'know how', the facilities, the staff and the desire and will to get on.

It was not very long after our move to Walton-le-Dale that it became obvious the steady and constant increase in the traffic we were being offered would require additional carrying capacity, and the question we had to answer was: should it be additional vehicles or larger vehicles of increased carrying capacity?

It must be remembered we were now operating under the 1933 Road Traffic Act and like most operators, had no experience of the Licensing Authorities, or what might be involved if we applied for additional vehicles. This would certainly lead to an objection by the railway and inevitably public enquiry. To be quite honest, I think I was a bit scared of perhaps having to appear in the Traffic Court to give evidence of need and deal with the Railway's objection, in cross examination by their solicitor, having in mind I was still suffering from my speech impediment. The Road Haulage Association had an excellent solicitor who acted for members in our area, a William Blackhurst of Blackhurst, Parker & Blackhurst. He acted for us on many occasions later. However, after much discussion and enquiries from vehicle agents and distributors we found we could now replace the 2-ton carrying capacity Dodge vehicles with 3-ton vehicles which only weighed 8 cwt more unladen each. This meant we could increase the carrying capacity of the 10 vehicles by 50% without any licensing problem at all.

While making our enquiries we found that a firm in Walton-le-Dale, Hardman Bros., had recently been appointed Dodge dealers. They were a long established family firm of wheelwrights and builders of horse-drawn vehicles, and now engaged in commercial vehicle bodywork, building and repairs. Having recently been appointed by Dodge Motors they were keen to do a deal for a bulk order for 10 vehicles and build the bodies to our design and specification.

The outcome was we ordered the 10 three-ton vehicles at $22\frac{1}{2}$% off list price and they took the 10 two-ton vehicles from us at the written down price in our books. I often wondered if Dodge themselves were involved, or if Hardman Bros. made anything on the deal. I was very pleased. It was a really good bargain for us, and gave us the extra capacity we so badly needed.

A large proportion of the increased traffic was brought into the depot in the daytime by all kinds of firms from all over the country. This proved without doubt that Preston was an excellent centre and being so near the A6 main road was an additional advantage.

Extra staff were now employed unloading, checking and sorting goods brought into the depot by customers, and the goods being collected by our own vehicles were increasing to such an extent that the vehicles were now unloaded and goods sorted into the respective loading bays by a permanent night staff, who started work at 7.00 p.m. and 9.00 p.m. and finished 5.00 a.m. and 7.00 a.m. Day staff in the depot and drivers started at 7.00 a.m. Monday to Friday, with a rota of skeleton staff on Saturdays. The depot was, therefore, now operating 24 hours per day 7.00 a.m. Monday to 5.00 p.m. Saturday.

Our move to Preston was also taken as an opportunity to change completely our records and delivery note sheets and system. Previously deliveries had been entered on sheets of 20 deliveries on which signatures for goods delivered were taken. With the increasing number of vehicles and routes being operated this was no longer the ideal system, so around mid-1936 we changed over to a single delivery note for each delivery and one of the night staff's main duties was making out and sorting the delivery notes for next day. We also were now able to keep more correct records of the number of collections each day, the number and weights of deliveries each day, and other information in regard to traffic volume and flow.

I had realised soon after the 1933 Road Traffic Act became fully operational that the grant of extra 'A' licences for additional vehicles would depend to a great extent on the amount and quality of the factual evidence which could be presented to the Traffic Courts. We had, therefore, set up a system whereby the evidence we needed was collected each day, week and month, and sheets prepared showing the growth in the traffic handled. The value of this was proved in early 1938 when we took the bull by the horns and entered an application for three additional three-ton Dodge vehicles. This was published in Applications and Decisions and we duly received an objection from the Railway to the grant of any extra vehicles. By this time the Traffic Courts were operating fully and in order to save time there had been set up a Road/Rail Traffic Committee, on which sat representatives of the Railways, the Road Haulage Association and an independent member.

The idea was that if the applicant for extra vehicles wished, he could present his case and his evidence to this Committee and that, depending on the evidence, the Railways or other objectors might withdraw their objection, in which case the vehicles might be granted automatically by the Traffic Commissioners, or if the Traffic Commissioners did want to see and hear the evidence there was a 90% chance the application would succeed and the extra vehicles be granted. It was occasions such as this that I used to worry about my speech impediment, and whether I could possibly do my job justice. It is said, 'The day of miracles is or is not past'; also, 'better be born lucky than rich'. I have had above my share of good luck or miracles, but none so important to me as what happened early 1938.

I have mentioned earlier our home, Walton House, had a large hall and curved staircase, at the foot of which was a very big cast iron heating radiator, enclosed by a fancy cast iron frame; the top was a marble slab 6 feet long, 2 feet wide and 2 inches thick. On this slab we had the telephone instrument, directories, writing pad, etc. One evening Alice had gone to the local shop not many doors away and the 'phone rang. I answered. It was a customer making an enquiry about a special delivery next day. I was having difficulty speech-wise in dealing with the query when Alice came back. She had her umbrella in her hand as it was a wet night. I was leaning on the marble slab with both elbows, with my backside stuck out, I suppose. Anyway, as Alice passed behind me she must have heard my difficulty and in fun or otherwise gave me such an almighty smack across my backside with her rolled up umbrella. I dropped the 'phone and straightened up like a shot, and right away without any difficulty said, 'What's that for?' Luck, miracle or what, I have not stammered since, and no one can tell me why.

I duly attended the Road/Rail Committee and with the factual written evidence together with my oral back up, the Railway withdrew their objection, the Chairman congratulated me on the way our case was presented and the Traffic Commissioners granted us the three extra vehicles without a Public Hearing.

What a relief! I owe Alice a debt I can never repay, for this incident alone. In a few seconds her action had solved or cured a problem I had endured for 30 years that I could remember. It seemed like the start of a new life for me; my family, relations, business and social acquaintances were as surprised or amazed as I was, oh what a relief!

It was not many weeks later I was invited to a supper and meeting at the Victoria and Station Hotel, Fishergate, Preston, to give a talk on road transport, multiple delivery problems, vehicle maintenance and fleet standardization. I spoke for nearly one and a half hours, without any speech problem at all, the audience between 30 and 40 were all interested in road transport and I made some very useful contacts.

Road transport continued to develop and expand. We were now receiving enquiries for storage and distribution facilities on an increasing scale. It was soon apparent that the storage space available in the depot would limit our ability to cope. By this time most of Flatts Mill had been sold, by Mr. Outhwaite. Ribble Paper Mills had bought a large portion, including our depot on lease, and they had set up a paper making plant, using mainly recycled paper in 1938. Howarth and Airey, Wine and Spirit merchants had bought most of the rest of the Mill on Flatts Lane and had it renamed 'Winery Lane'; their section included a Customs and Excise bonded store.

The question of vehicle maintenance facilities was also bound to arise, as the expansion of the vehicle fleet took over more of the depot space. We were indeed fortunate that above the depot a firm of textile manufacturers had taken space as Rity Linen Co., which was somewhat less than half the area of the depot. We were lucky in being able to have this unused space added onto our lease, now with Ribble Paper Mills as owners. We were also very fortunately able to lease workshops and open yard space behind the depot. The vehicle entrance to the workshops and yard space was directly off the main A6 road through the main mill gates and yard. The lay out of all this additional space was ideal. The workshop, while entirely separate from the traffic depot, was accessible on foot from the depot through a doorway we opened out in the dividing wall, direct into the workshop.

We also put in a staircase from the depot loading deck to the new storage space above. We were also able to open up the floor above the loading deck, a six foot square to enable goods going in and out of the store to be hoisted up or down straight off a vehicle or on to the loading deck.

We put in a travelling hoist of 10 cwt capacity and had slings and trucks to use which enabled goods to be brought out of storage and put in the various loading bays behind the vehicles with the minimum of handling.

It was now two years since we moved from Lytham, and the progress made in this short time fully confirmed we had made the right decision in moving. We now had an excellent depot, storage facilities and workshops and lots of room for expansion. We were the only 'smalls' operator covering every day the whole of Lancashire including Ulverston and Barrow-in-Furness and Kendal and Windermere in Westmorland. It was the perfect set up of which Alice and I were very proud. Our nearest competitor was Blackburn Parcels Express whose operations covered mainly Manchester, Central and East Lancashire so they did not normally affect our activities. The two nationwide smalls operators were Suttons and Carter Paterson, London based with depots in Manchester, who in Lancashire were mainly concerned with delivering goods sent into their Manchester depots from London, Birmingham, etc.

One of our early substantial storage and delivery customers was British Creameries Ltd., Hull, manufacturers of cooking oils and fats for hotels, bakeries, chip shops, etc. It appeared their traffic manager was at the meeting which I had addressed and their problem was the delivery from Hull to the Lancashire area of consignments between 1 and 5 cwt. So far rail had been used, and not proved very satisfactory. What could we do?

Well, the Bridges' luck turned up again. In our village, Walton-le-Dale, a general haulage business had been started soon after the 1914/18 war ended with the purchase of two ex-army W. D. vehicles. Ted Hankin, the proprietor, had three sons, all in the business and they were now operating Leyland six wheel heavy haulage vehicles and draw bar trailers. They had quite recently started running a regular twice weekly service between Lancashire and the east coast port, Hull.

The outcome was British Creameries used Hankins for the bulk haulage of between 10 and 20 tons each week from the works at Hull to our depot, we stored it and distributed in consignments of between 1 and 5 cwt throughout the area covered by our services. This meant British Creameries could give delivery anywhere in Lancashire within 24 hours of them receiving the order. Normally the order came to us by post, which we received before 7.30 a.m. so they could go out that day if required. This type of activity increased and it, of course, meant we were now receiving at the depot goods which we had not collected on our normal vehicle routes, and again extra vehicles were needed.

We entered an application for three additional 3-ton Dodge vehicles, which duly appeared in the publication Applications and Decisions. The Railway objected and the application came before the Road/Rail Committee. This time the Railway would not withdraw their objection and the application was listed for Public Enquiry at Morecambe Town Hall. Mr. William Blackhurst took our case, and we very carefully prepared our figures and general information to support our case. We cited, of course, the increase in traffic such as British Creameries, which we did not collect, the general increase in all our activities and so forth.

British Creameries were so concerned that our application should succeed and so enable us to continue to handle their traffic, that they sent their traffic manager over from Hull to give evidence in our support. He cited the delays in delivery of small consignments from Hull to Lancashire and the problem which arose in hot weather, and the constant demand from customers for quick delivery to enable them to operate with lower stocks.

I was fairly confident, having in mind the case we had prepared, that we would succeed but it was early days under the 1933 Act and there had not been any application for three extra vehicles in the Preston area.

At least I now had one main worry less. I could talk and I think I rather looked forward to the questions I was sure would be asked of me by the Traffic Commissioner himself and the Railway solicitor.

In the event all went well. I dealt with all the verbal queries. Mr. Blackhurst did a good job with the statistical evidence and I felt we had completely demolished the Railway objection, and so it was the three additional 3-ton vehicles were granted for operation from our depot at Walton-le-Dale to the North West region mainly Lancashire for consignments mainly under 5 cwt, general goods.

Our fleet was now 18 vehicles with a carrying capacity of over 50 tons, more than double that when we left Lytham in 1936. Alice had by now overcome her grief over the loss of Joyce. Charles, Nancy and David were attending St. Leonard's School, Walton-le-Dale. The depot was now well organised, with workshop, repairs and maintenance staff, day and night staff in the depot and storage staff. Goods were now being brought into the depot from all over the country, both by operators who had set up regular services to the North West, like Charles Alexandra and Youngs Express from Scotland; Blands, Leicester; Pecks, Nottingham; Ripponden Motors, Yorkshire; Hawkers, Bristol; Collins,

A photograph of myself taken for an election leaflet in 1938, when I stood as Conservative candidate for the Walton-le-Dale Urban District Council.

Birmingham; Brevitts, Willenhall and many others. Amongst these was W. G. Greenwood Ltd., Burnley, a subsidiary of Bouts-Tillotson the London and nationwide operator.

Bouts-Tillotson accepted traffic in London up to 4.00 p.m. It was trunked to Greenwood's Burnley depot during the night, and they delivered to our depot about 6.00 a.m. Then we delivered the same day, often before noon, which was under 24 hours from London to most main North Lancashire towns at what we were given to understand was less than half the railway rate for the same service.

While all this exciting development was taking place, we had our home and private life to run and enjoy, not without its ups and downs, of course. One was that Alice, expecting another baby in May 1938 fell in the garden. She did not appear any worse for it. Dr. Wagner came from Lytham, was very concerned and tried to persuade Alice to go into hospital for examination, particularly as Alice was over a week overdue.

As usual Alice would have nothing to do with going to hospital. She said, 'I have had my five children all at home and I am not going to hospital with this one which is to replace Joyce and will be my last, I hope'.

However, the time came, 14 days overdue. Nurse Cartmell and Dr. Wagner attended and there were problems. Dr. Wagner called in another doctor and after 24 hours the child was born. It had it appears been a choice of Alice or the baby, as Alice would not go to hospital and the baby did not survive. Dr. Wagner, Nurse Cartmell and all of us were very sad, but at the same time very thankful that Alice had survived the ordeal.

Dr. Wagner was so surprised that Alice could possibly have given birth to such a large baby that he sent for his daughter who was studying medicine in Edinburgh to come and see the baby before it was taken away for burial at St. John's Church, Lytham, with Alwyn Joyce. Dr. Wagner felt his daughter should actually see the child with her own eyes, which she did. Alice made a remarkably quick recovery. She was to have had the baby, a boy, called Richard, but this was not to be. It was a great pity that while Alice was not able to go out, St. Leonard's School, Walton-le-Dale held their Annual May Rose Queen Festival at the school. Nancy had been chosen as May Rose Queen and was duly crowned Queen amongst all the other festivity and jollification, which unfortunately Alice could not attend.

I had become involved with the Ex-Servicemen's Club, and the Conservative Party Club in the village, and also in starting an Old Folks Annual Party, which was and continued to be a great success.

Alice and I were also nominated and elected to the St. Leonard's Church Council, so that we were becoming part of the village community. These interests and also perhaps because we now had around fifty employees led to my being asked to allow my name to be put forward as the Conservative candidate for the Walton-le-Dale Urban District Council. This was nothing in my line, but I was eventually persuaded to stand. It was experience in a new field for me. The local party appeared to be well organised, and while they appeared confident, I had my doubts. Here I was, a newcomer only lived in the village two years, and totally ignorant of any sort of political activity, apart from being a member of the Club about 12 months. My opponent was the current councillor, an accountant, about my age and who had lived in the village many years.

I had nothing to do with any of the arrangements for printing leaflets, meetings, or the like, other than approving what was arranged. One of the first items I was asked to suggest was a slogan or catchword that I thought might be appropriate. After much deliberation with Alice we came up with the Lytham St. Annes Corporation motto on their coat of arms. We both and our business wholly had been in Lytham around 20 years and it seemed to us very appropriate. It was: 'Solus populi Suprema Lex' in Latin, which, I was informed, translated into English something like 'The Welfare of the People is the Supreme Law'.

This motto in heavy block blue capitals duly appeared on the front of a leaflet with the translation underneath. Inside the leaflet was a brief history of my background and career, and what my views were on local government etc. On the back of the leaflet in heavy block type was printed, 'Vote for Bridges and fair play'. I queried this and was told it had something to do with events in the

Alice, Freda, Charles, David and Nancy in a slate truck, on holiday at the farm in Wales, 1939.

past and I need not worry about it.

The usual meetings in the evenings were held mainly in schools about four in all. It was at one such meeting I had to do some quick thinking, which I well remember. As usual after a meeting questions could be asked, which I answered all right. The last meeting was at Bamber Bridge and when question time came I was asked 'Does Mr. Bridges *think* his opponent is not playing fair?'

The questioner had evidently thought that the 'Fair Play' referred to my opponent, whereas it was meant to refer to past events. However to gain time to think quickly for a suitable answer, I said, 'Will the questioner please repeat the question slowly exactly as asked'. Back it came – 'Does Mr. Bridges *think* his opponent is not playing fair?' My reply was, 'Mr. Bridges has a perfect right to *think* whatever he likes but must be very careful what he says'. End of meeting.

Election day came and my opponent beat me by 35 votes, which was only to be expected, as he stood as an independent and was the sitting member. As events arose the following year it was a good job I did not win; war clouds were gathering over Europe, and if war did come, I expected not to have any time for outside activities such as the local council.

Alice and I had planned as soon as we could to take all the family on holiday together but could not decide where to go, until talking to 'Old Bert', my first employee. He said a brother of his who lived in Cheshire went to a farmhouse in the Welsh Hills, which might suit. All arrangements were made and off we went to Glyndyfrdwy between Llangollen and Corwen. We had a lovely 10 days on the farm. The family consisted of mother, two sons and two daughters; only the elder daughter could speak English fluently, the others just a few words.

All the food was local produce, the mother baked bread in a large brick built oven out in the yard. They made a fire inside the oven, raked it out and put the bread in to bake. It was all in 4lb loaves, and very tasty.

We could go down to the river Dee at the low end of the farm to bathe; all the children loved it. In the hills above the farm was a working slate mine, most interesting and unusual. Normally slate is extracted from open quarries like stone; this one was totally underground. The only lighting, big candles stuck on the rocks. The slate was brought out in huge blocks on trolleys to be cut and split into slates by hand. The slates were loaded into small waggons about 4 feet long by 3 feet wide with high sides, about five of the waggons were coupled together and they went down to the main railway line in the valley to be loaded into the main line trucks. These small waggons travelled down entirely by gravity, with a man to work the brake. Where the line gradient was too steep, the waggons were lowered down the steep slope by a winch and cable or chain, to a lower easier gradient for the gravity run. The waggons were hauled back up to the mine when empty by horses, and hauled up the steep slopes with the same winch which lowered them down. Stores and equipment etc. went up to the mine the same way, sometimes a horse or two pulling one small waggon.

On several occasions we all had a ride on the waggons from the mine to the railway in the valley below, and walked back to the farm about two miles, all the family enjoyed our Welsh holiday and we made arrangements to go again in August/September 1939.

Back at the depot all had run smoothly while we were away. My brother, Frank, was in charge and had the full support of a keen, loyal, hardworking staff in all departments.

The profit sharing scheme was, I am sure, in many ways creating the feeling that all were part of the firm, and all could and did make their contribution for the good of all. The scheme was based on complete and total mobility of labour between various departments within the capabilities of the staff concerned. All members were graded according to their job and capabilities, drivers mates or van boys, junior office staff and the like were Grade 1; drivers, checkers in the depot, unskilled workshop staff and so on Grade 2; charge hands, senior drivers, fully skilled mechanics Grade 3; department heads Grade 4. Each employee was allotted one unit according to the grade, multiplied by 50 which roughly represented the weeks worked in a full year. So a driver had 2 x 50 units (100) to his credit if he had worked the full year.

All the units of all the staff were totalled and this total divided into the sum we were to set aside to the scheme based on the audited accounts for the previous year. This gave us a figure per unit, which multiplied by the employee's grade total for the year gave us the entitlement of each employee in the scheme. This was paid out on a weekly basis during the 50 weeks of the following year. No employee could join the scheme until he had one year's service with the company and if an employee left he had no entitlement to any share after leaving.

We had various rules on our right to suspend payment of the bonus to any employee guilty of misconduct, vehicle accident for which he was to blame, damage to goods in transit through carelessness and so forth. The whole scheme was drawn up in collaboration with the staff, and no union was involved in any way. Very few of our employees were union members; those who were in a union were those who made collections from and deliveries to big warehouses and docks in Liverpool and Manchester, where they might be asked to show their union card. If they did not have one, they might refuse to unload or load the vehicle. So far as I am aware we were the only operator in the North West with a profit sharing scheme of this nature and I am quite sure it was one of the main reasons for our expansion.

During early 1939 international affairs on the continent of Europe looked increasingly serious, and it was no surprise when there was talk of a national emergency which might call for road transport control and fuel restrictions.

The Road Transport Associations were asked to form committees to discuss and make suggestions on how this might best be brought about, through National, Regional and District Committees. I was invited to act as the representative of the operators engaged in multiple deliveries in the Preston district, and attended monthly meetings, where we put forward ideas, talked over various schemes which had been suggested, which were then sent to the Regional Committee.

Meanwhile the business continued to grow and we were considering an application to add an additional vehicle to our 'A' Licence. We felt certain we would get an objection from the Railway, so were preparing our case carefully for Public Enquiry when we received an enquiry for distribution of an entirely new line of traffic over the northern half of Lancashire.

The Maypole Dairy Co., who were part of a large nationwide group of retail provisions shops, had recently started an egg collection scheme in the Fylde area of the North West. Maypole vans collected the eggs from the many poultry farms in the Fylde, brought them into a depot in Adelaide Street, Preston, where they were graded, sorted and code marked. Packed 18 dozen in square cartons marked Grade A, B or C they were then taken for distribution several times weekly to the Maypole Dairy retail shops in the area.

The Maypole would deliver to us each day, with detailed lists of addresses numbers and grades to be delivered to each shop. It was agreed address labels would not be required, all the cartons were the same size and clearly marked Grade A, B or C. There were several hundred cartons to deliver each week, so on the strength of this we entered our application for two extra 'A' licensed 3-ton vehicles. The Railway objected and when we appeared before the Road/Rail Committee, we had such a good case overall for the extra vehicles that the Railway withdrew their objection and in due course the Licensing Authority granted the application and we became the operators of 20 'A' licensed vehicles all engaged on multiple deliveries in the North West. We were now averaging over 1,000 deliveries per day at an average weight per delivery of around $1\frac{1}{4}$ cwt with around 60 employees. All the new vehicles we had acquired were painted royal blue and lettered in white and for recognition and operational purposes numbered 1 to 20; while not over superstitious we did not have a number 13, but 12A instead.

The railways were very active in their anti-road policy and advertising and I thought we should have a short snappy phrase or logo. We had all manner of ideas and suggestions put forward and in the end adopted four simple words: SEND IT BY ROAD. This eventually appeared on all our vehicles, stationery advertisements, etc. and was still in use with additions 25 years later.

The old Austin 12 car I bought secondhand in Lytham was still in regular use by office and workshop staff, and Alice and I thought it was time we had a proper car big enough to take the family out. I mentioned this to Hardman Bros., the Dodge dealers in the village and a week later they came along with just the job. It was a demonstration model of one of the largest cars built by Dodge. It had only done a few thousand miles. It had a lot of extra optional equipment and Dodge Sales Department had sent it to Hardmans to be sold. In view I suppose of the fact that we had bought 20 Dodge vehicles in the past three years, we eventually bought it at about half list price.

1939 school holidays came and we had decided to go to the farm in Wales towards the end of August for 14 days, eight of us in all: Alice and I, Alice's mother and sister and our four children. We had a wonderful first week, lovely hot sunshine every day, and we all had a really good time around the farm in the hills and the River Dee.

Some days Alice and I and the children went off in the car. Freda and her mother stayed at the farm. The car was fitted with a very good radio set, which when the car was stationary was very clear, and in view of the worsening international situation on the continent we always listened to the news. So it was we heard the declaration of war, while on holiday in the Welsh hills. Alice and I decided we had better get back home next day. There would be so much to see to around the business. We left the rest of the family and arranged to return for them at the weekend. On the way home we heard on the radio the news of the first U-boat victim, a passenger liner sunk by a German submarine.

One of the first jobs at the depot was arranging for the 12 large windows along the side of the depot to be capable of being blacked out completely at night, as our night staff worked all through the night five nights a week. Luckily the village joiner had his workshop on the opposite side of the road, and he made 12 shutters to cover the windows, held in place by two bolts through the window frame. We put these in place each evening and removed them at daylight next morning.

The large sliding door entrance to the depot was a bit of a problem which we overcame by shielding the lighting opposite the door so that no light shone directly out. Fuel rationing was introduced at once. My brother, Frank, was appointed to look after the scheme as it affected us and other operators in the Walton-le-Dale area. Broadly speaking the scheme was that each operator received a basic issue of petrol coupons based on the size and number of vehicles operated. This basic issue was a right, but it was so small that application could be made for supplementary coupons. These were very strictly controlled, and issued solely on the basis of how important the work to be done was to the war effort.

Applications for supplementary coupons were very carefully vetted by those in control and none were issued if the work was not considered important to the war effort. My brother, Frank, and our depot office was the point where the

107

coupons were actually physically issued to the applicants. We had nothing to do with who or how many were to be issued. Each applicant had to describe fully the kind of work the vehicles would be engaged on, the area and mileage involved. It was quite a task, which had to be done – no coupons, no petrol.

Our activities were described as multiple collections and delivery throughout Lancashire and the Lake District of foodstuff, medical and veterinary supplies, ships stores to vessels in ports of Preston, Fleetwood, Heysham and Barrow-in-Furness, raw materials, manufactured and semi-manufactured goods to munitions works, firms and companies engaged on War Department Contracts, etc. etc. It was expected that if the foodstuff and medical supplies were considered essential for the war effort, then our case was a good one, and so it proved; we never had any real fuel problem, no doubt due to our type of operation. The war soon began to have its effect on the operation of many of our vehicles. With the likelihood of air raids, the Ministry of Food began to disperse stocks of foodstuffs from Liverpool and Manchester to all kinds of what were called buffer depots throughout Lancashire and I expect other adjacent counties.

Large quantities of cartons of tinned milk, milk powder, dried eggs, Canadian cheese and other supplies imported from abroad, instead of following the normal practice of being stored in warehouses in Liverpool and Manchester, were dispersed into all kinds of empty buildings. We were asked to store, and did, hundreds of chests of tea and tons of margarine for the Ministry of Food – the margarine came from Lever Bros., Port Sunlight and Crosfield, Warrington. It was no longer branded, the different sorts were code marked and we delivered on Ministry of Food delivery orders.

The whole pattern of food distribution changed with the introduction of food rationing. We were now receiving orders to collect, say, 400 cases of tinned milk from a buffer depot and deliver them to instructions perhaps to 20 different points. The same applied to other imported foods dispersed from Liverpool and Manchester. There was, therefore, a need for us to have a much heavier flat body vehicle not a van like the 20 we had. Our application for one additional 6-ton Dodge vehicle was granted without objection so the fleet was now 21.

One of the early problems we had was young men being called up for National Service. It was possible to apply for exemption, if the person was considered essential in his civilian job. We managed to keep replacing those called up with older men, or those who had not been passed fit for military service. Very few exemptions were granted and usually only for a limited period to allow a replacement to be found. My brother, Frank, was called and went into the Navy, then two workshop managers were called up in succession and went into the Royal Air Force.

The premises at Lytham leased by H. Worswick Ltd. were now unoccupied, the firm having closed down when the lease ran out. One of our new wartime customers was the Navy, Army & Air Force Institute, who had canteens and other leisure facilities for troops in the many barracks and new training camps set up in the area, mainly in the Northern half of Lancashire. We collected from various NAAFI stores and warehouses and delivered to the barracks and camps where NAAFI facilities existed.

When the bombing in Liverpool and Manchester increased we were asked to provide storage facilities for all sorts of NAAFI hardware, crockery in crates, pots and pans, tables chairs, cutlery in cases and so on. Our storage facilities at Walton-le-Dale were already being used to full capacity, so we opened the property at Lytham as a part temporary measure. We really wished to sell the property but knew if we did not agree to let it to NAAFI they would have it compulsorily requisitioned, probably for the whole of the war.

As things turned out the problem was solved for us about 18 months later. A firm had started in Lytham in a small way, making aircraft parts for the War Office and were looking urgently for larger premises. We sold the whole of the Lytham property to this company, Clifton Aircraft Ltd., subject to the NAAFI occupation, and it was not long before they had full possession. I suppose aircraft parts had big priority over NAAFI storage.

As soon as Clifton Aircraft Ltd. agreed to buy the property, we had a problem in so far as the underground petrol storage tank we had installed in 1929 and used till 1936 had 500 gallons of petrol in it, and Clifton Aircraft Ltd. wanted to buy. It would have helped their petrol ration and coupon allocation immensely. They offered to pay a lot over the market price for it, and use it in their own cars. We had taken delivery of this 500 gallons just as the war started. The tank was empty, petrol rationing was coming and it would be a very handy fall back if we got short of petrol or coupons at any time. Strangely enough we held it quite legally – it had actually been delivered just before the petrol rationing scheme started. When the scheme started we had to declare stocks held where the vehicles were operated which was of course, Walton-le-Dale.

We were not having any problems getting the coupons and petrol we needed, so I decided the best thing to do would be to get the petrol company to take it back and credit us. We were lucky in that we were still dealing with the same petrol company. They wished to take a sample to test which they did. It was O.K., so later they pumped it out of our tank and took it away and passed us a credit note which showed quite a good profit.

With the increase in the intensity of the bombing on Liverpool and Manchester which usually started soon after dark, the drivers were all instructed to be out of Liverpool and Manchester well before the raids started and if there was an air raid warning to get out at once. At this time we usually had three vehicles delivering in Liverpool in the morning and collecting in the afternoon.

One day there was an earlier than usual air raid warning. Two of the vehicles got out alright, the third had a rear wheel puncture on Scotland Road, Liverpool. They were actually changing the wheel when the siren went, so the driver, John Rawsthorne, and his mate spent the next two hours under the vehicle as the only cover immediately available.

Luckily for them the raid that night in that area was mostly incendiary bombs, and while none actually struck the vehicle, there were many near misses. The bonnet and cab were splashed all over with metal, from incendiary bombs. The amount of bits of metal lying on the roads from bombs and anti-aircraft shells caused a higher than normal number of punctures on the Liverpool and Manchester vehicles during the years of the heaviest bombing.

We did, in spite of all sorts of problems caused by the war, maintain all our regular daily services. The depot in Walton-le-Dale became the Air Raid Warden's Post for the northern half of the village. It was ideal for this as due to our normal operations our telephone was available 24 hours a day on five days a week.

Our children, Nancy, David and John, were all attending St. Leonard's School, Walton-le-Dale, gas masks and all! Charles was at Giggleswick. Alice had taken on the job of making a number of regular weekly calls in the village to collect subscriptions for the British Red Cross. Freda spent all her spare time knitting socks etc. for various forces' welfare agencies. Alice's mother had gone back to Willenhall to live with her eldest daughter, Edith, who had lost her husband, killed in action in France. Air raid shelters were now the order of the day; brick built shelters were erected in some streets in the towns. Anderson shelters were provided for erection in gardens and many other methods of improved air raid shelters came into use.

We made our own shelter in the cellar at Walton House. It was fitted out with steel wine bins from floor to ceiling, and was directly under the main staircase and the hall which had a very strong concrete and tiled floor, so made an ideal shelter. We had electric light and heating, water, and cooking facilities in the cellars, so when fitted out with bunks and blankets it was O.K. We had very many air raid warnings due to the German bombers passing over on their way to Liverpool and Birkenhead. The nearest high explosive bomb fell bout 200 yards away in a disused brickworks. It was a fairly large one by the sound of the explosion and the crater it made. No damage was done.

A great number of incendiary bombs were dropped around Lostock Hall and Leyland, a good number falling in open country, allotments and parks, though none were near the depot.

We had a concrete pill box on the main road side in the village manned by the Home Guard at night, who checked on anyone passing on foot during darkness. It was about 50 yards from Walton House one way and 50 yards from the depot the other way. The main road in front of Walton House, the A6, was a long wide straight road for about 250 yards and was a favourite place for

Army vehicle convoys to stop on the roadside for a break in their journey. This was the occasion for all the houses on the roadside to be brewing tea, cocoa and coffee for the vehicle crews before they moved on.

On the advice of our accountants, due to the continued growth of our activities, we formed a new Limited Company to operate all our storage and ancillary work. This had certain considerable tax advantages, quite legally, and was operated as a separate company until 1950 as Walton Vale Storage Ltd., very successfully. Extra vehicles on our 'A' Licence were applied for and granted as the business continued to expand and it was obvious that it would not be many years before we would be needing larger premises, both for our distribution, warehousing and collection and delivery services.

It was, therefore, with interest that we learned that Stone Mill, Bamber Bridge was for sale. It was owned by Ridings Corn Merchants, Preston. Mr. Riding had died and the two acre site, with a large single-storey weaving shed and four-storey mill, was on the market for a quick sale. The big snag was it had been compulsorily requisitioned by the War Department and was in use as a billeting and training depot for the armed forces.

We felt it was reasonable to assume the war would likely be over within three years, when the site would be released. Also we could not visualise any move until the war was over so in the event, we might buy it cheap now and await long term developments. We would be drawing a rent and the site was ideal in size and location for future development and expansion which we visualised once the war was over.

There was quite a problem in arranging for us to visit the site and inspect the buildings and for our architect and surveyor, Mr. A. T. England, to do a survey of the site and state of the buildings. This was eventually arranged amicably with the military commander's office.

On one of my visits Alice came with me. We were shown round by a sergeant of the Military Police. In the course of our tour of the ground floor, we came to a door marked 'Showers'. The sergeant threw the door open wide and in a parade ground command gave 'Party Ten Shun' and there they were about twenty young soldiers in a line under somewhat primitive showers, standing stiffly to attention and stark naked. We did not go any further than the door. The sergeant turned to Alice and said, 'Sorry about that, ma'am'.

However, we eventually bought Stone Mill, Bamber Bridge very reasonably and felt very pleased that we had secured our future depot site.

In 1938 Alice and I had decided that Charles was now of age to go to boarding school and in due course he entered Catterall House, Giggleswick. After the war started Alice was not too happy about it and Charles was not so keen either; we were a very happy, close knit family. The war was now raging all over the world, and it was, therefore, not really a surprise after a little over two years that Charles wanted to come home.

We did our best to try and persuade him that it was in his own long-term interest that he should have the experience and benefits that an education at Giggleswick would provide. However, Charles would have none of it. The only thing about Giggleswick that he really liked and was very keen on was the cricket which he did enjoy. However, he must have decided he would be better at home and left the school three times in attempts to get home.

The first occasion he did not get far. I think one of the school staff saw him in Settle and took him back to Catterall House for a good talking to by the Headmaster, Mr. Partridge. The second time he did get further, but again returned to the school and this time I think the punishment was made to fit the crime. The third time Charles somehow got to Lytham and was picked up by a police sergeant whom we knew very well, and, seeing a young lad in Giggleswick School outfit, cap and all late at night, acted promptly by phoning us at home.

Alice and I went to Lytham Police Station and found Charles having a cup of cocoa in the office. We took Charles home and subsequently Alice and I went to see Mr. Partridge, the Headmaster at Giggleswick. He said it was no use Charles being returned to the school. He was determined to be at home to work, and he was sorry. Later talking over the matter with Alice and Charles, it appeared Charles' wish was to be at home to work in the family business. He did comment, 'Dad left school when he was 13 and now has over 80 employees working for him'. What could I say to that? So Charles started work in the mechanics workshops, to learn the basics of vehicle repairs and maintenance.

The German bombing raids were not so heavy or frequent now; instead we had the occasional flying bomb or doodle bug as they were nicknamed. One or two exploded out in open country not far away. It was quite eerie to hear them, going over, with a loud humming or whining noise, then a few seconds complete silence while the bomb was falling and then the big bang. Luckily none fell on Walton-le-Dale. By now the American armed forces were in evidence all over the North West with a big base at Burtonwood, near Warrington, and another between Lytham and Preston, for the U.S.A. Air Force.

The progress of the war was now very much more encouraging and we began thinking and talking about plans for 'after the war' and our intended new depot at Stone Mill, Bamber Bridge. We were kept very busy all year round and as we required and applied for extra 'A' licensed vehicles they were granted.

So in 1945 came the news everyone was praying and longing to hear, V. E. Day, the war in Europe was over. Thank God, V.E. day, 7th May 1945. Our early thoughts were on how soon the War Department would de-requisition Stone Mill and we were pleasantly surprised when this happened fairly soon. But before the actual effective date, it was requisitioned by the Ministry of Works as a training depot for ex-soldiers to be trained as building trade workers.

We were assured this would not be for more than two years, by when it was hoped more permanent training arrangements would be made. It appeared this might just tie in with the lease of the depot at Walton-le-Dale which was due to expire in 1946. In the meantime, a portion of Flatts Mill, including our depot and Walton House, had been sold and part fitted out as a paper manufacturers, Ribble Paper Mills Ltd. The new owners were prepared to extend the lease of the depot on a year to year basis at an increased rent, but wanted to have possession of Walton House in 1946 as a residence for the paper mill's manager. This meant we had to seek a new home and once again fate, luck, or just pure coincidence came to the rescue.

Chapter Seven

Salwick Hall, Dixon Bros

THE Salwick Estate, 1,200 acres and Salwick Hall, on the death of Mr. Magee came on the market to be sold. Mr. Magee had lived there, as owner, with a housekeeper and butler for many years and it was the estate on which I was gamekeeper's boy at 10s. 0d. per week in 1913/14 and 5s. 0d. per week in 1914/15. It was to be sold by auction, and all estimates seemed to indicate it would sell at around £100 per acre, which was far beyond our reach having in mind our business plans for the future. Alice and I went to the sale and saw it sold to the Duchy of Lancaster for £84,000 – £70 per acre.

It was indicated at the sale that the farms would continue to be rented to the present tenants but the Hall, with the fishing, shooting and sporting rights over the whole 1,200 acres, would be on lease. This set Alice and I thinking. The Hall was, of course, far larger than we would require. My only hobbies were shooting, fishing and gardening and we could see plenty of scope for that. Negotiations with the Duchy of Lancaster's Office in London through the local agent resulted in me taking a 21-year lease of the Hall and sporting rights over the whole estate on a very reasonable rent, with no rent review. In fact, due to the run-down state of the shooting, the Duchy agreed a reduction for the first few years.

Well, what do you think about that for the wheel going full circle, game-keeper's boy returns after 30 years – as squire! 'HA HA'.

Most of the farm tenants had been at school with me at Clifton School near the windmill, and I knew all the woods, ponds and boundaries quite well even after 30 years. We were responsible for all inside maintenance of the Hall and the Duchy looked after the outside and main walls, roof, chimneys, etc.

There followed a time of great activity. We put in a new kitchen range, had all the rooms we intended to use decorated, a lot of rewiring was done by the

Alice crowns the Rose Queen at Newton Blue School, Newton-with-Scales, 1950/51.

Duchy and they replaced part of the heating installation. There was a very large orchard and kitchen garden, greenhouse and vinery and all the outbuildings associated with a large country house, two gardeners, one of whom, Bill Lindsay, acted as part-time gamekeeper. The other, elderly, had a son who was at school with me in 1913. The kitchen garden had a 9 ft high brick wall on the north and east side, on which were trained plum and pear trees.

We very soon got organised with a hen cabin and 20 hens, and two young pigs to fatten and kill for our own use, had a two-acre paddock ploughed and sown with oats, to provide feed for the poultry and pigs; animal feed was still rationed.

Salwick Hall to Preston journey time was about 15–20 minutes, and during school term we all went together by car. Charles and I to work, Nancy and David and John to school, and home together after work.

It was not long before Alice and I were elected to the St. John's Lund Parochial Church Council, later I was Vicar's Church Warden for 10 years. Alice was treasurer of the Mothers Union and John a junior sidesman at the Church. The four children went to church with me every Sunday morning. Alice and Freda went every Sunday evening, and we all took part in our different ways in various church and village events and activities from 1946 to

1957, of which more later.

With the ending of the war, there was the task which faced the government and the nation of rebuilding all the war damage. Also no homes had been built for eight years so the prospects for the building trade at least were very promising. The first thing one thinks about in building I suppose is bricks, and so it was when I was introduced to a venture to take over a small brickmaking and agricultural field tile works in Blackburn.

The business had been run for many years by two brothers. One of the brothers had died and the two employees they had were approaching the age of retirement, so the surviving brother wished to sell out and retire. The business had carried on through the war as their main activity was making field tiles for military camps, airfields, etc. which had to be drained during the war. They also had a small trade in special hand made bricks.

There was only a small amount of rather primitive machinery in the works, the main asset was 16 acres of clay bearing land almost in the centre of Mill Hill, Blackburn. I had to admit I did not know the first thing about brickmaking, the only real connection I had with bricks was carrying them 8–10 at a time up a ladder when I was a bricklayer's labourer in 1920/21.

However, having made all the enquiries I could about the possibilities it seemed a reasonably sound proposition which after talking over with Alice I decided to back financially, for up to £25,000 which it was estimated would see us through the rebuilding and re-equipping into the first year's production.

The Ministry of Works introduced a scheme of subsidy for firms which did get into production in 1947 so we had a target date to strive for.

The biggest job was to build a new brick firing kiln, which was duly accomplished together with machine house and drying tunnels. One big problem was obtaining the new machinery we required; all the brickmaking machinery builders had, of course, been on war work. Scores of brickworks had been shut down and were now looking for new and modern machinery to start up again. We did eventually acquire what we needed, mostly secondhand, including a 100 h.p. electric motor from Thos. Dryden & Son Ltd., Preston. Several of my friends became interested in the project and took shares.

We registered the company as Dixon Bros. Brickworks Ltd., Registered Office 12 Park Street, Lytham, on 20th March 1945. Eventually, after many delays and hold ups we got into production and had no difficulty in selling at the going rate all we could produce, in a short space of time we had three different works managers and none of them could reach the target figure of 120,000 saleable bricks per week.

One of the problems apparently was the clay was of an unusually fine grain, and required a considerable quantity of coarse sand mixing with it, otherwise excessive shrinking occurred in the drying process before the bricks went into the kiln to be fired. This sand had to be bought in and machines provided and installed to mix it with our clay, which all added to the production costs, delays and problems. It was, therefore, with no surprise that we realised we were running the venture at a loss, and decided the losses being incurred called for drastic action, even a shutdown of the works. About this time the National Coal Board, who had a number of brickworks throughout the country, were extending their interest in brick making by buying firms in certain areas, and they approached us on these lines.

At their request, to facilitate the negotiations, I bought out all the other Dixon Bros. shareholders, some in full at £1 0s. 0d. per £1 share, others on a payment on deposit, with the balance to be paid if and when the firm was sold. Negotiations were proceeding satisfactorily with the National Coal Board when it came to their notice that there was a distinct possibility the whole 16 acres of land might be the subject of a compulsory purchase order by the local authority for housing in the not too distant future.

This put the N.C.B. off altogether and all negotiations ceased. So I was the sole shareholder of a company operating at a loss with a trading loss of around £40,000 on its balance sheet. At least I was the boss and could take what action I thought was needed without delay. After long talks with Alice I decided to shut down at once, all employees except the works foreman, Fred Baron, were discharged, stocks of all materials sold and Fred Baron employed as caretaker, to prepare plant and equipment for sale and just keep the company ticking over, which would enable the company to carry the operating loss forward each year. We were fairly successful in disposing of most of the heavy machinery and the rest was sold for scrap.

Some revenue came from clay sales and from parking commercial vehicles. The problem was what to do with the company and its £40,000 trading loss. If we could find activity for the company on a profitable basis the £40,000 loss would mean the first £40,000 profit would be tax free. Examination of Dixon Bros. Brickworks Ltd. Memorandum and Articles of Association showed that after brick and tile manufacture, builders and plumbers merchants were included, along with related activities. This set me thinking: could we set up a builders and plumbers merchants business at Stone Mill, Bamber Bridge? There was ample room in land and buildings, and I set about making enquiries about the possibilities and what would be involved. Once again Bridges' luck came to the rescue. During the course of my enquiries I found that a Mr. Dewhurst operated in Tulketh Brow, Preston, as Preston Builders Supply, a private non-limited company. Mr. Dewhurst was a bachelor, no family, getting on in years and ready for retirement, and had been in the business at that address many years. The company owned the land and building freehold in an excellent position, with a showroom on the main road, Tulketh Brow, with ample yard and warehouse buildings. Negotiations with Mr. Dewhurst proceeded very amicably and I bought the business, land and buildings, lock, stock and barrel for around £30,000, which included the stock at valuation. The accounts showed the business had been operating at a useful profit margin, which I was quite certain could be increased by higher turnover. Mr. Dewhurst had been quite happy to have a quiet, easy carry on at his age, and had not pushed the business at all. We put Mr. Dewhurst's assistant, Tom Green, in charge on a day to day basis and later he became manager, a very quiet hard working young man, who did a good job.

We installed a 30-ton weighbridge in the yard near the offices, and bought a tractor digger for loading sand and gravel, etc. Later we acquired premises next door which had been Bambers Motor Engineers for use as a cement and plaster store.

The land and the remainder of the machinery at Blackburn were sold, and in due course the shareholders who sold their share to me on deposit were paid out in full. Thus ended a venture which had caused me a lot of headaches and worry. Everyone outside my family had been paid out in full, and we now had a business which was showing a good profit which could be improved and expanded.

Looking back, in 1920 and 1921 I got paid for carrying bricks 10 at a time in a hod up a ladder; in Blackburn we lost a lot of money making bricks, now I hoped to, and did, make money buying and selling bricks; so be it.

Dixon Bros. Brickworks Ltd. continued to trade very satisfactorily as builder and plumbers merchants and on 16th May 1961 the company name was changed and registered as Dixon Bros. Builders Supplies Ltd., with Alice and myself as directors.

Chapter Eight

1947 Transport Act and 'the Plan'

MEANWHILE, amongst all the activity and problem of moving to Salwick Hall, and the brickworks venture at Blackburn, Harold Bridges Ltd. was very much in the Road Transport scene. The General Election in 1945 gave the country a Labour Government with a majority in the House of Commons to ensure they could pass the legislation the Labour Party favoured of restrictions on and nationalisation of Road Transport. At first we did not worry too much, thinking it would most likely only apply to long distance heavy haulage.

We had after the war ended made our first acquisitions of two other operators. The first was a one vehicle business, operating a daily parcels service from Kirkham to Preston and return each day with a 30 cwt vehicle. The owner was in poor health and we bought the vehicle and goodwill, which included the operator's 'A' licence. This the Licensing Authority transferred to our licence, without problem and we promptly replaced the old vehicle with one of twice the carrying capacity and only 8/9 cwt increase in unladen weight.

The second acquisition was a three vehicle local general haulage business based in Bamber Bridge operated by Jack Cowley who was ready for retirement. On this occasion for taxation purposes we formed a new company, Transport Factors Ltd., which took over and operated the vehicles. Again we took advantage of the provisions in the 1933 Road Traffic Act where on a change of vehicle an increase in unladen weight of less that 10 cwt on any one vehicle was allowed without enquiry. On this occasion we were granted 'A' licences for four vehicles in place of three with a much larger increase in carrying capacity. This was because one of Cowley's vehicles was a big old Leyland heavy articulated vehicle tractor unit and trailer. There had always been very strong opposition by the Railways to any increase in unladen weight above that allowed in the 1933 Act, or to any increase in the number of vehicles

119

on an 'A' licence.

We had now got full possession of Stone Mill, Bamber Bridge, to be the site of our new postwar depot, and as the premises at Walton-le-Dale were quite inadequate for the 36 vehicles we were now operating, while planning for the new depot we made alterations at Stone Mill of a temporary nature to ease the pressure.

The first job was to have demolished a very tall factory chimney which stood right in the middle of all the buildings, so could not be felled in the normal way at one go. The steeplejacks worked for a few days at a time dropping the rubble brickwork down the sides of the chimney, and we had an old tipping lorry carting it on to land for foundations for the open vehicle parking ground planned for.

Thomas Croft & Son Ltd., Preston, built a loading deck inside the main building ground floor which enabled us to unload, sort and reload 12 vehicles at any one time. Part of Stone Mill was a large, stone-built, four-storey building. The old lift to take goods above ground floor was obsolete and beyond repair. The demand for storage and warehouse space was increasing all the time so we installed a 10 cwt electric hoist to serve all four floors. We also used the large single-storey weaving shed to store several hundred tons of animal feeding stuffs brought in by heavy haulage contractors, and collected by animal food merchants, and we bought our first Clarke fork lift truck.

Everything looked to be in our favour for an exciting prosperous future. When the 1947 Transport Act came into force, the industry as a whole knew that there were certain to be restrictions on the operations of heavy haulage long distance operators, but I do not think anyone had the faintest idea the restrictions and the powers to acquire operators would be so widespread and all-embracing, as indicated in the following:

Part 3 Section 39 Subsection 2 reads:

(2)   In this Part of this Act, the expression 'ordinary long distance carriage' means, in relation to an undertaking, the carriage of goods by the person carrying on the undertaking for a distance OF FORTY MILES OR UPWARDS in one goods vehicle or a succession of goods vehicles, in such circumstances that the vehicle, or, as the case may be, one or more of the vehicles, is at some time during the carriage, more than TWENTY-FIVE MILES FROM ITS OPERATING CENTRE.

Part 3 Section 39 Subsection 3 reads:

(3)   The distance of forty miles mentioned in subsection (2) of this section shall notwithstanding anything in section thirty-four of the Interpretation Act, 1889, be measured along the route actually taken by the vehicle or vehicles in question.

Subsequent sections and subsections excluded some traffic like bulk liquids, livestock etc. and permits could be applied for to carry outside the 25 miles radius of base, or 40 miles by road. During the period 1947 to 1954 I never heard of any operator being granted a permit. So what now? The Act was the law of the land, so the first thing I did was to get two copies of the Act from H. M. Stationery Office, one for the office for anyone to study and one for me to study at any time.

Part 3 of the 1947 Transport Act covered Transport of Goods by Road. It had 24 sections and 101 subsections, 88 pages in all so there was a lot of studying to do, to try to decide what was the best course to pursue in the best interests of our customers, employees and the whole future of the family business, built up with so much hard work, devotion and loyalty to the firm by our employees, very many of whom had worked for us all their working lives, and were known along with their families to Alice and me personally. We knew there would be compensation but as near as I and the company's accountants could make out this would be about half what it was worth to the family.

Not that we were alone; oh no, there were throughout the country thousands of small firms, fathers and sons, with a few devoted employees who had worked hard since the war to build a business and livelihood, now to lose it all and for what purpose? Only to bolster up the railway system which could not meet the competition from its young rival, road transport.

However, the Act was there. It was the law of the land, and we had to plan accordingly. Inevitably the industry was dumbfounded by the foreseeable consequences for thousands of operators.

Meetings of protest were held all over the country. I attended several in the Preston district at which all sorts of protests were suggested, including blocking all the main town roads and traffic routes, withdrawing services and so forth. I could now speak and talk without any problem. I did speak at every meeting I went to, I always put forward the obvious fact the Act was the law and we could not do anything to alter that. What we must do is so arrange our affairs, that we received the maximum amount of compensation allowed under the Act. We might also see whether by exchange of customers, some activity might be continued even if on a much reduced scale.

Preston and district and, in fact, any operator whose base was on the coast, was in a very poor position as around half the 25 miles radius was in the sea, Fleetwood and similar ports were in a still worse position. Permits to operate outside 25 miles could be applied for, which were never granted if the operator was one the Transport Commission wished to acquire.

It appeared all our schemes and dreams for the future were gone with the wind and our 28 years' hard work would be brought to a sad and very unsatisfactory end, unless some legal way could be found through the 88 pages of the Act which would enable some form of activity to be continued. To this end I read the Act through and through many times, drew 25 miles circles on maps, talked about it with anyone in or out of the industry who was interested and formulated my own plan, which Alice and I talked over at great length time and time again.

The firm opinion of all those who had studied the Act and had experience in road transport or who were in the legal and similar occupations, was that while my plan could possibly work practically, and as a viable scheme. The fact that it entailed the Bridges' family starting a new business exactly similar in every way to the one acquired by compulsory acquisition meant that the Transport Commission would undoubtedly use all means at their disposal to stop us.

Briefly my plan would be in operations soon as ever possible after we were acquired, possibly before we had even received our compensation payment, we would be in direct competition with the old company on the same routes, exactly the same type of traffic, over the same areas. The plan could not, of course, come into full effect at once. It would take a few years to develop. I was approaching my 48th birthday. I had three sons, a wonderful wife and daughter and all willing to have a go, so get planning.

The first decision was that by every legal and practical means, we must delay the actual date of our acquisition as much as possible. We were able to do this by the very nature of our operations. We were now with Transport Factors Ltd. operating 36 vehicles, all except one were engaged in the collection and delivery of small consignments from a few pounds weight and up to 4 cwt; the average weight per delivery was under 1 cwt.

The distance the goods were carried varied from five miles to 100 miles, and while we had some information it was almost a practical impossibility to decide whether we were in 1946 engaged in long distance haulage of goods for hire or reward as defined in the Act. The representatives of the Commission came to the depot many times, but like us could not really convince themselves or us what our position was regarding compulsory acquisition or not. This went on for some time and we agreed to try and assemble information in the future to enable an agreed decision.

This delay was just what we were playing for. Our next move was to apply for permits to operate outside the 25 miles radius if we were not acquired. We did not apply for all the permits we needed at the same time. Each application took a few months to process, as each application was refused we made application again for another area, and so the delaying tactics went on. All quite legal and above board and great fun.

There were several reasons why we wished to delay acquisition as long as possible. The main one was the effect of delay on the amount of compensation we would receive. Broadly, compensation was to be based on the commercial value of all fixed assets, land, buildings, vehicles, tools, equipment, etc., and on the average nett profit over the three years immediately before the acquisition.

The average nett profit was reduced by 3% of the value of the assets and this figure was then multiplied by not less than two or more than five being the goodwill figure based on the type of operation on which the acquired under-taking was engaged. Our nett profits were increasing each year, so the longer the acquisition could be delayed the higher the three years average would be multiplied by the goodwill figure of 2 to 5.

We also took steps to reduce to the practical minimum the value of the assets, which would be charged with the 3% before arriving at the average nett profit for the last three years.

No new vehicles were ordered, surplus vehicles held as stand-bys were sold, as were all items of a capital nature not required during the year in which acquisition would take place. The effect of our delaying tactics were that although the Act came into force early in 1947 the Notice of Acquisition we eventually received was to take effect on 14th August 1950, three years' delay. It was very hard to believe that a piece of buff coloured paper, 10" x 8", could take away from a hard working family the results of 29 years' work, and we were not alone. In anticipation of the acquisition, Walton Vale Storage Ltd. and Transport Factors Ltd. had been merged with Harold Bridges Ltd., further increasing the nett profit on which the goodwill compensation would be based.

While all this activity in the business was taking place home life at Salwick was very relaxing, peaceful and enjoyable, and it sometimes seemed hard to believe that 30 years before I was the gamekeeper's boy on the Salwick Estate for 5s. 0d. per week. Now I was arranging to rear wild duck and pheasants, to stock the ponds and woods, and have shooting days with friends in due course.

I had always, thank God, enjoyed very good health, now and then a bad cold or tummy upset, probably through over-eating, until mid 1948 when I suddenly started with terrible pains in my abdomen about midday. I drove home and went straight to bed, thinking I would be O.K. next morning. Instead I was awake all night. It just felt as if someone was inside me with a pitch fork. Alice sent for Dr. Gibb from Great Eccleston on whose panel I was. I had never met him before. His examination only took a few minutes, then he said, 'Hospital at once, acute appendicitis, maybe burst appendix'. Alice 'phoned the depot for a car, the doctor 'phoned the Royal Infirmary, Preston, spoke to Cunliffe Shaw the surgeon, and in an hour I was in the hospital, and another half-hour later I was going to the operating theatre for a three hour stay.

Alice had gone with me and was still there when I came round and was conscious. It had, I learned later, been a very close call. Apparently I had during the past few years had appendix problems, several times. Each time the appendix was weakened and this time it had burst, acute peritonitis the result.

Cunliffe Shaw, the surgeon, told me later that when he made the incision to open me the green fluid spurted out, and he had looked at Sister Hampson and shook his head. It appears that the reason the operation took so long was they were trying to clean up the mess in my abdominal cavity, and it was this cleaning up process that kept me in hospital for five weeks.

I was also told that I was not expected to live more than 48 hours after the operation and that the two things that saved my life were a very strong constitution and the fact that I had massive injections of Penicillin every four hours for eight days, a case of kill or cure and it was a good job I was not allergic to penicillin. I had about a month's convalescence at Salwick and not had any ill effect since. Had things gone wrong there would not have been any story to tell after 1948 as none had been told up to then, or any diaries kept.

Salwick Estate of 1,200 acres was far from ideal as a sporting estate; it was about eight miles from Preston where there was the usual number of the poaching fraternity. On the south, east and north the land was all owned by individual farmers, and there was in consequence no game reared and no gamekeepers to keep the poaching activity under control. There were no game birds and the farmer occupiers probably thought the poachers were one way of keeping the rabbit population under control.

On the west of the Salwick Estate was the Treales Estate of Lord Derby, later sold to the Church Commission. On Treales game was reared; two gamekeepers were employed, whom I had known 30 years before, and naturally we joined with them in efforts to thwart the poachers.

The first few years we had lots of incidents, which tailed off when I suppose word got around that Salwick was no longer a happy hunting ground. It was so easy for poachers as the railway line from Preston to Lytham ran right along the south boundary; in fact, the railway was the boundary, the Preston to Lancaster Canal and its towpath ran right through the middle of the estate from south to north and the estate also had two roads south to north and two roads east to west, all of which gave easy access and escape, either on foot, bicycle or car.

We only had three incidents with night poachers using long nets 2–3 hundred yards long, set up in the fields alongside woods. On these occasions we were usually in company with one of the Treales gamekeepers, the local police constable, Bill Lindsay, my gardener gamekeeper, and myself.

On the two first incidents we did not get the poachers; it was a pitch black night and they just scattered in the darkness, on each occasion there were three poachers. They had, of course, abandoned all their long nets and 2 ft. long pegs and a bag of 12–15 rabbits in their getaway, so had a night's work for nothing and lost all their tackle. I think they gave Salwick a wide berth after that.

The third occasion was sheer luck in how it came about. Nancy had been into Preston on the Viking bus in the evening coming home about 9.00 p.m., and there were two men on the bus with hessian sacks and they got off the bus at Salwick station. Nancy said they looked like poachers. So we got organised, four of us, and we went along all the woods on the Salwick Estate where we

Alice crowns the Rose Queen at Newton Blue School, 1952.

knew they would be likely to try as there were plenty of rabbits, but we drew a blank, no sign of anyone.

The Treales gamekeeper said, 'They must be on Treales, let's try the far side of the big wood'. He was right, it was a moonlit night and we came on them just as they had got 200 yards of net set up. It was a man called Sharples and his son. Luckily the constable knew him from a previous conviction and said, 'Hello, Sharples, no use running this time'. On account of previous poaching offences and this being night poaching, he got six months in gaol and all their tackle confiscated.

Daytime rabbit poaching was usually the poacher on his own with a ferret and purse nets, one over each rabbit hole. When we caught these we usually took all their nets and rabbits if they had any and told them to clear off. If we caught them again on Salwick we would take their ferret as well and prosecute them. This seemed to work. We never had a second or third offender.

There was occasionally to us an amusing incident which I am sure scared the poacher so much he would not come near Salwick again. We had a Land Rover and Lindsay used to do a tour round the roads at weekends. On one such occasion he saw a man leaving a wood near the canal. He watched him go to the canal towpath, get on a bicycle with a sack over his shoulder and ride off towards Preston. Lindsay came to the Hall, picked me up and we went to a canal bridge about a mile further along the towpath knowing the man on the bicycle would come along shortly. The Land Rover was on the road away from the bridge; we hid behind the bridge on the towpath.

Peeping out we could see the man on his cycle coming, just as he came from under the bridge Lindsay jumped out to grab him. The man must have been scared out of his wits; he did a bit of a wobble and fell backwards – cycle, bag and all – into the canal, which was about 4 feet deep.

We got him out, or he got himself out, cycle and bag, we kept his nets, and

three rabbits he had caught. He had no ferret. It had stayed down a rabbit hole. Lindsay got it next day. Lindsay wanted to take his cycle too but I said, 'No, I think he has had a lesson and will keep away from Salwick now'.

Another to us amusing incident (I was not involved) was when Lindsay saw a man come out of a wood near the canal with a gun. When Lindsay asked what he was up to the man started arguing. Lindsay said, 'Give me that gun.' And grabbed the barrels of the gun, a jolly dangerous thing to do as if it was loaded it might have gone off. However, after wrestling around for possession of the gun it broke in two at the stock grip. All this was on the towpath, near Salwick Hall. It must have been quite a tussle; when the gun broke the man was back to the canal and he fell into 5 ft of water with half his gun in his hand. Lindsay proudly brought me the other half of the gun. I said, 'I don't think we'll see him again.'

Alice crowned the Rose Queen one year at the annual event. This was a first for her. Another highlight at Salwick was when the King, H.M. George VI, the Queen and Princess Margaret came to Salwick to look at some of the farms on the estate which were owned by the Duchy of Lancaster. The farm tenants, about 10, Alice and I were assembled at Garlick's Wards House Farm to be introduced. The King and Queen were given the tenants' names, shook hands,

Alice at the microphone after crowning the Rose Queen, Newton Blue Coat School, 1952.

spoke very briefly to each one and moved on. Alice and I were the last in the line. We were introduced by the Equerry, Sir Norman Warwick as Mr. & Mrs. Harold Bridges, lease holders of Salwick Hall and sporting rights. We shook hands; the King looked hard at me and said, 'Bridges', where have I heard that name before?' The Equerry said, 'The Gamekeepers at Sandringham. Mr. Bridges' father and his three brothers, Fred, Wilfred and Ralph were all gamekeepers at Sandringham and their father' (my grandfather).

The King said, 'Oh yes, of course, poor old Ralph, he should have had that leg off years ago'. It appeared that Ralph had slipped into an open boiler of boiling dog food some years before and in consequence suffered very badly for years while the surgeons tried to save his leg. In the end Queen Mary, the Queen Mother, arranged for Ralph to go to London for treatment, which led to his leg being amputated.

Ralph lived at Appleton Lodge, a bungalow on the Sandringham Estate. The King seemed to know all about the Sandringham Bridges, he was a very keen and very good shot and would know them all personally from contact at Sandringham. Dad had three cousins: May married the Sandringham head kitchen gardener, Bert Southgate; Lily married one of the grooms at the Royal Stables; and Florrie married the Sandringham House postmaster, Fred Bunn. Dad also had a cousin, Bert Bridges, who was the Sandringham House carpenter all his working life, so the Bridges were very well represented at Sandringham.

It was some years before this that Alice and I went to Sandringham with the children for a holiday. We stayed at The Feathers, Dersingham. Cousin May and Bert Southgate and their two sons, David and George, lived at York Lodge, Sandringham. One afternoon we all went to May's for afternoon tea, and May told us Queen Mary might be calling but not to worry, we would be in the living room and Queen Mary would not stay long and would be in the front room.

Queen Mary was the Queen Mother and duly arrived in her big Daimler car with footman. Queen Mary's chauffeur, Fred, was Bert Southgate's brother, and had been chauffeur for many years.

May showed the Queen Mary into the front room, the communicating door was slightly open and we could hear the conversation. It was an unwritten law that in the presence of Royalty, one answered a question but did not elaborate on it. This is what was heard:

> Queen Mary: 'Have you had your holidays yet?'
> May: 'Yes, Your Majesty.'
> Queen Mary: 'Did you have good weather?'
> May: 'Yes Your Majesty.'
> Queen Mary: 'Where did you go this year?'
> May: 'Lancashire.'

Queen Mary: 'Oh, why Lancashire?'
May: 'I have a cousin lives there.'
Queen Mary: 'What did you like about Lancashire?'
May: 'The Lake District and Windermere Lake.'
Queen Mary: 'Did you go on the Lake?'
May: 'Yes, Cousin Harold hired a boat for three hours.'
Queen Mary: 'Do your cousins ever come to see you?'
May: 'Yes.'
Queen Mary: 'Where do they stay?'
May: 'At the Feathers in Dersingham.'
Queen Mary: 'Have they been this year?'
May: 'Yes.'
Queen Mary: 'Have they been to see you?'
May: 'Yes, they are here now in the next room.'
Queen Mary: 'Oh, I would like to meet them.'

So we were all introduced to Queen Mary. After asking the children their names and hobbies, the Queen Mother asked John, the youngest, about his hobby which was keeping an autograph book. She said, 'Have you got it with you?'

John said, 'Yes, Ma'am'.

She asked John if she could see it. John handed it over and she opened it and said, 'Oh dear'. The page she opened it at had the public executioner and hangman's autograph 'Pierpoint The hangman'.

She asked John if she might take the book to look through, which she did. Next day one of the footmen brought it back to York Lodge with her autograph. Before the Queen Mary left us she said to me, 'I must tell you a little story about Windermere'. She said, 'May tells me you took them on Windermere and what a lovely day they had. Well it is many many years ago – I was staying at Lowther Castle and a trip was organised to have a ride round Windermere in an open horse-drawn waggonette. It was a very misty day, rained most of the way, I did not see a bit of Windermere and I was wet through to my petticoat. May has been lucky'. So all that was a day to be remembered for all of us.

Little did I or any of the family know or think that some 25 years later I would be called to Buckingham Palace, London to receive from the then Queen Mother Elizabeth the OBE at the Investiture, 5th February 1974, more of that later. By now, 14th August 1950, our Nationalisation Day or Acquisition date, as it was officially described was approaching. We had taken all the steps we were legally entitled to, to delay the acquisition, and in the end decided to let the acquisition go ahead, and arrange our affairs accordingly.

Our family was now growing up. At 14th August 1950 Alice was 52. I was 50, Charles 23, Nancy 19, David 17, John 14. Charles, Nancy, John and I were all working in the family business, Harold Bridges Ltd. David was serving his apprenticeship as an automobile mechanic at Dunderdale & Yates Ltd., the Austin agents in Preston. David had won a scholarship from St. Leonard's School, Walton-le-Dale to Hutton Grammar School for two years. Nancy was working in Harold Bridges Ltd. general office to become my right hand and John had started work in the office. Charles was in the Depot Traffic Department, and helping out in the storage warehousing, and anywhere else so he was acquiring a wide knowledge of the whole job, and David would go to workshops. Long term, the family would have had a member in all the departments, but this was not to be, thanks to the 1945 Labour Government. Nancy and I decided we would stay with the new set up for six months as we were allowed while employed to see the collection of all moneys owing to the old firms and pay their creditors, and it would give us six months inside information on the new set up. John also stayed on with Nancy and I. Charles gave his notice to finish in four weeks for reasons which will be explained later.

So came 14th August 1950, a day I shall never, ever forget. It was a bright sunny morning. About 9.00 a.m. Nancy and I were going down London Road to Walton-le-Dale in the Austin 16 K.T.B. 300 when we met three of the firm's vans coming up the hill behind each other all in royal blue and white lettering across the front of each van:

Harold Bridges Ltd.
Transport Contractors
Send it by Road

I remember I said to Nancy, 'They are not ours any more. It's not right'. And I just could not help it – my voice broke and tears ran down my cheeks. After that first shock, I realised we still had a future, and that was what we must look to, no use looking back, let's get on with 'The Plan' and show the industry and the nationalisers what a Lancashire lad who left school at 13 could do with the willing backup of a very loyal, loving wife and family and a band of loyal workers. So into battle here we go, against the advice of all the experts – they all said in varying degrees of convinced judgement, 'They will never let you get away with it.' 'They' being the new National Transport set up. We had, of course, not been idle on the plan. When Charles completed his four weeks' notice the plan came into action at once (first stage). We had negotiated and purchased from two brothers Walmsley a general haulage business with three 'A' licensed vehicles based at Farington, Lancashire (near Leyland). The two brothers drove themselves and had one employed driver. The business was bought in the name of Charles Harold Bridges. I found the finance. So five weeks after the date of acquisition we were, or Charles was, in business with three vehicles. The conditions or descriptions of work on the three 'A' licences was 'General goods mainly in Lancashire' and the vehicles were three 5-ton carrying capacity. The base was Farington so the 25 miles radius to which the restrictions applied enabled us to collect and deliver within a 25 miles radius of Farington, Nr. Leyland, Lancs. This area included Southport, Liverpool, Manchester, Oldham, Rossendale Valley, Burnley, Nelson and Colne, Clitheroe, Lancaster, Morecambe, Blackpool, Fleetwood, all the Fylde and, of course, Preston. It was in effect the total area we wished to cover from the start and was an excellent beginning to 'The Plan'.

The three Walmsley vehicles were fitted with headboards on the front of the cabs. We had these relettered, 'C.H. Bridges Transport Contractor'. Walmsley's had mainly worked for clearing houses, and had really very few direct customers of their own. We very soon changed that by advertising and it was just fantastic how the work came in. In a very short time we acquired Miller's based in Chorley with three vans engaged on parcel work from Manchester, and Kenneth Greenhalgh based in Westhoughton, also engaged in parcel delivery from Manchester.

In each case we just painted out the previous owners name on the vehicles and lettered them, 'C. H. Bridges, Transport Contractor'. These were followed by acquiring Stewart & Hill, Blackpool, four vehicles, and N. A. Birkett Ltd., Morecambe with two vehicles. All these acquisitions were 'A' Licensed vehicles and in all could cover the whole area we operated previously, including Kendal and Barrow-in-Furness. The main consideration was that Preston or near Preston must be covered within each vehicle's radius of 25 miles allowed under the 1947 Road Traffic Act. It was only because our particular type of operation entailed the unloading of vehicles each night, sorting the mixed loads into the respective routes or areas for the delivery vehicles to load next morning, that 'the plan' was feasible; it could not possibly have been commercially employed for general haulage although it was tried in some parts of the country without much success.

Mention has been made earlier about the actual operating depot necessity and this was one of our early problems, we must have a secure place where we could unload the vehicles and sort the traffic into loads for next day, and where customers could bring traffic to us in their own vehicles for us to deliver anywhere on the territory next day.

We first rented some old farm buildings at Bamber Bridge not far from Stone Mill Depot. There was a very large barn-type building, we rigged up a sort of loading deck with second-hand timber and struggled on. By now my six months as 'temporary depot superintendent' at Harold Bridges Ltd. was up. What a title, but that was official and I was glad I stayed that six months to see what happened.

I, of course, had no say in any decision taking. I was the previous owner and just took orders like any other employee. What amazed me was how quickly changes were made which I thought were wrong. The first was that our profit sharing scheme was discarded, the average of the previous three years worked out and added onto the basic wage and called service bonus, so there was now really no direct incentive for employees to strive for the company's and their own benefit.

Another change was to our rule and practice over the past 29 years that there must be utter and complete flexibility of labour within the capabilities of the employee concerned.

I was instructed to prepare or have prepared a complete list of all employees, age, length of service, in what capacity employed etc. and finally exactly in detail what the employee's duties were, and instructed that in future, each employee was as far as practically possible to be kept to those duties, and to be made aware what they were. To my mind this was a lot of rot. There is perhaps little doubt it would be union inspired, and from calculations I made during my six months it increased our labour charges between 7 and 8 per cent. However, not to worry – it was none of my business, and thank goodness I had not agreed to stay 12 months after we were acquired.

Soon after we were acquired the Commission formed what they called the Lancaster Parcels Group composed of W. V. Greenwood Ltd. and Same Day Delivery, based in Burnley; Blackburn Parcels Express Ltd., based in Blackburn; and Harold Bridges Ltd., based in Walton-le-Dale, all engaged on parcel delivery or 'smalls'. Between them the Group would be operating between 80 and 90 vehicles, over the same routes and areas, as we intended to so we could expect some pretty fierce competition and opposition.

The manager of the Lancaster Parcels Group was a Granville Cooke. He had been the Managing Director of W. V. Greenwood Ltd. and Same Day Delivery Ltd., as an employee; these two parcel companies had belonged to Bouts-Tillotson Ltd of London and Burnley who had sold out or been acquired by the Commission. I knew Granville very well. We had done business together from before 1936 when we were in Lytham and often been together on committees in connection with Road Transport. Although he was an employee of the new set up, he was very sceptical of the future as he saw it developing.

He used to come to see me at Harold Bridges Ltd. every few weeks as part of his managerial duties. On one occasion he brought the North West Division Manager, a Mr. MacVie, to see the Walton-le-Dale and Bamber Bridge premises of Harold Bridges Ltd. Granville Cook had always admired out set up and the way we operated, having been handing traffic to us for delivery north of Lancaster from about 1934 to 1950, he was well aware of the way we had developed.

I think Granville was as amazed as me when after having seen both depots and had lots of explanations of our activities and methods of working, Mr.

McVie set about finding fault and trying to make out how things would be improved under the new management. MacVie had come from the Ulster Transport Authority to this job in the North West of England. He quite evidently did not know the first thing about parcel collection and delivery, at least that was the impression I got. I had only a few weeks left to serve and so could not help but had my say as follows:

> Mr. MacVie, all due respect to you, you are the North West Divisional Manager of the parcels activities of the Transport Commission, I am only temporary depot Superintendent of Harold Bridges Ltd. I started in 1921 with a model T Ford and a £1 note in my pocket. Your people have just taken my business with 36 vehicles off me. In that 29 years I have learned a lot, made a lot of money and I know what I am talking about; if you do as you say and make the alterations you have just mentioned in five years you will be losing money. I shall have started my business again. You or anyone else cannot stop me and we will run rings round you. I am not boasting or apologising, remember what I have just said.

Future events fully confirmed what I said.

Fortunately the depot problem was solved when premises in Miller Street and Adelaide Street, Preston came onto the market for sale. They were part of a previous cotton mill, from which we could operate about 20 vehicles, and the whole of the vehicles we had acquired could legally load and unload there. We had a loading deck built with access on each side from Miller Street and Adelaide Street, which were side roads from New Hall Lane, one of Preston's main thoroughfares, so we now owned the depot from which we operated. A little later we acquired adjoining premises on New Hall Lane, with offices and warehouse room, and more ground floor area which enabled us to extend the loading deck and connect it to the Miller Street and Adelaide Street section.

We also rented a disused school playground close by to park vehicles at night for which there was not room in the depot.

Nancy was now working in the office with me and John in the office, warehouse and depot as needed. The traffic we were now handling was such that we applied for and were granted additional 'A' licenses from time to time. There was no doubt 'The Plan' was working, and most important of all, I had been proved right in three separate cases, where operators had as we did started in business soon after acquisition. Two of the cases went to the Appeal Court and one to the House of Lords. In every case, at every stage the Transport Commission lost the day. The decision was that there was nothing in the 1947 Transport Act to stop an acquired operator starting again within the law the next day. This was certainly the 'All Clear' we needed and I felt we were now off to a flying start. Another very encouraging aspect was the long list of experienced, long service employees of Harold Bridges Ltd. who wished to leave and join us, and we took full advantage of this and were able to pick and choose employees in all departments, including office and workshop staff, whom we knew – some had worked for us at Lytham. This loss of fully experienced men by Harold Bridges Ltd. was their loss and our gain; drivers and mates who could and did multiple deliveries of up to 90 a day and then do 10 or 15 collections were not to be found easily if at all.

The men had been brought up with it and our methods, and we welcomed their return. I met Granville Cooke on occasions at Association meetings, and learned he was fed up with the new set up of Lancaster Parcels Group, the red tape, and everyone passing the buck to someone else, even though he would soon retire. The outcome was, would you believe it, Granville Cooke, Group Manager, Lancaster Parcels Group came to work for us as General Manager. We had by this time decided the business was growing so fast and the financial side becoming rather involved, we should turn the whole job into a private limited company and the outcome was the formation and registration of Bridges Transport Ltd.

By this time we had, through the acquisitions, a very mixed variety of vehicles of various makes, sizes and unladen weights. I had always been a strong believer in standardisation as much as possible and we began to put this into effect by ordering 12/3-ton Austin vehicles from Dunderdale and Yates Ltd., Preston. While all this was going on, our accountants, William Latham & Co., Lytham, had been very busy dealing with the compensation side of our acquisition. We had received a small down payment in 3% Transport Stock, the balance when agreed also to be paid in 3% Transport Stock. All the tools, equipment, stock, vehicles property, etc. had to be valued and agreed, and there was for sure lots of room for disagreement and argument – after all, it was not a case of a willing seller and willing buyer negotiating a price, the job was being taken from us against our will and we knew from the terms of compensation in the Act that we would only get about half what it was worth to the family, and we could not do anything about that. We finally agreed everything except the multiplier – 2 to 5 years times the average profit of the last three years after they had deducted 3% of the value of fixed assets, subject maybe to some adjustment for any special circumstances. We or they could not agree even after several special meetings in Manchester and Lytham. In these circumstances the Act provided for a panel in London to hear both sides and suggest a settlement. If this failed it could go to Appeal whose decision was final.

It was known from the many acquisitions which had been settled that the Commission were very reluctant to agree a multiplier of more than four years whatever the type of operation, or prospects for the future.

Parcels or smalls operators like us, where a high degree of organisation was required, and where future prospects were good, did get in many cases a multiplier of four. I felt very strongly that we had a very good case for insisting on the five year multiplier and this eventually led to our going to London to argue our case before the Compensation Panel. I had with me David Denton, The Company's accountant and Fred Senior, the Companies' and family solicitor.

We met the Panel at 2.00 p.m. at their office in London and each side argued their case till about 5.00 p.m. when it was suggested by the Chairman of the Panel that we have a two hour break, meet again at 7.00 p.m. to see if we could reach agreement.

I said no to this, 'There is lots of time tomorrow. I suggest we meet at 10.00 a.m. tomorrow so that during the break each side could consider their position and give a final decision to the Panel'. This was agreed and we parted with us still sticking to our claim for a total of £128,000 which we calculated was the maximum we could claim under the provisions of the 1947 Transport Act even though we felt very strongly in our own minds that it was worth twice that to the family, due to the very certain expansion that would take place in the next five years if it was left with us. David, Fred and I had a long evening's talk weighing up the whole position. We decided we should and would stick to our claim for £128,000 which was based on the five year multiplier, the maximum allowed under the Act. When we parted at 5.00 p.m. the Commission's final figure was £125,000 so there was £3,000 difference between us.

It had been evident during the meeting that they were very much against the five year multiplier. Whether they had ever paid anyone out on this basis I could not find out but they did hint, without actually saying so, that they had never paid five years. My reply to that was, 'Well you can start now, use a five year multiplier and the job will be settled'.

However, we met next morning 10.00 a.m. and we explained our position and I restaked our claim at £128,000 and this was final. At this the Chairman of the Panel said, 'I hope you realise, Mr. Bridges that if we do not reach agreement today this case will have to be dealt with by the Appeals Tribunal set up under the Act for this purpose and there could be several months' delay'.

I replied, 'Yes I know all about that, and I am quite happy to wait, and also quite happy to appear before the Tribunal for a decision'. I also said, 'you will perhaps excuse me if I remind you and the gentlemen opposite that under the Act the Commission must pay to the acquired operator interest of 3% per annum on the total value finally agreed to be paid for the period from the acquisition date to the date of issue of the stock, and also if on the day the compensation is paid the stock market valuation of the stock issued is below par extra stock has to be issued to make up the shortfall. At the present time 3% Transport Stock is slightly below par and if interest rates rise, it will fall further and more stock would have to be issued to equal the total compensation figure. Do you agree?'

The Chairman said, 'Yes I agree, the longer the delay, the more interest will have to be paid, and the amount of 3% Transport Stock issued on final payment does depend on the market price of the stock on that day'.

I said 'Thank you very much, perhaps the gentlemen opposite will now consider whether in view of what has been said £3,000 is worth arguing about?' The reply to this was, 'We have considered very carefully all that was said yesterday, and our own decision is to agree £128,000 as the total compensation to be paid. In our calculation we have not included five years multiplication, the figure we have used is rather less; in order to reach agreement we have increased the compensation for the 36 vehicles acquired by £3,000. We hope Mr. Bridges will agree.'

I was quite agreeable we were to get our £128,000 and they had preserved their not using a five year multiplier – what a game to save face.

We caught a train at Euston Station about 2.00 p.m. very glad that the matter was settled. We had achieved the maximum compensation we would under the Act, and could now look to the future and 'The Plan'.

Immediately we had confirmation of the amount of stock we were to receive, we arranged with our bank to sell it forward as there was a tendency for 3% Transport Stock to decline – we did not want to hold 3% Stock when we could make the money earn 15% in our own business. The sale of the stock forward resulted in a loss of ¼per cent, but extra stock to cover the market value had been issued to us, so we ended up with around £128,000 in a new account at the bank. Perhaps not so bad for 29 years work by a lad who left school at 13 and was not 50 years of age. Through all the years since 1937 scores of times my thoughts went back to the days of my speech problem and the way it was solved, and I wondered how I would have coped if it was still with me.

Alice and all the family were as pleased as I was that this worry was now out of the way and we could now really get cracking on 'The Plan'.

When Granville Cooke joined us as General Manager, he brought the business of several good customers with him, on occasions the same happened when a driver left Harold Bridges Limited to join Bridges Transport Limited, all to the good. Bridges Transport Limited introduced a Company Profit Sharing Scheme which applied to all employees with over one year's service. In my own mind there was not the slightest shadow of a doubt but that it was due to the PSS that we kept forging ahead, traffic was increasing all the time and once again we were facing the depot problem. We were now approaching full economic capacity at Miller Street and Adelaide Street, and if we were to continue to expand, the decision what we were to do about it could not be delayed.

My dream was a purpose built depot on a virgin or open cleared site in or very near Preston. Enquiries to Estate Agents and the like only revealed old cotton mills and factories of various sorts, none of which had the area I envisaged we would require, and in any case would require demolition site clearance etc. before building could start.

Once again was it? Bridges luck came to the rescue, someone mentioned a site which had quite recently been completely cleared of an old cotton mill, Raglan Street Mill, off Eldon Street. Charles and I went to have a look at it, decided there and then this was it. Making enquiries we found it belonged to Preston Corporation. The mill had been demolished, the site cleared and, would you believe it, they were prepared to lease it on a long lease on favourable terms to industrial or commercial firms to develop. The site was just under two acres bounded on the east by the main line railway, on the north by Eldon Street, on the west by Raglan Street and on the south by Maynard Street. What a site to have: streets on three sides, open ready to build except for a very high factory chimney which had not been demolished, as it was thought it might be used by a new lessee. This I found out when I went to the Town Hall to get details.

Alas, there were going to be problems. It appeared the terms of the Compulsory Purchase Order when the site was acquired were it was to be leased to firms, not to one lessee only. I expect the idea was to help a number of small firms. At the time of my first meeting at the Town Hall they had no other enquiries about the site which had, it appears, been vacant some time. I explained we required a site about two acres and Raglan Street Mill site would be ideal for our purpose, but they could not let us have it all and said they would get in touch with us when they had another enquiry.

We had in mind the continued expansion of our warehouse facilities and we toyed with the idea of forming a separate limited company to operate the warehousing and storage side of our activities, so there would be two firms on the site to satisfy the conditions.

However, about two weeks later our luck was in, the Corporation officer concerned 'phoned me to say they had another party enquiring about a very small portion of the site, were we still interested? It appeared a firm of electrical goods and equipment distributors, Lionel Robinson & Co. Ltd. were prepared to take a lease of a plot on the corner of Eldon Street and Raglan Street for a distribution depot showroom and offices, etc. The area they required was so small compared to the whole site that it would not make any material difference to our plans and, luck again, the mighty big factory chimney was right in the corner of the site where they wished to build, so that was their problem.

It did not take long to agree the terms and conditions of the lease, which was a ground lease for a long term, with no rent review provisions. Now we could get busy, we soon had our architect and surveyor, A. T. England of St. Annes, on the job, plans drawn and passed by the Corporation. Thomas Croft & Son Ltd. of Preston got the contract for the main depot building and offices, around

£35,000 for the first stage, and building our new depot started, Raglan Street Depot, Bridges Transport Ltd. The main depot building was 240 ft. long in three spans of 50 ft or 150 ft wide which would enable us to unload and load 60 vehicles at the same time all under cover and any vehicle being able to enter or leave its loading bay without having to move any other vehicle, and no pillars or stanchions where the vehicles moved.

Purpose built workshops were ready when we occupied the depot – refuelling installation and a 32-ton weighbridge and office, so that every vehicle entering and leaving the depot was weighed.

While all this activity was taking place other events of dramatic impact on our plans took place. The Labour Government of the day elected in 1945 brought in the 1947 Road Transport Act and nationalisation; then another Labour Government followed so the 1947 restrictions carried on until a Conservative Government was elected and brought in the 1953 Transport Act, which abolished the 25 miles radius restriction as from the end of 1954 in Section 8(i):

> 8 (i) At the end of the year nineteen hundred and fifty-four section fifty-two of the Transport Act 1947 (which provides for restricting the use of goods vehicles more than twenty-five miles from their operating centres), any such condition in a licence as is provided for by the said section fifty-two and sections fifty-three and fifty-six, subsection (ii) of section fifty-seven, section fifty-eight, subsections (i) and (iii) to (vi) of section sixty, and sections sixty-one and sixty-two of the said Act (which contain various provisions supplementary or incidental to the said section fifty-two) shall cease to have effect.

We were now free to carry on within the limits of 'A' licences issued under the 1933 Act of which we had over 20 years experience and was no worry at all. We had one scare about the time we were preparing to move into Raglan Street. The Suez Canal crisis developed and we were to have fuel rationing as during the war. The scheme introduced was that the first and subsequent basic issue of fuel coupons would be based on the fuel delivered during the previous full calendar month. We had a 1,000 gallon underground storage tank in Adelaide Street, our nominal average consumption was about 2,000 gallons per month.

The form which had to be sent in simply asked, 'How many gallons of road vehicle fuel was delivered to your premises last month?' Well, well, would you believe it, in the last month the new fuel installation at Raglan Street had been completed and we had had 2,000 gallons of fuel delivered to Raglan Street, and the usual 2,000 gallons to Adelaide Street, so we answered the question quite honestly, 4,000 gallons, so we did not have any worry about fuel coupons whilst the Suez crisis lasted. When we moved to Raglan Street the premises in New Hall Lane, Miller Street and Adelaide Street were sold to Preston Farmers

Ltd., who had their corn mill in Adelaide Street next door.

We were now all set to go ahead, 'The Plan' had worked just as I thought it would while the 25 miles radius restriction was on. Now we were free, which gave us a great deal more flexibility in the use of the different companies' vehicles, as any vehicle could go anywhere on the area covered by our services. We resolved to take full advantage of our new freedom of operation, and having the required depot facilities to expand as rapidly as possible. Granville Cooke had now retired, so I now became more involved in the actual day to day operation of the undertakings. The businesses of Stewart & Hill Ltd. and N. A. Birket Ltd., were now merged with Bridges Transport Ltd. and we set about looking for operators with 'A' licences who were prepared to sell as being the quickest way to expand rapidly. We were very successful in this, in that we acquired Dean & Pounder Ltd., Morecambe, Globe Parcels, Ltd., Liverpool, Hargreaves Delivery Services Ltd., Blackburn. The acquisition of these three limited companies added 20 vehicles to our fleet and were followed by a number of single vehicle operators, in and around Preston. The Globe Parcels Ltd. acquisition was particularly useful as their 'A' licence entitled them to collect and deliver general goods throughout the whole of Lancashire and Cheshire.

Our services were, therefore, extended to cover the whole of Lancashire and Cheshire five days a week, and some local deliveries on Saturdays. All this seemingly frantic business activity did not mean Salwick did not exist.

Chapter Nine

'The Foundation' and Sale to Tayforth

TIME passes and changes in home life as elsewhere take place. Freda had gone back to the Midlands to look after her eldest sister, Edith, a widow who lost her husband in France in 1915. Edith had been a diabetic for some years and this has caused her to recently have a leg amputated. Nancy was now married and living at Broughton, near Preston. Her husband, A. D. Milne was from Aberdeen, employed as a sales representative by Dunlop Rubber Co., Ltd.

David had been called to military service when his apprenticeship to Motor Engineering was complete. He was in the Royal Electrical & Mechanical Engineers, REME for short, and was attached to the 3rd Independent Parachute Brigade in Cyprus at the time of the Suez crisis.

Charles had married and was living at Bamber Bridge, so this left Alice, John and me at home, in a very large country house.

All the time we were at Salwick Alice had a domestic help, two days a week, who lived near Chorley. She had to leave home about 6.00 a.m. to get a bus to Chorley, catch another bus to Preston, and then the Viking bus to Salwick. She arrived about 8.30 a.m. and left on the 5.00 p.m. bus Salwick to Preston, so by the time she got home it was a 13 hour day. Mrs. Woods was a hefty lass, about 40, and she could knock the washing about. We had no electric washer, tumble dryer or the like. Alice and I decided to look for a small place near Preston, as Mrs. Wood had intimated she would not intend to or be able to come to Salwick after the spring of 1957.

I first of all had to see the Duchy of Lancaster about the lease of the Hall and Estate which had around another 10 years to run. I was prepared and very willing to retain the shooting lease on the Estate if they would release me from the Salwick Hall lease. They agreed to try and in a few weeks the Hall lease had been transferred to a cotton manufacturer from Chorley, a Mr. Craven. In

Myself, 1957. Taken in Robson Byers Solicitor's Office, Hastings Place, Lytham.

the meantime, Alice and I after much searching and inspecting properties, found 'Ashburne', 346 Garstang Road, Fulwood, and we moved from Salwick to Fulwood in April 1957.

When John, our youngest son, was leaving school at Walton-le-Dale in 1950 he had the usual medical inspection and we were informed he had a very slight heart murmur, that it was nothing to worry about but it would be advisable if he had an examination annually to check his heart. Later I was taking out some life assurances on my own life and took John along to Manchester to be checked over, on the basis of life assurance for John. The outcome of this was that I was accepted as a first class life, but they would not consider John at all after he had been examined. I asked what would be the best thing to do about it, who to see and so forth. They advised me to try and get an appointment with Sir Russell Brock, later Lord Brock, in London. The family doctor was a Doctor Gibb from Great Eccleston and he made arrangements for us to see Sir Russell Brock in Harley Street, London, so in due course off we went on the train to London.

The appointment was for 2.00 p.m. which would enable us to catch a train home around 5.00 p.m. Sir Russell had a long chat with us while X-rays were taken of John's heart and he then told us all together that John had a serious heart fault that would gradually worsen and if nothing was done John's life expectancy could not be beyond 35–40 years, that it would be advisable not to indulge in any sport or activity which entailed physical exertion of any kind, or even to marry.

Sir Russell went on to say the fault could be corrected by operation; if the operation was successful John would have a first class life. The snag was that it was a difficult and intricate operation and at the present time the mortality rate in the operation was around 24% which was rather daunting.

Sir Russell advised having another examination in six months. If John followed his advice he would take no harm, and as the techniques and experience in this particular operation improved the mortality rate was bound to come down and no harm would result from waiting, provided John did not run upstairs, play tennis, football or other physical exertion.

So followed two further visits at six month intervals and at the last one Sir Russell informed us the mortality expectancy was now around 10%. After explaining it all to John he asked John what he thought. John said, 'You say if I come through I will be 100%, if I don't, well I will not know anything about it, so get on with it as soon as you can.'

Sir Russell Brock soon made arrangements for John to go into Guys Hospital, London, for the operation which Sir Russell carried out himself.

The operation was a complete success. John was home in under three weeks and after two later checks at six month intervals John was passed O.K. first class.

Some time later John had a further check by the Life Assurance medicals and they were completely satisfied and would now accept John as a first class life. Oh what a relief! Alice and I and indeed all the family and our many friends were delighted beyond words. Alice and I felt we ought to show our gratitude to the medical profession in some tangible way, and we later asked Sir Russell if he had any particular aspect of his work which we might be able to support to show our gratitude and appreciation. He informed us he would very much like to set up a fellowship at the Royal College of Surgeons in London for research into cardio-vascular and heart problems, surgery and treatment. Alice and I agreed we should do something about it.

There followed a lot of suggestion, discussion and so forth between Sir Russell, the RCS and our solicitors and accountants, the outcome was that the RCS would require a sum of £100,000 to invest and use the income to fund the operation of the fellowship. After much more discussion, Alice and I decided we should set up some form of charitable trust and provide the funds to start the Fellowship at the RCS and when this was accomplished to donate the income to charitable purposes, mainly in the North West, where our success had enabled the funds to be generated.

In due course, a trust deed was agreed; the trustees were to be the Trustee Division of Williams Deacons Bank Ltd., Manchester. The charity was named The Harold & Alice Bridges' Charity, Regd. No. 236654, established 14th October 1963. For operational purposes the title Harold Bridges Foundation

Raglan Street depot, 1964.

was used in later years. It was June 1970 when the accumulated income of the Charity reached £100,000. This was duly handed over to the Royal College of Surgeons to establish The Harold Bridges Fellowship, the first Fellow appointed was Dr. Edward Proctor. Alice and I were very pleased indeed and we agreed that we would transfer to the Foundation further assets as and when it was possible and advisable tax-wise, such sums to be capitalised and the income donated to charities. We always had in our minds our debt to the medical profession. My peritonitis in 1948, Alice's last child in 1938 and now John and his successful heart operation – three lives had been saved. If I had died in 1948 and it was a very near do, there would have been a much different story to tell after 1947. The trust deed laid down broad guidelines to follow, in considering the donations to be made.

Meanwhile at Raglan Street Depot the increase in the demand for our services and the amount of traffic we were handling was just fantastic. We, or I at least, had 40 years 'know how' in the job, by nationalisation all our Road Transport assets had been turned into cash and we had so arranged our affairs so that our cash flow was extremely good. We were showing a net return to capital employed of 30% and in spite of or because of our rapid expansion we had no need to resort to loans, bank overdrafts or hire purchase.

The credit control staff were under very strict instruction that on no account was any account to become overdue more than two weeks. Payment was due before the end of the month following collection of the goods, so for goods

Raglan Street depot, 1964.

collected the first week in the month they could get eight weeks credit, goods collected the last week in the month could get four weeks credit, which I felt was quite long enough. We had to pay for all our vehicles and equipment on the same terms, wages had to be paid every week, licences, insurances of all kinds had to be paid twelve months in advance.

In the few cases of slow payers we insisted on the customer paying us an estimated sum in advance, based on the average of the previous three months; if they did not like this, well, it was just too bad, and we did not want their traffic. We only slipped up once, when a customer who had always been a good payer suddenly without any warning called a meeting of creditors and eventually went into liquidation owing us about £250 for eight weeks work, four weeks of which was due and four weeks due before the end of the next month. Very fortunately we had a tip off of what was to happen two days before the end of the month. I was alerted, we made our collections on the last two days of the month but did not deliver the goods, they were not perishable and worth around £2,000. Our conditions of carriage of which every customer had received a copy and signed for it when we started to do business with them made it quite clear we were entitled to hold any goods handed to us for delivery until the account for the charges was paid. We notified the liquidator we intended to hold the goods until our account was paid. After quite a bit of argy-bargy on the 'phone and correspondence, he was left to sort it out. The outcome was when the statement of affairs was produced at the creditors meeting Bridges Transport Ltd. was right at the top first in the list of preferential creditors, before the Inland Revenue and wages due.

The liquidator explained the position to the meeting, that if he was given permission to pay our account £250 we would deliver the goods and he would collect around £2,000 for the goods. This was readily agreed to and in due course we got paid and delivered the goods.

The only other accounting problem we had was in collecting our charges for odd mostly one-off jobs, where the customer did not have an account; the charge might be anything from 5s. 0d. upwards. We could not have the collecting or delivering drivers collecting cash and we used to send out about 40–50 of these 'sundry accounts' as we called them, daily and they varied usually between 5s. 0d. and £5. Around 75% would pay, some later, some not at all, and it was not worth chasing the lower amounts.

We, therefore, made a minimum charge of £1 for items usually charged up to 10s. 0d.

'High Load' – Raglan St. depot warehouse, 1964.

with an offer that if the account was paid within seven days they could deduct 10s. 0d. This did the trick for the smallest charges, higher charges were graded on similar lines, with a 100% surcharge and a 50% reduction if paid within seven days. This worked remarkably well, and we had no further problem collecting sundry accounts.

The demand for warehouse space and storage facilities, with the resulting distribution of the stored goods continued and it was not long before Thos. Croft & Son Ltd. were back building a new two-storey warehouse along the Maynard Street side of the depot area, and installing another 32-ton weighbridge by W. T. Avery Ltd., who told us they did not know of another road transport depot in the United Kingdom which had two 32-ton weighbridges in the depot yard.

The weighbridge office had windows on each side facing the weighbridge platforms and the mechanism of each weighbridge issued a printed card showing the date, time and weight of the vehicle. Other details on the card entered by weighbridge staff showed the driver's name, fleet number of the vehicle, registration number, route for the day, the number of deliveries being

My address at the Bridges Transport Ltd. annual dinner, 1953: someone getting ticked off!

taken out, amount of fuel and oil put in the engine that morning, and signed by the driver. On the reverse side of the card which was used when the vehicle came back to the depot, the weight was printed, the number of collections entered, and a vehicle report showing all O.K. or reporting any faults, again signed by the driver. The workshop night staff worked on these reports during the night. The information on all the cards was next morning transferred onto master sheets and totalled, so that by noon I knew what weight, how many deliveries had been made, how many miles covered, and a whole host of relevant information, which was invaluable in our costing procedures and also very important when we made, as we regularly did, applications for additional 'A' licensed vehicles.

The master sheets totals were transferred to weekly, monthly and annual totals and formed the foundation of our case for extra vehicles, which were invariably opposed by the Railway and British Road Services, the Parcels Section. It was very satisfying to me and my staff that in all the applications we made we never failed once, and were on several occasions congratulated by the Traffic Commission on the detailed way our case had been prepared. My right hand in all this was John Daly, who in total was an employee for over 26 years. John had joined us at 15 years of age, and been through all the aspects of traffic operation, he was a most loyal and hard working employee.

When the final compensation was received, Alice and I decided all the employees of the old firm, Harold Bridges Ltd., who had rejoined Bridges Transport Ltd. should be rewarded for their service and loyalty in the past, by a bonus of £10 for each complete year of service over two years with Harold Bridges Ltd. This came to several thousand pounds. 'Old Bert' the longest serving employee from 1923 to 1950 received £250 for his 27 years up to nationalisation.

Our current profit sharing scheme was very greatly appreciated by all concerned, paying around 20% of current wages and I am quite certain it was a considerable contributory factor to our continued expansion and success.

In 1963 Alice and I thought we had so many long service employees we should

My address at the Bridges Transport Ltd. annual dinner, 1953: 'business can be fun!'

have our own pension scheme, which might include life assurances. Following much discussion with the Company solicitors and accountants, a non-contributory Pension and Life Assurance Scheme was set up with a leading Life Assurance Company. This was entirely non-contributory, and would apply to all employees after two years' service with death benefits applicable immediately. Pensions were to be graded according to wages or salaries and death benefits likewise. This was naturally very well received by our employees, particularly as no medical inspections were called for.

Our night foreman at this time was Jack Mayson, he had been with us as a driver for many years, with his brother, Robert, and his duties as night foreman usually ended between 6.00 a.m. and 7.00 a.m. He was a North End football fan and followed North End to all away matches. The first football season after the pension scheme started he went to watch North End play Derby County at Derby. About half way through the match he had a heart attack and died on the

Bill Thomas, gamekeeper at Salwick Hall.

stand. He had never been off work through illness and it was a great shock to us all. His widow received £800 death benefit from our new scheme for which she was grateful and expressed this to Alice and myself personally.

I have no doubt that the pension scheme being non-contributory further cemented the good relations between employees and management, following the benefits now being received regularly by all employees from the company's profit sharing scheme. 95% of the traffic we collected was unloaded, sorted and checked by the night depot staff, now numbering between 40 and 50. They started work at 7.00 p.m. and usually finished around 6.00 a.m. This included depot office night staff responsible for checking consignment notes and making out thousands of delivery notes where we did not receive them from the sender.

The whole vehicle fleet of all vans and two flat lorries were painted in our usual royal blue and white lettering, Alice's choice in 1923, and on each side of all the vans was our new slogan adopted when we started again in 1950 in plain block letters:

Send it by Road
It's Better by Road
And Best by Bridges

The only advertising we did at any time was a full single page in the Motor Transport Goods Guild. This was an annual publication giving very full details of operators throughout the country, A4 size, 12" x 8" and very well laid out. Our advertisement round the edge had illustrations of many types of bridges and many famous ones, London Bridge, Forth Bridge, Sidney Harbour, etc., about 10 in all and also illustrations of a bamboo bridge, rope bridge, clapper bridge, etc. The typed matter was in the centre of the page and read something like the following, some in heavy black type:

All Land Transport even the Railway depends on Bridges
There are Bridges of Stone, Steel, Concrete, Wire, Wood, Bamboo and Others,
but only one Bridges Transport

147

To offer you daily deliveries 5 days a week throughout the whole of Lancashire, Cheshire, Cumberland & Westmorland.

Send It By Road
It's Better by Road
And Best by Bridges

Full details on request. Bridges Transport Ltd., Raglan Street Depot, Preston.

Lytham Hall, 1950s. From the left: Tom Croft, Arnold England, Jack Schofield, myself, Michael Clifton and his son, Rupert, John Kennedy (Clifton Estate Agent), two I cannot name, Norman Whewell and Bill Thomas, Gamekeeper.

We were now covering the whole of four counties everyday, Monday to Friday and without doubt the leading express parcel operator in the North West. It is said, 'All work and no play makes Jack a dull boy' (maybe?) While I was very actively engaged now in the day-to-day running of the undertaking I had my simple pleasures and leisure.

'Ashburne', our home, had a fairly large garden area front and back, lots of

*'A cold winter's day':
Abbeystead, Trough of
Bowland. From the left:
Maurice Rose, Tom Croft,
myself.*

shrubs and I had my kitchen garden and greenhouse, lots of borders, roses, etc., which I enjoyed looking after immensely. I also still had the shooting rights on the Salwick Estate; my gamekeeper was Matt Roskell from Lord Derby's Treales Estate next to Salwick which had been sold to the Church Commissioners. Matt was a gamekeeper at Treales when I was the gamekeeper's boy at Salwick in 1914. He was a grand dedicated keeper and was on the Salwick Estate for me until he retired, when I engaged Bill Thomas, formerly at Lytham Hall. I used to go over to Salwick every week and from October to January we had a shooting day every other week, when I had five or six friends with me for the day. This led to me being invited to shoot on other estates which I enjoyed very much. There were days at Lytham Hall Park with William Latham, the Estate Trustee and friends, or at Winmarleigh, Whitendale or Croasdale with Tom Croft, Brock with Bernard Blackburst and Abbeystead, Lord Sefton's Estate, with Terence Whalley, the Estate Agent; all very happy days and good friends.

I was one day invited to have a walk round the Lytham Hall Park shoot with Mr Latham, the Trustee and the Home Farm Manager to meet at the Home Farm at 2.00 p.m.

When I arrived Mr. Latham's car was there and the farm manager's Land Rover, but no one about. I went across to the farm buildings and found them in a loose box with a heifer having its first calf. The manager said that in mistake or accident the heifer had been served by a big Friesian bull, so it was

149

a very big calf and he might have to send for the veterinary surgeon. However, I said, I know all about this business, the first calf I helped to be born on my own was when I was about 14 about 45 years ago so I will give you a hand if you wish.

Mr. Latham and the farm manager had the usual knotted ropes on the calf's feet which were just showing, but had not been able to make any progress with the delivery, so I would give them a hand. With the three of us all we did was

'5 hours at Burrow Mill Pool', 1962.

pull the heifer along the bed of straw in the loose box. There was only one thing we could do; we roped the heifer's head to the door and after much effort managed to get the calf, and that was O.K.

After we had cleaned ourselves up I found my braces were busted so Mr. Latham said, 'Get yourself a new pair'. It will look very well in the Clifton Estate Accounts, 'to one pair of braces for Mr. Bridges, 10s. 0d.'

I had also at the invitation of an old friend, Norman Whewell, taken to fishing. Norman was at St. Cuthbert's School, Church Road, Lytham, at the same time as me around 1910. His parents had been in the drapery business for many years and also in farming, and he had stalls on market days at Preston, Blackburn, Southport and Fleetwood, so when I started in 1921 in Lytham he was one of our early regular customers. His family owned Scorton Fell, Nr. Garstang and during the war years he invited me to the shooting days he organised and he was usually a guest with me at shooting days on estates I have mentioned and at Salwick at my invitation. He set about teaching me to fish on

'It's so easy when you know how' – or is it? The Bothy Burrow, Robert Taylor and his son. Myself in doorway. 1967.

Wyresdale Hall Lake, and the Lake at Abbeystead where we fished at the invitation of Terence Whalley, Lord Sefton's agent. Later I joined Wyresdale Anglers Association at Scorton and fished in the River Wyre.

When Alice and I went to Scotland for a holiday near Aberdeen, as we did for quite a number of years, I fished in the Dee and the Ythan. I found it a quiet relaxing sport or hobby which I enjoyed. So when 1¼ miles of fishing rights in the River Lune at Burrow, two miles south of Kirkby Lonsdale, were to be sold by auction I was interested enough to have a look at the river and about two acres of land round a derelict water wheel driven sawmill, which had not been used since 1936, about 25 years. All well informed opinion seemed to indicate it would sell for around £12,000 maximum, which would be a record.

The Lune was a very famous salmon river and there was little doubt there would be keen competition at the sale, and there was. Mr. A. T. England, the Company's architect and surveyor, who was a keen shooter friend of mine, went with me. He was also a very keen fisherman. When we were leaving Ashburne for the sale Alice said, 'If you want it you get it bought. We will rebuild the old sawmill and go there to live when you retire'.

The sale was at the Castle Hotel, Hornby, and the room was packed solid. Bidding started at £10,000, very quickly reached £18,000 and stopped and I put in my first bid of £18,500. It then went up in £250 bids and knocked down to me at £20,750.

It turned out it was the highest price ever paid for fishing rights in the River Lune, the press made great fuss of it, both locally and nationally, nearly £10 a yard along the river bank, over £3 a foot, 5s. 0d. an inch and all that. Little did they or I know or imagine that in 1979/81 I would sell it for over 3½ times what I paid for it without the value of the two acres of land, quite a good deal and 20 years' immense pleasure and happy memories for my friends and me. Up to 1968/69 when the salmon disease reached the Lune, my friends and I normally caught between 80–100 salmon each year and 200 brown and sea trout. This gradually tailed off in the next five years, by which time I was 75 and fishing very little, so I decided to sell in three separate lengths. We rebuilt the old sawmill as Mill Lodge and resided there from 1965, of which more later.

So much for fun and games, now back to work. Still going ahead full throttle, we made another very useful acquisition, Whitesides Haulage Ltd., St. Annes on Sea, 10 vehicles on 'A' licences, only three of the vehicles were working, the other seven were parked at Whiteside's farm, grass growing on them and hens' nests in the cabs when we took them over. We scrapped nine of the vehicles and kept one tipper which was on contract to Lancashire County Council Highways Department. The nine vehicles scrapped were replaced by two new tippers which we hired to Dixon Bros., Builder Supplies Ltd. and seven replaced by vans for Bridges Transport Ltd.

We were now operating around 70 vehicles on our regular daily services. Thomas Croft & Sons Ltd. had been back again and built another extension to the depot part, two-storey – upstairs for storage and ground floor extension to the loading deck.

We had secured an important storage and distribution contract with the Shell Oil Co. Ltd. for the storage and distribution of all their automotive lubricating oils and grease, also various equipment used on Shell filling stations in the North of Lancashire. This entailed bringing in the stock from Ellesmere Port in barrels, drums, cans etc., on average around eight tons per day, and the return of returnable empty barrels, drums etc. to Victor Blagden Ltd., Trafford Park, Manchester, the drum reconditioners. It entailed the storage of around 100 tons of various automotive products, most of which were then distributed on our regular services, mainly in the northern half of Lancashire. We had erected around 400 ft of 10 ft high racking to hold the stock, some inside the depot, and the barrels and 45 gallon drums outside. We were very fortunate that the east depot side was just far enough from the railway embankment wall to allow room for the storage racks and a forklift truck to operate to load and unload the racks. Two new fork lift trucks were purchased and we designed and had made forks which enabled us to handle 1, 2 or 3 45 gallon drums at once with the fork lift trucks. This new contract was new business. It had formerly been handled from Ellesmere Port and we had no difficulty in having three extra 'A' licences granted to handle it.

When the Royal College of Surgeons made the Press release in 1963 about the £100,000 donation there was a lot of publicity and scores of letters and messages from all over the country. Amongst these was one from Harold Wilson, Prime Minister, 10 Downing Street, London. It was addressed to Mr. Burgess and did not have a stamp on it. We had double postage to pay (8 pence), so much for the 'dynamic' efficiency he had been talking about the previous week!

Amongst the messages was a telegram from a T. Atkinson, Burnley. This seemed to ring a bell but I could not just place it till I recalled I had seen the name on letter headings of Caledonian Transport Ltd., a Scottish operator who had a depot at Longton, near Preston. We had on occasion delivered consignments for Caledonian and we had similarly handed traffic to them for Scotland.

I sent a note of thanks for the telegram to Mr. Atkin and he later 'phoned me to ask if he might have a look at our depot about which he had heard so much, and he commented wherever he went in the North West he seemed to see a dozen of Bridges Transport Ltd. vehicles any day. I invited Mr. Atkin to come and have a look at our set up. As he was apparently a director of Caledonian Transport Ltd., the Scottish operator there might be a chance to discuss a joint operation to Scotland. When Mr. Atkin came we were in a bit of a turmoil. Thos. Croft & Son Ltd. were extending the depot again and we were having a lot of extra storage racking erected. However, Mr Atkin said it was the best parcel depot he had seen and he would like to bring along one of his co-directors to see it as they had extension or re-building in the planning stage at Scottish Parcels Ltd, Glasgow.

We arranged to leave it for a while until we got tidied up. Crofts were now engaged on the fourth extension to the depot since we moved in, at that time we had ample car and vehicle parking space in the depot yard. This was now fast disappearing and being replaced with buildings, so once again the question of depot space, warehouse space and our capacity to handle the constantly increasing traffic efficiently and economically came to the fore.

There was a row of six terraced houses along the Maynard Street side of the depot. We had acquired these over the years we had been at Raglan Street, so when we had the last one we demolished the lot and added the extra land onto the depot yard. The car and vehicle parking problem was solved when we purchased the Empress Cinema in Eldon Street only about 50 yards from the depot. At the rear of the cinema was a very good car park, which we put to use at once. We then applied for planning permission to convert the cinema building into a two-storey warehouse, but this was refused, mainly as Eldon Street was a very busy street. However, there was no problem in our using the car park as there was no change of use, and once again our luck was in. The cinema had been unused for some time with big TO LET notices on it. We took these down when we were applying for planning permission, and within four weeks we had let the cinema building on an annual tenancy as a bingo hall.

This did not help us with warehouse space, we could not find anything suitable in Preston, so in desperation we bought a very large building in Dock Road, Lytham, which Lytham Shipbuilding & Engineering Co. Ltd. had built during the war and had been unused since the shipyard closed down. It was a very big, high, fine building with high wide doors and a large parking area in front at the road side, just the job for us, but it was 12 miles from Preston. However, it would serve as a temporary measure; we did not want to turn business away if we could help it. I mentioned earlier we had workshops built at Raglan Street for the repair and maintenance of vehicles – there were now around 90 vehicles being operated daily in addition to the three forklift trucks, workshop, van and two company cars – and all had to be maintained. Our maintenance schedule called for each vehicle to be in one day in 25 for routine checking and maintenance, so every day there were four or five vehicles in the workshops apart from unscheduled repairs. Our type of operation with an average of 80 stops and starts per day per vehicle called for a strict maintenance routine to be adhered to.

It was obvious the space occupied by the workshop buildings and parking area would before long be under threat by the expansion of the traffic and warehouse requirements. As a temporary measure again, to avoid any maintenance problem, we bought all the shares in Merigolds Ltd. and Preston Embee Motors. These were very old established family businesses in financial difficulties, a creditors' meeting had been called, the creditors' meeting statement of affairs showed they had been trading at a loss for some time and there were many unsecured creditors. We were interested really because Merigolds Ltd. had a large workshop and public garage repair shop and Preston Embee Motors Ltd. had in the past been lorry and coach operators and acted as carriers agents and depot, more of this later. This relieved the workshop in the depot yard; we re-organised the procedures so we managed very well as a temporary measure. It was not long, however, before Crofts were back again altering the workshops and building on the parking area and this was to be the last alteration or extension we could do at Raglan Street.

On the home front, we were very happily settled in at 'Ashburne', Fulwood. David was home from his military service, so I had my three sons, Charles, David and John in the business with me.

Earlier, Nancy's husband, Duncan Milne, could not see very good future prospects for him at Dunlop and was having thoughts about starting on his own in the wholesale and retail tyre factor business. His father had been operating a similar business in Aberdeen, Scotland, as Tyre Scotland Ltd. in a fairly big way. I am not sure if he was the owner, partner or just an employee, so as he was now a relation by marriage, I asked him what he thought about Duncan's plans, and whether, as I would likely finance the venture, it would be financially viable in a reasonable time, and also to be quite candid about it. I knew from my own experience as a buyer of around 300 32 x 6 and 34 x 7 tyres a year that competition was very fierce between the big tyre companies and I had my doubts. I did not wish to become involved in another Dixon Bros. brickmaking fiasco.

'Sandy' Milne, Duncan's father said, no he would not advise it, as the big tyre companies were buying up tyre factors and distributors who were well established, and he thought this would make the competition greater. 'Good for the operator'? Duncan had been trained by Dunlop and the India Tyre Co. Ltd. as a sales representative. I had a long talk with Alice and Duncan about his future. He was married to my only daughter and we all wished to help him if we could. It was suggested he might be useful at Bridges Transport as an outside representative, to call on customers, when needed, to discuss rates, claims and other matters which arise in an expanding successful family business, with good prospects for the future, and where good personal contact is to be desired. The idea seemed a good one. We all agreed and Duncan joined us willingly. He did not know anything about the actual practical side of our activities, so it was agreed he should have a few months in the different departments, to put him in the picture, get to know the staff and how we ticked.

Some weeks later Tom Green, the Manager at Dixon Bros., Builders

Supplies Ltd., informed me he wished to give four weeks' notice to leave. He had decided to have a go on his own, he had rented a small yard and office in Ribbleton Lane, and felt he could better himself that way. Alice and I talked this situation over and decided we should offer the job to Duncan. While he probably did not know anything about the building trade as such, it was a 'selling' job which might suit him. I talked this over with Nancy and Duncan, they agreed and Duncan was appointed as General Manager of Dixon Bros. Builders Supplies Ltd. in 1961.

Charles, Nancy, David and John all had a small number of shares in Bridges Transport Ltd. and in Dixon Bros. Builders Supplies Ltd., and I thought it wise for the shareholdings to be arranged so that Nancy had more shares in Dixon Bros. and none in Bridges Transport Ltd., and Charles, David and John had more shares in Bridges Transport Ltd. and none in Dixon Bros. There would then be no clash of interests. In the course of the redistribution Alice and I transferred some Dixon Bros. Shares to Nancy, and Duncan bought some for cash. This ended in my having overall control, Alice next, as a major share-holder then Nancy and Duncan with a minority holding.

Duncan took up his new job gladly and said he would do his best to succeed. Dixon Bros. bought two new tippers, to replace the two hired from Bridges Transport. These were sold and replaced by two vans. I saw Duncan frequently during the week and most weekends, and all seemed to be going very well, he had about six staff who had been with Mr. Dewhurst before we bought the business so Duncan could devote time to going out 'selling' which he did. One prominent builder in Preston whom I knew very well, commenting on the new manager, Duncan, said to me, 'That son-in-law of yours could sell snowballs to an eskimo!' Progress at Dixon Bros. was slow but steady in a very competitive business, and increased as Duncan got the hang of the job he had to do.

In the meantime Bridges Transport kept battling on; in due course Tom Atkins of Caledonian Transport Ltd. and one of his co-directors came to inspect the depot and our activities and were very much impressed. In the course of the conversation which followed over a cup of tea in my office, I learned that they were both also directors of Tayforth Ltd., a Scottish Holding Co. based in Falkirk, Scotland, who had recently been acquiring transport operators in the North of England and in particular they were interested in parcels operators similar to Bridges Transport. Then came the bomb shell, 'Would you be prepared to consider negotiations to sell to Tayforth?'

I said, 'It has never entered my head to sell, why should we, I am only 64, we have a most successful family business, three sons in the business and still expanding. We are showing a return to capital employed of 30% after direc-tors' fees before tax. It's a gold mine'. T. Atkin replied, 'Will you think about it, you may hear from others on the same lines, if you do don't forget Tayforth,

Raglan St. depot, 1964.
Albion 'Claymore': over
40 of this type were
operated. Note under-floor
engine, low cab entrances.

we can meet any competition'. Well would you believe it? Only 12 years roughly since Bridges Transport Ltd. started. That was something to tell Alice and the boys and gave us all something fresh to talk about.

For some time after moving from Salwick to Fulwood, Alice and I went over to Lytham every Thursday, Alice to visit old friends from when we lived in Lytham, and to shop at Stringers and E. H. Booth Ltd. The car we had then was an Austin Princess with a Van Den Plas body, a big heavy car with very wide doors. One Thursday when I drew up to the kerb in front of E. H. Booths where there was a lot of camber on the road, I was getting out and holding the heavy door open against the camber when I twisted my back somehow, it took my breath away. I managed to slide back onto the seat and wait till Alice was ready, managed to drive home with great difficulty and get to bed. The doctor next morning said, 'slipped disc; put a board in the bed and don't get out until I tell you'. I was in very severe pain, my left leg was numb. I could not sleep, eat or read for two weeks, after which it was X-rayed at Mount Street Hospital, Preston. The X-rays confirmed the damage, so it was another three weeks in bed, then to St. Annes for three visits to be stretched on the rack.

Dr. Mackie of Great Eccleston was my doctor, and after eight weeks let me resume a normal routine. He did a marvellous job, for which I was most grateful, my back has not given me any trouble at all since. Good show, Doctor!

Meanwhile at home we had decided to consider rebuilding the derelict

Burrow Mill on the banks of the River Lune at Burrow. Mr. England, the Company's architect, drew up plans to rebuild it as a fishing lodge. Friends said, 'you'll never get planning permission on the bank of the Lune in open countryside'. The first reaction of the Planning Office was 'What is your definition of a fishing lodge?' We said, 'The applicant owns 1¼ miles of fishing rights on the River Lune for which he has paid £20,750 and will be paying over £400 a year in general rates'.

'The fishing lodge is a place where we can have a meal in reasonable comfort, a kitchen will be needed to cook a meal, sometimes a fisher may fall in the river and need a hot bath, and if we are sea trout fishing at night and wish to stay the night we will want a bedroom as well as a bathroom.'

It all sounds a bit far fetched now but it worked, planning permission was granted, subject to all reconstruction and new work to be in natural stone. We engaged John Edmundson & Son as builders, we got most of the stone we needed apart from the old building out of Leck Beck and the River Lune. The builder did a first class job, the planners were very pleased with the result, and we had no problem in later years when we applied for an extension to enlarge the lounge and add a second large bedroom.

Alice and I had our 1963 and 1964 holidays at Mill Lodge, Burrow, and in the fishing season I had my days fishing with friends.

In 1965 Duncan's family, father, mother, brother, Douglas and sister, Margaret, were coming to stay with Nancy and Duncan for two weeks. They had not enough room for them all so Alice and I went to Mill Lodge for the two weeks and the Milne family used 'Ashburne'.

Alice and I enjoyed our 14 days at Burrow so much we decided to take up permanent residence there. Nancy, Duncan and family moved into Ashburne as their permanent home. I could now fish whenever the weather and the river was right. We had outbuildings built and laid out the lawn and border and a good kitchen garden. I went to Preston four days a week, Alice went with me one day and on Thursdays we went to Lytham, shopping, visiting friends, etc. We were very happy in our new surroundings, 200 yards down our private road from the main road and 40 minutes by car to Preston.

It was now around 12 months since Mr. T. Atkins had mentioned the interest of Tayforth Ltd., when he 'phoned me, saying he would like another chat about Tayforth and Bridges Transport Ltd. and he came with his co-director and one of their depot managers, who said he had never seen anything anywhere to compare with our depot.

I was informed that Tayforth were really very keen for some progress if I was willing to talk. We had, of course, talked this over many times, Alice and I and the boys, and we had decided no harm would be done if we were to find out what sort of arrangements Tayforth had in mind. To this end we instructed our accountants, W. Latham & Co., Lytham, to supply Tayforth's accountants with such information as they thought desirable in the strictest confidence to enable Tayforth to make an offer entirely without any obligation on our part.

I gave Tayforth a brief outline of what had happened since Harold Bridges Ltd. was nationalised without disclosing any of our future plans. In about a month we had a letter from Tayforth saying the information we had supplied appeared to indicate £850,000 as being a figure around which they would be prepared to negotiate. My own view on this, and the family agreed, was that it was far below the figure at which we might begin to even consider selling. I informed Tayforth of this and suggested that they await our annual accounts for the current year's trading which I knew would reflect our expansion and increase in nett profit, and they could then if they wished make a much improved offer. They agreed to this and expressed their continued interest.

The business was continuing to make steady progress, each year we were applying for and being granted additional 'A' licenses, for the extra vehicles we needed, and we had now set our sights on operating 100 vehicles by 1965.

Fortunately, the workshop problem of the distance Merigolds was from the depot was solved when premises in Eldon Street, about 50 yards from the depot, came on the market for sale and we bought them. They had previously been the depot workshops of Scout Motors Services, a bus and coach operator. They were ideal for our purpose, so we now had the new workshop, the parking area for cars and vehicles at Empress Cinema and the depot almost next door to each other. This enabled us in due course to dispose of the Merigolds and Preston Ember Motors properties, which we did at a handsome profit.

In 1963 when the Harold Bridges' Foundation was registered, Alice and I also set up a family trust for our eight grandchildren living in England, briefly to pay income to them from the age of 18 for life, then to their children, if no children then to the other grandchildren. This settlement was started in a small way with the intention of adding to it and to the Harold Bridges' Foundation as and when funds became available.

In due course we heard again from Tayforth after they had another set of our annual accounts, which as I expected reflected our continued progress. They asked for another meeting, two of Tayforth's finance staff came to the meeting with David Denton and Frank Greathead of our accountants and myself, held at our accountant's office, 12 park Street, Lytham.

Tayforth were very agreeably surprised and pleased at the results shown in our last accounts and were now prepared to negotiate around £1,100,000. They did express the view that as Raglan Street Depot was now fully developed it was rather difficult to see how any further expansion could be expected, and it was rather difficult for me to argue against this, having always expressed our efficiency in operating Raglan Street to its full capacity in operating and coping with the expansion. The outcome of this meeting was that I would see what Alice and my three sons thought about it and I would be in touch with

> 001140   T A Y F O R T H   L I M I T E D.   83-02-06
>
> 5 ST. ANDREW SQUARE · EDINBURGH 2
>
> 3   31 · 3 · 1966
>
> A/c Payee Only
>
> **National Commercial Bank of Scotland Limited**
>
> ST. ANDREW SQUARE OFFICE 42 ST. ANDREW SQUARE EDINBURGH 2
>
> PAY   Messrs Byers & Senior   OR ORDER
>
> One Million Three Hundred & Fifty Thousand Pounds
>
> £1,350,000 · 0 · 0
>
> No. 1 ACCOUNT   For and on behalf of TAYFORTH LIMITED
>
> Walter A. Alexander .... Director   R. Johnston .... Director Secretary
>
> ‖83‖0206‖ 270 934‖

them in a few weeks' time.

We had several meetings at Ashburne with our accountants, Alice and my three sons and the outcome was, we could not see any answer to Tayforth's doubts about further expansion. Someone at this meeting mentioned that we had a Labour Government and who knows what they might do, even re-nationalise road transport. Should we get out now? It was also pointed out that in 1950 we had 36 vehicles operating, by mid-1966 we expected this to be three times as many, certainly over 100. Tayforths were offering us over eight times as much for three times as many 'A' licensed vehicles. One could say, of course, this showed how low and how wrong the acquisition compensation was and it was compulsory. However, the outcome of all our deliberations was that Tayforth should be informed that we were prepared to negotiate and that it be left to me to seek the best terms, above £1,250,000.

Would you believe it? It is true, the Bridges' luck came to the rescue in no small measure. Right opposite Raglan Street Depot on the corner of Raglan Street and Maynard Street was a Cotton Mill, Maynard Street Mill, the main entrance was 20 yards from the Raglan Street Depot entrance. It was around two acres, and when we went into Raglan Street, was operating as a cotton mill. It closed down and was for sale at £65,000. I arranged to inspect it with the Company's architect and surveyor in the morning, made an appointment to meet two of the directors in the afternoon and bought it. We immediately applied for planning permission for a Road Transport Depot and builders

After negotiation, we agreed on a sale price of £1,350,000 for the whole of the issued share capital of Bridges Transport Ltd. The payment was made by certified banker's cheque to the family solicitor, Byers & Senior.

merchants depot on the site, and this was granted. What unbelievable luck, right next door a two-acre site, we could build an exact replica of Raglan Street with improvement and operate another 80–100 vehicles or expand the storage and warehousing activity which was still in great demand.

Whilst all this was going on, I kept stalling further negotiation with Tayforth and I think at one stage they thought we had another buyer in the offing, though this was not so. The acquisition of Maynard Street Mill was only the beginning, a two-acre cotton mill with hundreds of iron pillars and low headroom was no use to us as it was, the site would have to be cleared, and a purpose built depot erected.

We were in the process of getting prices for demolishing the mill, including a very high chimney, which every cotton mill had, and clearing the site, when one weekend we had a very bad freak storm and about a tenth of the mill roof was very badly damaged, a lot of it ended up on the mill floor. The mill was, of course, insured for storm damage, and the insurance company assessed the damage at £14,500 which we accepted. We were not under any obligation to repair the damage, and did not do so. Thomas Croft & Son Ltd. carried out the demolition and clearing of the site, they took all the salvaged materials, hardcore, etc. and charged £15,000. We left the main walls along Raglan Street and Maynard Street standing to enclose the site, the greater part of which had a stone flag floor. Now we had the answer to Tayforth's doubt and our own, we had the site, with planning permission to build and possibly double the size of the operation in the next 6–8 years.

In due course I got in touch with Tayforths, told them there had been a new development and that I felt we had had more than enough meetings with accountants and finance experts, would Ronald Alexander, Chairman of Tayforth meet me at Mill Lodge, Burrow, for a final make or break meeting.

This was agreed. Ronald Alexander and I had a long talk in the afternoon. He stayed the night at the Royal Hotel in Kirkby Lonsdale, garaged his car with the hotel garage. Next morning he found his car radio had been on fire in the night and fortunately burnt itself out.

Further negotiation that morning resulted in our agreeing a sale price of £1,350,000 for the whole of the issued share capital of Bridges Transport Ltd. I would be asked to stay on for two years and any of the three sons also if they wished. One snag developed which I would not agree to was that in acquisition of this size it was normal for half the payment to be made in Tayforth shares and half in cash. I would not agree to this at all, payment must be made in full £1,350,000 certified banker's cheque to the family solicitor, Byers & Senior, 8 Hastings Place, Lytham. Ronald said he could not personally agree to this, he would be going down to London on Monday to see the people in control and he would 'phone me on Monday around 2.00 p.m. and the cheque would be in the post 31st March 1966 – £1,350,000 for 15 years' work 1951–1966. How's that! John, my youngest son, and I stayed on for two years, my salary was £7,500 and John's £1,500 per annum. I was to be at the depot four days per week the first 18 months, reducing to one day per week in the last six months when I would be 68.

Charles and David decided not to stay, they had other plans in mind. Needless to say, the family all agreed fully with the settlement, and the arrangements which had been made in view of the possible sale. The main one was that as the share capital of Bridges Transport Ltd. was £1,000 in 1 shares this should be increased to £10,000 by a rights issue of 9 for 1 at £1 per share. Alice and I did not take up our full allocation, we arranged for 2,000 £1 shares to be issued to the Harold Bridges Foundation and 2,000 £1 shares to be issued to the Family Settlement, each received £270,000. Alice, Charles, David and John received £135,000 and I received £270,000 from the sale of the shares.

A letter from the manager of Bridges Transport Ltd. after my retirement.

The 1965 Labour Government budgets brought in the new Capital Gains Tax and in due course we had a right old argument with the Inland Revenue about tax on the increase in the value of the business between 5th April 1965 and the sale on 1st April 1966. They argued it had increased in value by a considerable amount or Tayforth would not have increased their offer by £250,000. Our counter to this was that yes, there had been an increase in the value of the business but not to that extent, the reducing factor was that the £1,100,000 did not represent the true value of the business at that time, hence our not accepting it.

In the end David Denton of William Latham & Co., our accountants, and myself went down to Wimbledon and argued all afternoon at the Inland Revenue offices. The outcome was we reached a compromise, we had some Capital Gains Tax to pay on the increase but far far below what had been demanded.

We had been very fortunate in the case of many of our acquisitions of limited companies that there had not been any Capital Gains Tax. In several instances we

> H. Bridges Esq.,
> Burrow Mill Lodge,
> Burrow,
> Via Carnforth,
> Lancs.
>
> Dear Mr. Bridges,
> . . . As a matter of interest you will be pleased to learn that we have exceeded 6,000 consignments per day delivered on a number of occasions recently and we have high hopes that soon we will achieve 6,500. The 'bank note printing machine' which you established, continues to pour out profits to the amazement of the rest of Tayforth and it looks as though we shall have achieved a 50% return on capital for the last period.
> Anyhow, I look forward to seeing you in the near future when I can give you more details, for I quite sincerely believe that a great deal of this credit belongs to you and I feel it is only reasonable that you should be kept in the picture.
>
> Yours truly,
> Alan Monighan.

had taken over Limited Companies with trading losses brought forward in their accounts, in the case of transport operators probably due to the 25 mile radius restrictions between 1947 and 1954. In such cases we carried the companies on as they were by buying the whole of the shares the 'A' licenses were held by the company, we operated the companies in their own names, very soon had them making profits, then when all the losses had been absorbed, we put the companies into liquidation, had the 'A' licenses transferred to Bridges Transport Ltd. and distributed the proceeds to the shareholders with little or no tax to pay.

One of my most important decisions or resolutions I made when I really got going in the mid 1920s was that at no time in any shape or form must there by any kind of tax fiddle for me or my family's benefit; if there was tax to pay, well so be it and my word, we did pay some over the years. At the same time I always had in mind that famous law judgement in a tax case: 'Anyone has a perfect right within the law to so arrange his affairs that he attracts the least amount of taxation'. And we made full use of this wherever and whenever possible, in many cases this benefited the Harold Bridges Foundation capital assets. For a while my position as manager at the depot seemed rather strange. I had no or very little decision making to do, what was planned for the future of Maynard Street had not been decided.

Tayforth appointed a secretary accountant and extra office staff to supply the information required monthly in the form they needed it. Later and well before my two years was up, a manager to follow me was appointed, Alan Monigham, if I remember correctly. He had not been in parcels operation; rather the opposite, with Beck & Pollitzer in London, a tall rather likeable chap, keen to carry on my success for Tayforth and he was accepted by the employees as my successor, with good grace. We had men working for us who came to us as lads 30 years before, we had several fathers and sons, and three lots of three brothers, who had been employees for around 20 years, so it was quite a change for these old hands, not old in age, but in service.

The name Bridges Transport carried on unchanged. Tayforth were most emphatic about that; there was no indication anywhere on vehicles or paper work that there had been any change. The idea that I should gradually reduce my days at the depot over the two year period worked very well for all concerned and Alan Monighan, the new manager, was able to pick up the reins and carry on the good work.

Tayforth did ask me to draw up a plan for Maynard Street, to which I had already been giving some thought and I submitted my suggestion in due course. We had felt for some time that around 100 vehicles was the maximum which could be economically and efficiently operated from one depot, when the whole of the traffic was being collected from all over Lancashire, Cheshire, Westmorland and Cumberland and sorted during the night ready for the delivery drivers to load next morning. With a double side loading deck, 50 vehicles on each side, allowing 9 ft. for each vehicle meant a loading deck 450 ft long (150 yards) along which some traffic had to be moved from the collection vehicle to the delivery vehicle. In our case we had always done this by the night staff with various forms of hand trucks, working 2–3 truckers with one charge hand. About 30 were employed on the night staff who normally worked 7.00 p.m. to 5.00 a.m. The depot was open on a three shift basis from 7.00 a.m. Monday to 5.00 p.m. Saturday, continuous 24 hours a day.

My suggestion to Tayforth for Maynard Street was to build a somewhat similar building to Raglan Street, with rather different facilities in some respects for the unloading of heavy articulated vehicles and trailers. Maynard Street would be used wholly for traffic brought into the depot, by other operators or by our customers' own vehicles, and all the traffic which came out of our own storage facilities. This traffic would normally all be in the depot by 4.00 p.m., a lot of it before noon.

By using demountable bodies which could be loaded as soon as a load for a particular route was ready for loading between 4.00 p.m. and 5.00 p.m. no night staff would be needed. Had we carried on at Bridges Transport we had intended to try this system out on an experimental basis at Raglan Street. The great advances being made in hydraulics, fork lift trucks and mobile cranes made such a system quite feasible and viable.

It was rather a remarkable coincidence that when I sent my suggestion to Tayforth they said that one of their subsidiary companies, Watson, of Spennymoor, Co. Durham, were already experimenting with demountable bodies, and suggested I go over to Spennymoor, which I did, and found that Watsons was a very similar type of operation to ours, covering the North East counties as we covered the North West. Before my two years were over we had set up a joint operation for an interchange of traffic between our areas in the North West and Watsons in the North East. Nothing developed at Maynard Street and when my two years expired I retired from the scene after forty-seven years in road transport parcels operations, one vehicle in 1921 to 106 vehicles operating in 1966.

The only communication I had with Bridges Transport after I retired was a letter from Alan Monighan, the manager, dated 7th November 1968, that is six months after I retired and two years and six months after Tayforth acquired Bridges Transport Ltd.

I was very pleased to have this confirmation that all was going well. 50% return on capital fully justified my argument with Tayforth and confirmed what I had told Tom Atkins in 1963, 'It's a gold mine'.

In the event as it turned out Maynard Street was never developed, the powers that be decided to move the whole operation to a new depot at Leyland, supposed to be the last word and described in publicity material as 'The most modern parcels depot in the North West'. I was rather hurt at the time that I was not invited to the opening ceremony, but not to worry. I did learn later they had installed at great expense some new fangled mechanical trucking system on the loading deck, which was not up to expectations and eventually was discarded to revert to our system of manual sorting and trucking on the loading deck.

I never saw the depot at Leyland and I do not know what went wrong but it made me very sad to learn that the profitability of the business fell away to such an extent that by 1988 it had been closed down completely and the depot sold; that was the end of Bridges Transport. But I am glad to say not the end of my story *As I Remember* 90 years in the 1990s.

To any reader interested in Road Transport, I suggest they try and obtain a copy of an excellent book by Charles S. Dunbar, *The Rise of Road Transport 1919 to 1939* published by Ian Allan Ltd. 1981. I met Charles Dunbar many times during the formative years of Red Arrow Deliveries and The National Conference of Express Carriers, which probably led to the following extract in Chapter 4, page 23:

> Harold Bridges of Preston left school at 13 and after a great struggle managed to raise £250 to buy a model T Ford in 1921, leaving himself with £1 working capital. The parcels business he slowly built up was nationalised in 1950 for £128,000. In 1951 he was able to start up again and eventually sold this second business in 1966 to Tayforth, a subsidiary of the British Transport Commission, for £1,350,000. But this is looking a long way ahead and Bridges' success cannot be regarded as typical. Many thousands got no further than their first lorry and that was often repossessed by the finance companies. [Reproduced with permission from *The Rise of Road Transport 1919 to 1939* by Charles S. Dunbar, published in 1981 by Ian Allan Ltd.]

Chapter Ten

Five More Companies

IN 1923 when my brother Reuben and I were driving the two Vulcan vehicles I had then, one delivering and collecting each day in Preston used to call at a firm then on Preston Dock, Thos. Kirkham & Son Ltd. They dealt mainly in timber, imported into Preston Dock, and in wire netting, barbwire, roofing felt, corrugated sheets and similar materials used by the booming poultry farms between Preston, Freckleton, Warton, Kirkham and Lytham in 1922 onwards. This was before factory farming, hen batteries, deep litter houses and so forth. They also dealt in all kinds of H. M. Forces surplus disposal goods and the vehicle which called on them each day usually collected some consignment to deliver on the way back to Lytham. This continued over the years, and when we moved to Walton-le-Dale in 1936 they would 'phone us when they wished us to call. In later years they had a very large warehouse and yard outside the Dock area on the main dock road, next to the dock office.

After the 1939/45 war they went into the forces disposal sales business in a big way and had also developed a manufactured joinery business on the timber side, and also were selling more goods and materials which in some instances was in direct competition with Dixon Bros. Builders Supplies Ltd. This did not bother Dixon Bros. very much, they were forging ahead under my son-in-law Duncan Milne's management, and had only one set back when in 1965 a fire destroyed a part of the three-storey warehouse and stock. Luckily it was fully insured, including loss of profits following fire, and they were soon in full swing again with no loss of profit.

Now I had finished at Bridges Transport Ltd. Alice and I would come to Preston once a week to Nancy's at 'Ashburne' for lunch, Alice would do some shopping and visit friends, and I would visit Dixon Bros.

Duncan was just as keen as I was about credit and slow payers and willingly accepted my instruction that if an account is not paid and becomes four weeks overdue we should stop supplying, and this applied to famous national firms in the Preston area, whom we knew could pay, and perhaps had no reason at all for not paying other than slackness somewhere along the line. Duncan felt as I did, 'You have not sold anything until you get paid, if you don't get paid you have given the goods away'.

Before supplies were stopped on account of non-payment Duncan was under instructions to consult me before taking action. It so happened that Thos. Kirkham & Son Ltd.'s name cropped up from time to time as slow payers and Duncan agreed with me that surely this could not be on account of financial problems, it must be slackness in the office. With a little pressure we always did get paid, we never actually stopped supplies, I knowing we had been trading with Kirkham's for 44 years, was quite happy to carry on. Duncan was not so sure and wondered now that Mr. T. Kirkham was no longer managing the business if they had problems. However, much to our very great surprise, when we had been pressing them for payment of an account under £50 we received notice from their accountants calling a meeting of creditors, as it was felt they could no longer continue trading.

The information supplied with the notice revealed a hopeless trading situation, and no wonder they had called a meeting of creditors. Duncan and I went to T. Kirkham & Son Ltd. before the meeting, met the manager and senior staff, some of whom Duncan knew, and had a good look round. It was a fine site with offices and workshops, the offices far, far too big for Kirkham's business, and car parking for about 50 cars. What amazed me was that the site and building were shown in the list of assets at £16,000 which was obviously to my mind a very old valuation. Also the figure shown as stock was to my mind much below realisable market value. The amount of stock comprised what is known as Government surplus was really staggering; it was piled so high and in such a haphazard way and fashion that it would be quite impossible to take any kind of stock figure as being anything other than guesswork.

Before the meeting I put it to Duncan, 'Can you manage Kirkhams as well as Dixon Bros.?' Duncan said, 'I am quite willing to have a go provided Nancy and I can have some shares. We can use some of the offices right away for Dixon Bros. As you know we are very cramped'. So we talked all this over Alice and I, Nancy and Duncan and it was decided Duncan and I should go to the meeting.

The creditors meeting was held at the offices of T. Kirkham & Son's accountants, attended by about 15 creditors. The chairman explained that the current position was due to poor trading conditions, answered a few questions and emphasised that an early decision was needed, otherwise the position could only get worse.

It appeared Mr. T. Kirkham and a member of his family had already made substantial loans to the company and were not prepared to put in any more. After some further discussion the chairman said it appeared a liquidation could not be avoided, and would someone propose a resolution to that effect, unless anyone present had any other proposal or suggestion to make. I had so far not said anything, but this was an invitation to the meeting so appeared to me to be my chance to speak.

I mentioned briefly the amicable trading relations I had enjoyed with T. Kirkham & Son Ltd. going back to 1923, around 44 years, and I felt personally there was something sadly wrong somewhere, possibly with management to give rise to the present position, and I asked would the present shareholders consider disposing of all their shares for a nominal sum, in which case the new shareholders would then be responsible for all the company's trade creditors shown on the statement of affairs, who would all be paid within 28 days. This would avoid liquidation and enable T. Kirkham & Son Ltd. to continue trading under the new ownership.

This naturally gave rise to the question of the unsecured loans made by the directors and family to the company. My reply to this was I would have to have access to further details and information on the company's activities over the past four/five years, before I would commit myself to repaying any of the loans, or any proportion of them. If my offer was accepted, this very old established Preston company would continue trading, all the trade creditors would be paid and the only losers would be the present shareholders and anyone else not a trade creditor who had made loans to the company. The present position was they had lost their shares value and their loans anyway, so they had nothing to lose, and maybe some reduction in their loss by accepting my offer.

I also wished to defer stating the actual figure I would pay for the shares, pending receipt of further information and details, but I did visualise at that moment it might be around 1s. 0d. per share for 30,000 £1 shares. This offer by me gained the instant unanimous approval of all the representatives of the trade creditors, and the shareholders' representatives said they would have a meeting with the shareholders as soon as possible and report back to me with the decision and the extra information requested.

The meeting then adjourned after I had been thanked for putting forward my proposals. Many, if not all, of those present knew me personally, and knew Bridges Transport Ltd. and Dixon Bros. Builders Supplies Ltd., in many cases being customers, either for sales or purchases, over many years.

In due course I received the additional information I had asked for and was informed the shareholders were prepared to consider the scheme I had suggested at the meeting.

Following meetings with our accountants, W. Latham & Co., Duncan, Nancy, Alice and I decided on the information we had before us that it would be, or could be, made a viable and worthwhile acquisition provided we could buy the £1 shares for 1s. 0d. each and make a token payment in discharge of the loans. At subsequent meetings our offer was accepted. I am recording this event 21 years later without any diary, notes or written record of any kind but if I remember correctly we paid 1s. 0d. each for the £1 shares and made token payments of 10% in repayment of the loans, which again if I remember correctly, were around £20,000 in total, and we, of course, as the new shareholders were responsible for all the trade debts and liabilities of the company which had been disclosed to us.

One other condition included was that the present general manager's employment by the company would cease on the day the sale and purchase of the shares was completed without any compensation for loss of office.

All this went through according to plan, a new bank account was opened with Williams and Glyns Bank Ltd. and as there was a negligible amount of cash in the company's old bank account to transfer, on the 2nd December 1969 I signed an overdraft guarantee for £10,000 at 5% interest on the amount of the overdraft on a daily basis. My guarantee was cancelled on 17th November 1971 as it was no longer required. When the transfer of the shares to the new owners was ready, Alice and I agreed with the advice of the family accountants and solicitor that in view of my age, nearly 70 and Alice 72, that I should only take 1,000 shares and Nancy and Duncan 14,500 each. They had in mind the effect of estate duty if as we hoped in a few years the shares would have increased in value. This was in spite of the fact that I was guarantor for the £10,000 bank overdraft facility. However, in the long run all went well and in June 1977 the shares were sold to the newly formed holding company, Grommet Holdings, Ltd. and I received £3,000 for my 1,000 shares for which I had paid £50 in December 1969. Duncan was appointed Managing Director and I as Chairman and Director and Nancy a Director.

Duncan and I now had a challenge on our hands. I had, of course, finished employment at Bridges Transport Ltd. in April 1968 and had no other business ties. We decided first the whole stock should be gone through. We had found from our enquiries there was army disposal stock from the 1914/18 war and a lot of it maybe valueless. There were also large quantities of army, air force and naval forces disposal stocks from the 1939/45 war, as well as all sorts of goods and materials bought at factory closure sales and the like, with no records at all.

The car park at the rear of the warehouse had an entrance from Calder Street and from the main dock road. When we took over it was almost full of all kinds of mainly ex-service disposal stock, wooden furniture, iron bedsteads, stoves ladders, etc., etc. Some went to the metal scrap merchants, a lot to the Corporation Cleansing Department tip and what was saleable was later moved into the warehouse, so that for a start we had space to park around 50 cars off the street.

The warehouse stock was much the same, piled high and no record at all, a small portion of the warehouse near the offices was used for current new stock coming in and as the sales area. Eventually the warehouse was sorted out. We did have a few lucky finds; one was when we moved about 20 bales of forces mens underwear we found 42 strong heavy wooden boxes marked with the W. D. Broad arrow and the date 1918. In each box was a brand new unused 6" engineer's bench vice wrapped in brown greaseproof paper. We sold the lot to Brown Brothers Ltd., the garage equipment factors.

Another good find was nearly a ton of copper rivets in $\frac{1}{2}$ cwt. hessian sacks, but what do you do with 30 kegs of army camouflage paint marked 1917 except send it to the tip?

However, everything got sorted out after a lot of hard work, and Duncan had the chance to show his salesmanship expertise and he did. Dixon Bros. Builders Supplies Ltd. accounts department was moved into Kirkhams offices and Duncan had his own office for the two companies.

While all this activity was taking place, Duncan was at the same time gradually introducing new saleable stocks ancillary to Dixon Bros. Builders Supplies Ltd. and more on a D.I.Y. basis for retail trade. Dixon Bros. had a small retail trade, but their main business was with builders, civil engineers and property repairers, and the building and estate departments of the many large firms in the Preston area.

By now we had begun to get some idea why T. Kirkham & Son Ltd. had got into financial difficulties, through our sorting out of the stock. I still felt that this was not the only cause and as I now had lots of time on my hands I brought three years goods received books and all the purchases and sales invoices for the same period home to Burrow, and began a lot of cross checking. The first year was not too bad although there were quite a number of invoices for goods which were not in the goods received books, and for which I could not get any explanation other than whoever received the goods must not have entered them.

The position in the 2nd and 3rd years was much worse; invoices had been paid for goods not entered and which no one could remember seeing; some invoices had been rendered to Kirkhams for goods supplied elsewhere, and it appeared the whole job had been a bit of a shambles from an efficient business point of view. The outcome of my investigation was that Kirkhams recovered around £9,000 in corrections. In the meantime we had an up-to-date valuation of the property and site which was £45,000. This confirmed my surprise at the valuation of the property for the creditors meeting at £16,000. Later the accounts to 31st January 1973 showed the freehold land and buildings as nett book value £55,000, total fixed assets £60,019, nett current assets £52,988 and profit before tax and directors' fees £30,358. So we had made substantial progress since December 1969 and great credit must go to Duncan Milne, my son-in-law, for this, not forgetting H. B. and the employees!

Dixon Bros. Builders Supplies Ltd. were also making good progress in a very competitive business. They had leased an additional area of land to add to the yard area from the owners of the adjacent Preston to Kendal Canal and purchased an additional building next door from Bambers Motor Engineers, which was now used as a cement and plaster store.

If I now look back 48 years to 1921 when I began my first road transport service, I had arranged with Mrs. knowles, the landlady at the Derby Arms pub in Lord Street, Preston, to use the yard behind as my Preston contact point for customers. Next door to the Derby Arms in Lord Street was a very old established iron and steel merchants, engineers suppliers, tools and all manner of hardware etc., T. C. Holden. It was owned by a Mr. Tom Pilkington. They had many customers along the Fylde Coast between Preston and Fleetwood and no vehicle of their own so all their deliveries were done by local carriers like me or hired vehicles for loads to large customers.

During the second week of my starting in 1921 a call had been left with Mrs. Knowles, landlady at the Derby Arms, for me to see Mr. Pilkington at T. C. Holden about deliveries to the Fylde Coast, which I did right away. It appeared that the carrier they used for the Fylde Coast was my competitor, John Eccles, based in Lytham. He came into Preston Monday, Wednesday and Friday like I did, his call point was Allsups yard near the Public Hall, Lune Street, which would be about quarter of a mile from T. C. Holden, and as he would not collect from Lord Street, they had to take the deliveries to him between 12.00 noon and 2.00 p.m. This meant a journey from Lord Street to Allsup's yard with a heavily built two-wheeled hand truck with anything up to 10 cwt of iron bars, and if it was a heavy load two men had to go. Luckily for them it was downhill or level all the way. My call point access was only 50 yards from T. C. Holden's warehouse, so I got the business and T. C. Holden was a customer of Bridges Transport interest and associated companies for the next 47 years.

Tom Pilkington was from 1948 one of my guests at Salwick Hall on shooting days along with several other Preston business men: Tom Croft, builder; Kenneth Atkinson, bedding manufacturer; A. T. England, architect and surveyor; Bernard Blackhurst, solicitor and deputy coroner and many others who were my guests at Salwick on different days. I also met Tom Pilkington on shooting days on various estates in the Fylde and at Whitendale and Croasdale grouse shooting with Tom Croft and his party of friends. It was on one such day early 1970 when Tom Pilkington said to me, 'I hear you have taken over T. Kirkham & Son Ltd., and that our overdue account is now likely to be cleared. What about T. C. Holden, my business. I am thinking about packing up?' (There was a compulsory purchase order on the Lord Street premises.) I said, 'O.K., we will have a look at it and see what we can do'. I talked this over with Alice, Duncan and Nancy and it was decided I should deal with the matter and Tom Pilkington.

T. C. Holden was not a limited company. I found it to be an entirely different proposition to Kirkhams. It appeared to be fairly well run, stocks were all good and records well kept and it was running at a reasonable profit, allowing for the sort of property in use. Lord Street, where the bolts, nails, screws, tools and all manner of hardware were sold, was a three-storey building with cellars and had been extended by the acquisition of several adjoining cottages; the stairs were narrow and steep and as I commented to Tom Pilkington when he showed me round the first time, 'You're a shooting man; this is like a rabbit warren'.

The Lord Street premises also housed the lighter bar iron and steel stocks, stored stacked on end, each bar had to be man handled in and out. The heavier iron and steel stocks were stored on horizontal racks in an old cotton mill weaving shed in St. Paul's Road, Preston. This would be about half a mile from Lord Street and the weaving shed was full of the usual iron pillars about 10 feet apart, which did not ease the use of a side loader fork lift truck which had to be used as there was no head room for any type of crane, except at one point where the floor level had been lowered and a small electric travel crane installed to unload vehicles bringing stock in.

My accountant and I were supplied with all the information and explanations we required, and in due course I made a verbal offer to Tom Pilkington which he said was not acceptable, as he already had two higher offers. He did not say what the offers were, I was not interested in anything higher than what I had offered unless circumstances arose to justify it, so the whole matter was left in abeyance.

A few months later I met Tom Pilkington again on a shooting day and said, 'Have you sold yet?' He replied, 'No'. Both the offers he had received depended on loans from the bank and they would not loan the cash required. A little while later Tom Pilkington 'phoned me to the effect that if my offer still stood he would accept it. After again talking the proposal over with our accountant, Alice, Nancy and Duncan it was decided to go ahead and the legal formalities were set in motion. While this was in progress a serious incident happened to delay our plans, luckily with no injury or loss of life to anyone.

The weaving shed floor was the usual old mill floor of stone flags about 3 ft. square and 4" thick. The roof was supported as usual by iron pillars about 4" diameter and 9 ft high. The racks for the steel stock were between the pillars and about 7 ft high, with three horizontal shelves at each side of each rack. The load on each rack could vary from three tons to 12 tons, and the fork lift truck moved between the rows of racks putting in or taking out stock according to demand. Heavy sections of steel beams and joists were stored laid on the floor where there were no racks.

One weekend the whole floor, the racks, the steel stocks on the racks, the weaving shed support pillars and most of the roof, collapsed into the space about 8 ft. deep below the weaving shed floor. What a mess it was, of course, all mixed up together and about three feet of water in the bottom of the hole. It appeared the mill weaving shed must have been built over an older mill lodge or cellars of some kind. There appeared to be brick bases on which the pillars stood, there may have been subsidence over the years and the weight of the steel stock had undoubtedly caused the collapse. Very fortunately it was weekend otherwise there could have been several men and the fork lift truck in the hole.

The mill in St. Paul's Road was owned by T. Pilkington, a new lower price for the mill was negotiated. I expect Tom Pilkington would collect the balance from his insurers, the stock was now open to the sky and very soon was very rusty and not in mint condition for selling. Some pretty tough arguments and meetings were held on how to resolve the question of the depreciation of the value of this stock. We did reach agreement and later T. C. Holden Ltd. made provision in their accounts for a possible reduction in the value of this stock of £10,000. By 1974 most of it had been disposed of at little loss, possibly due to rising prices and temporary shortage of some sections, which cleared the rusty stock. Now we had reached agreement we could go ahead with all the legal formalities.

A new limited company formed named T. C. Holden & Co. Ltd. with a capital of 2,000 £1 shares issued 900 each to Nancy and Duncan and 200 to myself. On 17th February 1970 I signed a guarantee for T. C. Holden & Co. Ltd. bank overdraft of up to £80,000 at 5% or more interest, this was discharged on 21st June 1974.

Again, as with Kirkhams, standing guarantor for £80,000 which was 40 times the issued capital, I should have had 51% of the shares, but again on the advice of the financial experts with estate duty and Capital Gains Tax in mind I agreed to their advice and took 10%. Duncan Milne was appointed Managing Director, I was Director Chairman and Nancy was a Director. T. C. Holden & Co. Ltd.'s accounts department was moved into T. Kirkham & Son Ltd.'s offices where there was ample empty space. Kirkham's also had a spare two-storey warehouse in Calder Street, part of the main site and building. All the Lord Street stock and activity of T. C. Holden & Co. Ltd. at Lord Street was moved to Calder Street.

While all this was going on we were looking for a site to which we could move the St. Paul's Road steel stock activities as soon as possible. The decline of the cotton industry came to our rescue once again when the site of a large cotton mill in Parker Street came on the market. A lot of the buildings had been demolished and the site cleared leaving once again a very tall mill chimney and a four-storey brick building and a small single-storey building. The site had a long frontage to Parker Street and was not far from Dixon Bros. Builders

Supplies Ltd. It was vacant after being used by Ribble Leathers Ltd. who processed hides and skins. Enquiries were soon complete and confirmation obtained from the Town Hall planning department that they could not see any objection to the site being completely cleared and a new steel warehouse erected. It appeared they were rather pleased at the departure of Ribble Leathers Ltd., as their processing of skins and hides had led to complaints of offensive odours. The purchase completed, a large new purpose built building was erected with a travelling overhead crane running the full length of the building, the very tall chimney was felled by experts and the whole site cleared except one building out of the way in one corner which was retained as it was fairly new and of a size which might be useful later. The whole of the steel stock was moved from St. Paul's Road to Parker Street and T. C. Holden & Co. Ltd. were in business with ample modern facilities and room for expansion.

To ease the bank overdraft, I personally bought the St. Paul's Road premises from Mr. T. Pilkington as long term they were no use to T. C. Holden & Co. Ltd. About the time the steel stock was cleared from St. Paul's Road a very old established commercial vehicle body builder and repairer, Stan Foster, in Fletcher Road, Preston was retiring and offered the goodwill of the business to two of his employees, Roy Ashcroft and W. Ball. Roy is a nephew of my brother-in-law, A Fryer, who married my sister Rose. This was mentioned to me by my brother-in-law and the outcome was I formed a new company, A. B. Coachcraft Ltd. A for Ashcroft, B for Ball and myself as Director.

Both Roy Ashcroft and William Ball were craftsmen panel beaters, sprayers and skilled in all bodywork repairs on any type of vehicle. We set up in the St. Paul's Road premises which I owned and after a while moved to part of another old cotton mill in Brook Street, Preston, where they made good progress.

I later sold my shares to Duncan Milne's two daughters, Heather and Alison, my grand-daughters, so this business also came under Duncan's control and my interest ceased.

Later a new building purpose built for A. B. Coachcraft Ltd. was erected on the Parker Street site and they moved in. Soon after I bought the St. Paul's Road site the Regional Health Authority enquired if I would sell the whole site to be cleared for parking vehicles as it was immediately opposite the Preston Royal Infirmary. I sold it to the Regional Health Authority at a nice profit subject, of course, to Capital Gains Tax.

There was only one condition attached to the sale, that as the whole of the site was to be cleared I could remove any building materials I wished and we did salvage quite a lot of useful material. That was the end of another Lancashire cotton mill which we had occupied.

Early in 1972 A. Messham & Son Ltd., Corporation Street, Preston, contacted Duncan at T. C. Holden to ask if they would be interested in negotiating to take over the company, which was a very old established dealer in non-ferrous metals, copper, brass, bronze etc. in sheets, bars and rods. They also had a small brass phosphor bronze foundry for casting.

The owner was retiring and wished to dispose of the business as a going concern. Enquiries revealed they owned the property on the corner of Corporation Street and Marsh Lane, they had been operating for some time in a reduced way and making a small profit, and they had work from the Admiralty for various naval dockyards and shipyards etc. and local engineering firms. Following several meetings agreement was reached and we acquired the whole of the 8,000 £1 shares, Nancy and Duncan 3,500 each and myself 1,000.

Once again on 19th February 1973 I signed a bank overdraft guarantee for £10,000 which was not required after 21st June 1974, my holding of shares as before kept low, always it seemed with an eye on the taxman!

To ease the bank position quickly I bought the property in Corporation Street, and the whole business was as soon as possible moved to the T. C. Holden & Co. Ltd. site in Parker Street, and I later sold the property to a buyer in Ireland. Duncan was appointed Managing Director. Is it fate, luck, coincidence or what, that by 1972 I had seen four companies taken over by my family, all four having been amongst my earliest customers in 1921/22, fifty years ago.

We had indeed been very fortunate in that the four companies in the group, whose activities were all closely related, were operating from splendid sites and premises, not very far apart, all acquired freehold at very reasonable prices. The offices of all the four companies were now at T. Kirkham & Son Ltd., Dock Road, Preston, which made for great economies.

Duncan was now Managing Director of four very well established profitable companies and I was the Director Chairman.

Chapter Eleven

Honours and Sadness

NANCY, Duncan and their two daughters, Heather and Alison came up to see Alice and me at Burrow most weekends, and much business discussion on general policy etc. took place, little of which would appear in the company minute books.

The four years since my retirement from Tayforth in 1968 had certainly not been without interest, excitement or knowing what to do in my spare time if I had any! I still had my fishing, not so good now as 1961 to 1969 – the disease in the salmon stock in all U.K. rivers had taken its toll, and catches on my 1¼ miles were down 50% with apparently no cure or explanation of how or what caused it.

The 21 years' lease of the Salwick Estate shooting and sporting rights expired in 1967. I renewed it with the Duchy of Lancaster for five years until 1972. During the later years my gamekeeper at Salwick was Matt Roskell, who had been a gamekeeper on the adjoining Treales Estate of Lord Derby. When Matt retired Bill Thomas, who had been gamekeeper on the Lytham Hall Estate for the Clifton family, came to be keeper at Salwick for me until the extended lease expired, he retired and that was the end of the Salwick saga in my life – 1914 gamekeepers boy 5s. 0d. per week; 1946/72 lessee of the Hall and shooting rights with my own gamekeeper.

Alice and I had now been living at Burrow seven years. I had got the garden and landscaping etc. to my liking, all stone walls, no hedges and a very good kitchen garden and greenhouse.

We had lovely views all sides of open country, the River Lune and valley, Leck Fell and the hills of the Trough of Bowland in the distance, an ideal setting and home for any couple who loved a quiet simple homely life – 55 years since Alice and I first met and 48 years since we married.

Unfortunately about early 1973 Alice's eyesight, which had been failing for some time, became so troublesome we saw an eye specialist, who diagnosed cataracts on both her eyes, which could be corrected by an operation.

In due course Alice went to Manchester Royal Eye Hospital and had an operation to remove the cataracts from both eyes at one go. The operation was completely successful and Alice would probably be home in about 14 days. The first week I went to Manchester each day, on some days Nancy or one of Alice's friends would go with me. Alice had her eyes completely covered for three days.

At the beginning of the second week, the sister in charge of Alice 'phoned about 8.30 a.m. to say that at 5.00 a.m. that morning a nurse had found Alice in the corridor outside her room and Alice had said she was looking for a bus to go home to Harold. Sister suggested I should get to the hospital that day, and stay until Alice was well enough to go home, they would find me a room close by.

I spent the remainder of the week at the hospital and at weekend Nancy and Duncan came for us. Alice made a quick recovery and her eyesight was restored to normal for her age, 75.

This was another debt we owed to the medical profession, and we were very pleased to feel we had done something tangible to show our appreciation; the Foundation Trustees had recently informed us that donations to April 1973 had totalled nearly £200,000. Good show.

While my interest in the Salwick Hall Estate and shooting had ceased on the expiry of my lease, I had many invitations to shooting days with my friends and many of them came to Burrow to fish in my length of the River Lune. The heaviest fish was caught by Morris Rose who had a stainless steel fabricating business. He hooked it right opposite Mill Lodge, he was fishing with fairly light tackle and it took over half an hour to land it, nearly half a mile downstream; it weighed 23½ lbs.

The heaviest I caught was 12 lbs. Leslie, a farmer friend, caught one 16 lbs. Towards the end of 1973 I received a letter from the Prime minister's office, 10 Downing Street, Whitehall, to the effect that the Prime Minister wished to submit my name to H. M. The Queen for inclusion in the 1974 New Year's Honours List, with a recommendation that I be appointed an officer of the Order of the British Empire (OBE) and asking if I was agreeable. When I showed the letter to Alice she was just as surprised and pleased as myself.

Following correspondence of formalities and arrangements I was informed the investiture would take place at Buckingham Palace on Tuesday, 5th February 1974 at which my attendance was requested.

Well, well, Alice and I had met Queen Mary, as Queen Mother at Sandringham and had quite a chat in 1947. In 1954 at Salwick we had met King George VI and the Queen and Princess Margaret, now we were off to London to see the Queen or Queen Mother. Nancy, Duncan, Alice and I travelled to London in Duncan's car and stayed overnight to be at Buckingham Palace before 10.30 a.m.

Only myself and two guests were allowed into the Palace, along with others to be invested with various honours. Duncan had to stay with the car in the Palace courtyard. There were lots of press photographers and reporters around, and we were eventually escorted to the rooms where the investiture was to take place. It was very interesting to us passing through the various rooms and corridors, the pictures, decorations, and guardsmen on duty.

It was all very well organised, guests were all seated where they could watch the proceedings. Came my turn, it was the 1974 Queen Mother who was taking the investiture, and as I stood before her and bowed, I thought what will she say, and what should I say? Thank goodness I could talk now, since 1937/38 my speech problems had not returned.

The Queen Mother's first words were 'Now Mr. Bridges, what is all this I hear about you'. I replied, 'It is a very long story, Your Majesty. It all began at Sandringham where my dad, his father and four brothers were all gamekeepers'.

I explained briefly what had given rise to the setting up of the Harold Bridges Foundation. She appeared to know something about it, and I also mentioned our meeting at Salwick 20 years earlier. She asked some questions about the Foundation, pinned the decoration on my lapel and wished me well, and expressed her admiration for what we had achieved from such a humble beginning.

So Harold Bridges was now O.B.E. Letters of congratulations came from all over the country, the local press also had write-ups, not all of which were just correct in detail, but no doubt well meant. I was particularly pleased to receive a letter of congratulation from Alan Monighan who followed me as manager at Bridges Transport Ltd. in 1968 and to note he was now six years later Managing Director of British Road Services Parcels Ltd. at their head office in London. His training in parcels operations at Bridges Transport Ltd. must have been good to get him to Managing Director of B.R.S. Parcels Ltd. in six years.

Another letter I received from Sir Daniel Pollit, head of National Freight Corporation on behalf of all members of the N. F. C. coupled with Bridges Transport Ltd. N. F. C. took over all British Road Services operations on privatisation, and have been very very successful.

In 1972 and 1976 Harold Bridges Foundation donated £19,000 to St. Martins Teachers Training College, Lancaster, towards the cost of building a new library for the college. Hugh Pollard was the College Principal, and in due course I was invited to lay the foundation stone of The Harold Bridges Library in 1974.

Alice and my sister Rose went with me and my mind went back 54 years,

Alice and myself, 1974, celebrating our Golden Wedding Anniversary at Mill Lodge, Burrow.

yes 54 years, when in 1920 I worked as a builder's labourer for William Eaves & Co. of Blackpool, on the St. Cuthberts' Victory Parish Hall, Lytham. Now William Eaves & Co. Ltd. were building the Harold Bridges Library and I was laying the foundation stone. It had taken me 54 years to qualify from labourer to stonemason!

I also recalled that all through the 1939/45 war as Harold Bridges Ltd. we had delivered all kinds of supplies to the same site and buildings when it was Bowerham Barracks, with a NAAFI Institute on site. A case of military barracks to civilian college not swords to ploughshares.

On completion the library was officially named The Harold Bridges' Library and opened by Dame Flora Robson, the famous actress and I have no doubt will be a great asset to the college for many years and generations to come. The Foundation Trustees informed me after the official opening of the Library that donations to date were over £250,000. 1974 was proving an eventful year with the by far most important event to come: the 16th September was our Golden

Wedding Anniversary. What can one say only, 'Thank God for 50 years of all one could wish for in our life together'. We had a quiet family celebration at Mill Lodge, the *Lancaster Guardian* came, took photographs and did a rather nice write up, followed by heavy congratulatory mail from relations, friends and acquaintances countrywide.

So passed 1974, and 50 years of happy married life and 57 years since we first met. 1975 was to be a different story. Early in 1975 Alice had at times seemed to lose her memory and as she was now 76 we thought it was advancing years, and the doctor agreed. However, one morning about 8.00 a.m. the usual getting up time, Alice could not move her legs and was talking far from her usual self. The doctor said she had had a slight stroke and to stay in bed a few days and he gave her tablets for which I took responsibility. In a few days Alice was up and about but far from her usual self, and this was the beginning of events which were to shape my life for the next 10 years.

A few months later a similar but more serious stroke left Alice more physically handicapped and mentally quite incapable in so far as she should really not be left on her own at all. Doctor arranged for the district nurse to call in each day, Nancy came from Preston as often as she was able and Nancy, Duncan and their two daughters came most weekends.

Golden Wedding Anniversary, 1974, at Mill Lodge, Burrow.

Alice's sister, Freda, and her husband, Robert, came from Wednesfield, Staffordshire, two or three times each year and stayed at Mill Lodge two or three weeks each time, and other members of our family came too. So between us all we managed fairly well to cope. When Freda and Robert were not at Mill Lodge, I was usually on my own as nurse, housemaid, housekeeper, gardener and general factotum, from Monday to Friday. Alice would not entertain any suggestion of going to hospital or nursing home for a period, all she wished was to be at home with me and the family at weekends.

About this time I was selling the property in Preston which I had bought from Messham Ltd. David Eaves of Reeds, Preston, had handled the actual advertising and sale, the Company's and the family solicitors since 1927 had been

Senior, Calveley and their predecessor, Byers Senior at Lytham. The sale was quite straight forward to someone in Southern Ireland with no complications, so I thought for this deal as I was so tied up I would use a local solicitor. The newspapers for Burrow were left in a box on the wall in the centre of the village, we collected our own papers anytime during the day. I used to collect ours about 9.00 a.m. and post letters when required, and had often met a Mr. George Clough collecting his papers. He lived at 'Keepers Cottage' at the far end of Burrow where the gamekeeper for the Fenwick family at Burrow Hall had lived before the estate was sold about 1945.

Mr. Clough I learned was a retired or semi-retired solicitor, who had practised in Bury as senior partner in an old established firm of family solicitors for many years. I learned from conversation when we met collecting our papers that he still did some part-time work for the firm and also as Deputy Registrar in various courts. In consequence I asked if he would handle the legal side of the property sale and he was quite happy and willing to handle the transfer. This entailed him visiting Mill Lodge several times for signatures and explanations etc. during which he met and chatted with Alice and was able to appreciate how tied up I was. He was a very keen fisherman so I told him to have a day's fishing any time he was able on my 1¼ miles of the River Lune. I was not able to fish now, only at weekends or when someone was at Mill Lodge to look after Alice. Mr. Clough offered to see if his wife would come and keep Alice company now and again, during midweek. Alice and I agreed this would be very welcome and so Mr. Clough and his wife, Joan came to Mill Lodge. Mr. Clough said, 'Call me George' and Joan said, 'And I am Joan'. So every Wednesday afternoon Joan came to Mill Lodge to keep Alice company for three or four hours. If George was away Joan would stay for tea and I was able to get on with jobs outside.

Joan and Alice got on very well together. Joan would be eight years younger than Alice. She had a son and a daughter, John and Patricia. John lived in Paris, he was European Manager for Clarkes, the American Earth Moving, fork lift and heavy machinery concern. Patricia was the *Times* correspondent in Rome for many years and later in Bonn, Germany. Patricia joined the new daily *Independent* when it was formed. It followed from this that Joan only saw her son and daughter intermittently during the year, so I am sure she did enjoy chatting to Alice, and they became close friends and confidantes. It was surprising how each time Alice had a stroke, after a few days in bed, she would recover a lot of her mental capacity, but physically very slowly got worse.

It was a few months after Joan's first visit she told me Alice had mentioned that she had a small lump in her left breast but not to tell me as I would only worry. Joan felt I should know, and let the doctor know, which I did. After a routine check of Alice's heart and chest, the doctor asked Alice how long she had known about the lump in her breast, she said, 'Oh, I don't know, I cannot remember, don't tell Harold'.

Doctor advised proper examination and X-ray which was performed at Lancaster Royal Infirmary. This confirmed the doctor's fears, breast cancer. Next day luckily Alice was in an almost natural mental condition, doctor explained the X-ray result and eventually after a lot of persuasion Alice agreed to go into hospital and have her left breast removed, as the only cure. The operation was at Morecambe Victoria Hospital and was completely successful. I think Alice should have been in hospital about three weeks, but after 10 days one evening Nancy, Duncan and I were at the hospital, Alice had been sitting in a chair for a while, when the nurses came to put her to bed Alice said, 'No I am going home to Burrow with Harold and Nancy'. We all did our best to try and get Alice to stay and be helped into bed, but she would have nothing to do with it. She was going home. The nurses brought the private ward sister, she contacted the matron, but no one could change Alice's mind.

Matron told me they could not let her go home, they had not the authority to discharge any patient, it was a doctor's decision. So after a lot of telephoning by the matron a doctor came, but it was no use Alice had made up her mind and that was that. Eventually, doctor agreed very reluctantly to allow discharge under protest. We arrived at Burrow nearly midnight, it was a very windy night, pouring rain and black as ink.

However, all went well. Alice's doctor called each day, a week later nurse took Alice's stitches out and she made a complete recovery.

One of Alice's physical problems was loss of balance and continually heavy falls. On one occasion she fell in the bedroom and the ensuing pain in her left thigh caused the doctor to arrange an X-ray at Mill Lodge, in Alice's bedroom. It was apparently a mobile X-ray machine and it showed a hairline crack in her thigh. Alice had to stay in bed about four weeks without putting any weight on the leg, which increased the problems. Joan came Wednesday and Friday, the district nurse every day, and again Alice made a complete recovery.

Among the many falls, Alice had two more which proved very awkward. The kitchen at Mill Lodge was very small, the door from the passage opened inwards; when in the kitchen you had to have the door shut. One day Alice went in the kitchen to fill the kettle. She shut the door and fell behind the door. What a job I had to force the door open by pushing Alice's body with the door till I could squeeze in. I promptly had the joiner to remove the hinged door and replace it with a sliding door outside the kitchen.

A few weeks later the same thing exactly happened in the bathroom, which was the same size as the kitchen and had a hinged door opening inwards, which I had altered to a sliding door next day.

This frequency of falls caused the doctor to arrange for a series of blood tests each day for ten days. The doctor took a sample each day, usually about noon, and I took it to Lancaster Royal Infirmary each day for the ten days and from the results the doctor adjusted Alice's medication. The falls also caused the doctor to arrange for Alice to have a walking frame, to help her walk. This gave rise to an amusing incident, when the doctor called later he asked Alice, 'How are you finding the walking frame? Does it help?' Alice replied, 'Oh yes. It's fine thank you doctor'. Doctor then said, 'Let me see how you are with it'. Alice stood up, picked the walking frame up like a suitcase and staggered about six steps. I was at hand or she would have been down. Doctor could not help but laugh, but at the same time he remarked about the strange lapses of mental and physical normality which occur with patients in Alice's condition, yet at times they have periods of normal mental behaviour, the physical failings do not alter.

I was not able during all this time to make my regular visits to the companies in Preston. We arranged to have annual general meetings for the four companies of which Duncan was Managing Director and I was Chairman Director at Mill Lodge, and any other occasional meeting which had to be officially recorded.

One other company of which I was founder Director Chairman was Heaps, Collis and Harrison, Air Power Centre, Blackpool Road, Preston, engaged in the repair, maintenance and installation of air compressors and ancillary equipment. It is strange how during my whole business career, some small seemingly unimportant incident is followed by a chain of events no one could possibly foresee and so it was with H.C.H. and my involvement.

For many years Bridges Transport Ltd. had been regular and very good customers of Brown Brothers Ltd., the motor accessory and equipment factors who sold every kind of equipment, spares, tools etc. used by the motor trade and road transport industry. They had branches in Preston and very many of the large towns in the United Kingdom. We had dealt with Brown Brothers Ltd. ever since they opened their Preston branch and we had also on occasions stored goods for them in our warehouse. I remember we once had about fifty lawn mowers in store for them all winter. I expect it was an end of season clearance by the manufacturer.

In all the years we had dealt with Brown Brothers I had never met or had a call from the Preston branch manager, until one day I was asked if I would see the new Brown Brothers manager, T. Dawson, by appointment at my convenience. I agreed, of course, we had a large monthly purchase account with Brown Brothers and might be able to arrange better terms.

In due course the new manager, Tom Dawson arrived with the local representative. We had a very interesting talk about various matters of mutual interest. I learned he had been with Brown Brothers from leaving school in Northern Ireland, his mother lived in Northern Ireland, my mother came from Southern Ireland.

While at Preston I got to know Tom very well. He was a very keen, eager and efficient manager and at the same time a very likeable personality. I learned he was a keen shooting man so I invited him to shoot at Salwick, which he enjoyed. He was a good shot and very well behaved safety wise, which is the very first golden rule in the shooting sport.

We met also at shooting days on other estates where we were invited guests, and so formed a friendship outside business affairs. It was not very long before Tom was promoted to Brown Brothers, Manchester branch, so I only met him on shooting days. Time passed and I had a 'phone call from Tom, could he come to Burrow to have a chat about a personal problem which had cropped up recently. Tom came to Mill Lodge, Burrow; he knew Alice and my sons, he had one son still at school or college.

Tom's problem was he had been offered a very lucrative promotion to Brown Brothers, London and would like to know what I thought he should do. He felt his increased salary would go in higher living costs, his son's education would be changed and other family matters caused doubts in his mind. After quite a long talk he asked me what I thought. I said, 'With your ambition and drive, your experience and capabilities you should be on your own, self-employed, or whatever you like to call it. You will never make a fortune working for Brown Brothers. There must be an opening somewhere in a job you know.' Tom said, 'Yes, I know, I have thought that , but I have no capital to speak of to risk, I am buying my home in Cheshire on mortgage otherwise I would have a go.'

After some further discussion, I told Tom to look around, delay his decision on the London promotion and if he could come up with a viable proposition I would consider financing him on a 50/50 basis of shares in a company he could manage. Tom was full of gratitude for this offer and my advice, and said he would be in touch. A few weeks later when we met again, Heaps, Collis and Harrison in Co. Durham was for sale – they were compressed air engineers and held the Ingersoll Rand Agency for compressors etc. in the North East.

We went over to the works several times and our enquiries showed there were financial problems and ageing owners, hence the offer for sale. The outcome was we bought all the shares and took the business over as a going concern. Alterations and improvements were made to the property, to increase capacity and improve efficiency which soon showed under the able management of Tom Dawson, now Managing Director of the company, and I was Chairman Director.

Tom's long connections in Lancashire while he was at Brown Bros. led us to consider opening a depot in Preston, and when this was decided premises were purchased in Blackpool Road, Preston, by Heaps, Collis and Harrison Ltd. and operated very successfully as the Air Power Centre. I was personal guarantor for the bank overdraft which was not required later, when I put £50,000 into the company by purchase of 50,000 £1 Preference Shares which

I gave to my son, David. By 1979 the company was firmly established and I sold my shares in the company to Tom's family and my interest ceased. The progress and success of the company was entirely due to Tom's keen business sense and drive. I did not know a thing about the physical or practical side of Air Power, and the only credit I can perhaps take is my hunch that Tom, given the chance, would succeed. I gave him the chance and provided the financial backing. I was very pleased it all went so well and the sale of my shares reflected my reward for providing risk capital.

Meanwhile at Mill Lodge Alice's condition, mental and physical, continued to deteriorate, frequent small strokes gradually took their toll. Duncan brought a folding invalid chair for Alice to be moved around in the house as she could no longer walk more than a few steps even with assistance, and could not use the walking frame.

There were two steps between the bedroom and living room. I made a sloping ramp so that Alice could be moved from the bedside to the living room in the wheelchair where there was a big bay window from which a long stretch of the River Lune could be seen, and the open countryside across and down the Lune Valley. Joan still came regularly each week and brought flowers or perhaps fruit or sweets for Alice.

Often during the week during the morning Alice would say, 'Will the lady who brings the flowers by coming today? I hope so, I do love her'.

It was very touching to me when Joan came into the living room. Alice would hold both arms outstretched in greeting and welcome. They would chat away all afternoon and it was remarkable how Alice changed during the afternoon from being quite clear and rational for a time and then would start rambling about her parents and childhood and wanting to go back to Willenhall to see her mother, who of course, had died over 30 years ago. When Joan or anyone else came I could get out and do some gardening and I had an odd job man to help out with the large area of grass mowing. Our vicar, Reverend R. C. Riley came often and Alice loved to talk to him about her school days and early years of employment in Willenhall. Alice tried to tell me that she did not think Joan was very happy at home, her husband, George, was away a lot and they seemed to be drifting apart.

I did not know what to make of this, they had, I think, been married about 40 years and I felt perhaps Alice had misunderstood Joan or was just rambling in her mind. Joan had been a school teacher and gymnastic instructor before marriage and travel abroad to Italy and Germany to see her daughter, Patricia, which meant she had lots of interesting experiences to relate. Alice had never been out of the UK and my only trip abroad had been to Germany in 1918/1920 in H. M. Forces of the British Army on the Rhine.

During the summer of 1976 I took Alice in the invalid chair to have afternoon tea in the garden at Keepers Cottage with Joan. On occasions George, her husband, was there and I had a feeling or sensed something was not just right or normal. However, it was none of my business. Joan had been very kind to Alice, which I appreciated and it was George who had brought them together. I hoped Alice's ramblings were in error, for which she could not be blamed, dear Alice, it was really heartbreaking to see the gradual worsening of her health.

In 1971 I was approached by the owner/occupier to buy Robinson House Farm, Burrow, 127 acres, which I did for £32,000 and in 1975 I bought a further 74 acres from Stowe Trust Ltd., which had been part of the Burrow Hall Estate, for £27,250, part of which was rented to Robinson House Farm and party to a local farmer.

Here we go again, backtrack to 1915 where I worked at Warton Hall Farm, Nr. Lytham for £15 for the year, and now albeit 60 years later I own 200 acres of very good agricultural land, close to home. I also bought the private road from Mill Lodge to the main road, about 300 yards, and the Mill Stream, which in the old days before 1936 had provided the water from Leck Beck to drive the water wheel driven mill known as Burrow Mill, now Mill Lodge. Included in this deal was some land adjacent to Mill Lodge and the land bought with the fishing rights in 1961; in all it made a very nice compact little estate, with which I was very pleased.

On the corner of our private road, named Mill Lane, and the main road was an old derelict stone building on about half an acre of land which was owned by the brewery who owned Highwayman Inn right opposite. This small plot of land had an opening onto the main road used when the building was stables and I had the idea if I could buy this plot I could make a road through it from Mill Lane to the main road, which would greatly improve the sight line as we came out of Mill Lane onto the main road. I approached the brewery. They agreed to sell and asked me to make an offer. I offered them £250 which they accepted, we cut a few trees down, demolished part of the old stone building and used the stone in the foundation of the new road, and we then had a very much improved exit onto the main road.

All this was before Alice's first stroke, they all turned out to be very good long-term investments, and gave me an interest in the outside world of agriculture and kindred activities.

So we passed into 1977. All the companies in Preston were continuing to make steady progress. Alice's condition continued to worsen, and the number of days she had to spend wholly in bed steadily increased. To her great credit she never complained once about anything. My daughter, Nancy, my sister Rose, the doctor, the district nurse and lots of friends were all very helpful and sympathetic and so on 30th November 1977 in the afternoon my dear wife of 53 years passed peacefully away to rest. Nancy and Rose were with me when Alice died, it had been expected for some days, but when death occurs that is it – finality. There is no coming back, and there is nothing so certain as death. The funeral service was at St. John's, Tunstall.

The church was almost full, amongst the mourners were many representatives from organisations which had benefited from the Harold Bridges Foundation, including a contingent in uniform from St. John's Ambulance Brigade.

Cremation took place at Lytham and Alice's ashes were laid to rest close to the church entrance and beneath a window of plain lead light glass, in which in 1979 a memorial stained glass window was dedicated, to the glory of God and in Alice's memory.

1977 Christmas, less than four weeks after Alice died, I spent at Ashburne, Fulwood with Nancy, Duncan and family and went to my sister Rose at Grimsargh on Boxing Day.

I was now on my own, and it was very heartening to me when I received so many expressions of sympathy from so many sources far and wide. Nancy and Duncan came most Sundays and Nancy made a hot lunch which was a change when I was not having lunch elsewhere. I was also invited and went to lunch on Sundays at the Vicarage with the vicar, his mother and his sister, Barbara, and on other occasions to friends in the parish.

Chapter Twelve

Joan, Tresco and Marriage

I T ALSO became a regular thing for me to be invited to lunch at Cloughs, Keepers Cottage, where George and Joan made me welcome. After lunch George and I would on occasions go for a walk up the north side of Leck Beck to Cowan Bridge and back along the south side to Burrow, when the weather was fair. It was during these lunches and walks I became more aware something was not just right at Keepers Cottage. It was a sort of feeling in the air, and I wondered if George's frequent absence from home during the week had anything to do with it, but as I have said earlier, it was none of my business. At the same time I was so sorry, they having been so good to Alice and me and made me most welcome. Being on your own after 53 happy years married is no joke. All the household chores must go on, amongst these the washing and ironing each week. We had a very good Bendix washer and dryer combined at Mill Lodge. I soon found out how to use it on my own and for some weeks into 1978 did the ironing as well, myself. This cropped up during conversation one Sunday at Keepers Cottage and Joan said, 'I have lots of time on my hands when George is away. I will come down to Mill Lodge afternoon or evening and do your ironing.' George was there and said, 'Good idea, and I will go fishing'. So Joan came each week to iron, made a cup of tea for us both, and we usually sat in the bay window and had a chat for half-an-hour. On occasions we would be joined by the vicar or the previous vicar, Ronnie Entwistle, or a friend of Alice's and mine calling to see how I was making out on my own.

I had, of course, talked with Nancy and Duncan and my youngest son, John and his wife, Jackie, about my future. I loved Mill Lodge and the Lune Valley. My dear Alice was laid to rest at Tunstall and I could not visualise leaving the district; at the same time I was 78 and could well afford to make such arrangements as were required to ensure I was looked after if need be.

It was one evening when Joan had finished ironing and we were sitting in the bay window having our usual cup of tea, when this problem cropped up and Joan said she had always envied the happy marriage Alice and I had enjoyed for so long, and that her own marriage was on the point of breaking up due entirely to their not having the love for each other that makes for a long, happy, enduring marriage.

Joan explained her daughter, Patricia, and son, John, were aware of the problem, but with them both being so far away Joan had no one to turn to and felt she could not go on much longer, and that she and George had talked about a separation. I said I was very sorry. I did not realise the problem was so serious although I had sensed there was something not just right.

I also said, 'You have two sisters in Clovelly, North Devon, would it be a good idea to have a few weeks' holiday with them, seek their advice, although they are both spinsters, and perhaps a few weeks apart from George might be of some use in mending the rift in the marriage'. Joan said George would not take her, she had not seen her sisters for years, and would love to have a few weeks' holiday with them, but it was a long difficult journey and 'I am 72'. Following some further talk on the problem I said I would take Joan and bring her back, if need be. I could break my journey at Wednesfield or Willenhall in Staffordshire where Alice had a sister and a niece and when we were travelling together an early start would enable us to complete the journey in the day. I said, 'See what George thinks about this and let me know next week'. Events arose in June 1978 which caused the idea I had suggested to be shelved on my part for the time being anyway.

On 16th June 1978 I received a letter dated 7th June 1978 from the Secretary General of 'The Most Venerable Order of the Hospital of St. John of Jerusalem' informing me my name and qualifications were to be forwarded to the Council of the Grand Priory of the Order with a view to its submission to Her Majesty the Queen, the Sovereign Head of the Order, with a view to my being invested as Officer of the Order.

Formalities followed and I received a letter dated 22nd August 1978 which informed me of my admission as an Officer of the Order as from 26th July 1978 by gracious permission of H. M. The Queen. The actual Investiture took place at the Grand Priory Church, London on 15th February 1979 when I received my decoration.

Very similar communications in 1982 and 1983 resulted in my being promoted to Commander in the Order as from 10th November 1982. The Investiture took place at the Grand Priory Church, London on 7th July 1983 when the Lord Prior, Sir Maurice Dorman, pinned the decoration on my lapel.

Joan was with me on this occasion and quite enjoyed the proceedings including lunch with the Lord Prior before the Investiture.

My second son, David, had been in hospital several times with an abdominal complaint which, growing steadily worse caused his death on 21st June 1978, age 45 years. While David had been ill for some time his death only seven months after Alice's was a great shock. David was a very happy go lucky type, married no children and matters were not helped by him not having made any will. However, all got sorted out, Joan was still coming to Mill Lodge to do the ironing and odd sewing jobs.

During 1978 I had all the wooden windows in Mill Lodge taken out and replaced by double glazed PVC framed windows by Croft Roplasto Ltd., Preston, and a very big improvement they were. Mill Lodge was improved beyond measure by the change, no painting, so easy to clean and much better from a crime safety angle and in case of fire from ease of opening and exit.

Towards the end of 1978 when these matters were being sorted out Joan informed me she and George had decided to separate. They had arranged or agreed any finance problems and she had arranged to go to Clovelly, North Devon and stay with her two sisters for a while, perhaps till New Year 1979.

If I remember rightly it was December 1st or 2nd 1978 when I took Joan to Clovelly. We called at Alice's niece, Winnie, in Willenhall for lunch on the way and arrived Clovelly soon after dusk.

Joan's two sisters, Thea and Meg, both spinsters, lived in two small thatched typical Devon cottages next to each other, both had a spare room. I stayed the night at a bed and breakfast farmhouse close by. Joan stayed at Meg's for a while and then moved to Thea's.

On my way home next day I called at Alice's sister, Freda, in Wednesfield and stayed the night as it was snowing and I did not want to be on the motorway in the dark and snow. December soon showed it was winter. We had quite a lot of frost and some snow, but I had no one to snowball!

Towards Christmas Joan 'phoned as usual each week and said they would like me to spend Christmas with them and by then she would have decided something about her immediate future.

During December I saw George Clough several times at church and he did not appear to

A letter confirming my promotion to Knight of the Order of St. John.

The Most Venerable Order of the Hospital of St. John of Jerusalem

```
                    Chancery of the Order
                       St. John's Gate,
                          Clerkenwell,
                      London, EC1M 4DA


                        10th June, 1991

Sir,
   I have the honour to inform you that
Her Majesty The Queen, the Sovereign
Head of the Most Venerable Order of
the Hospital of St. John of Jerusalem,
has been graciously pleased to sanc-
tion your promotion to KNIGHT of THE
ORDER OF ST. JOHN as from 15th May
1991 the date of Her Majesty's Sign
Manual.
   An announcement of this honour will
in due course appear in the London Ga-
zette.

            I have the honour to be,
            Your obedient servant,

               Secretary-General.
```

bear me any grudge for taking Joan to Clovelly. So two days before Christmas 1978 off I went to Clovelly. I stayed the night at Alice's sister Freda's in Wednesfield and arrived at Clovelly before dark, parked the Range Rover in a nearby farm yard, where I was to stay at night over Christmas for bed and breakfast.

Quite a lot of the farms in Devon appeared to do bed and breakfast business, mine was very comfortable, and kept by a very pleasant and homely couple. Joan appeared to be much more relaxed and more cheerful, being with her relatives after years apart had obviously done her good. During December I had now been on my own in most respects for twelve months since Alice died and it was no joy at all in spite of all the help and kindness shown by my family and friends, with some of whom I had talked about seeking a housekeeper.

Some were for it, some against, the job would be finding the right person. I was now nearer 79 than 78 so did not want a dolly bird and I was so well in general health and took such an interest in Mill Lodge, the garden, the river and farm etc. that I did not want to leave the district or go into an old folks home. The consensus of opinion, taking everything into account, was that I should advertise for a housekeeper under a box number and just see what, if any, response there was. I decided to do this in the New Year 1979, and in the meantime battle on. I was looking forward to spending a week in Clovelly at Christmas. My stay at Clovelly over Christmas proved to be a pleasant and restful change.

Joan's two sisters had both been in the far east, employed in some kind of social or missionary work and had many exciting and interesting experiences to relate. They both managed to get away during the war before the Japs moved in and on return to England had somewhat similar social work as employment. Naturally, I suppose during conversation Joan's problems and future arose and I mentioned my decision to advertise for a housekeeper in the New Year.

They all thought this was good idea and Joan said, 'You are well enough known in the Lune Valley, do use a box number or you will be swamped with "gold diggers" '. I said, 'Yes. That's just what I want to avoid, all I want is a mature, homely person, a good cook, oh yes – and preferably very practical not highbrow, fond of the country and garden and in good health. Tall order perhaps, but no rush, and I may change my mind, get a daily or part-time house help or battle on for a while'.

A day or two later Joan and I went to several places of interest on the North Devon coast in the Range Rover, on a very nice sunny day for December. We had lunch at a small country pub, and chatting afterwards in the lounge Joan said, 'About this housekeeper job. I know I am 72 but I cannot stay with my sisters, and have nothing to do all day, I am sure we know each other well enough to know we can get on together. George has told me I can take any of the furniture and chattels from Keepers Cottage if I so wish. If we can agree on terms, I can apply for the job'.

We talked this and relevant matters over and the outcome was that Joan would go back to Burrow with me and take up her duties as my housekeeper as early as possible in 1979, possibly immediately after we got home.

We had a good journey back to Burrow. Joan's sisters were sorry she had to leave them, but at the same time were very pleased that her future was more settled, and had, I learned later, expressed their complete approval of their sister's future employer. We very soon got sorted out; my handyman, Ernie Allen, took the Range Rover and trailer to Keepers Cottage with Joan and collected all her own personal belongings, and anything else she and George had agreed.

Joan had an Austin Mini, her own car, and as I had the Range Rover our double garage was O.K. Joan went shopping to Lancaster every Thursday and for her weekly visit to her hairdresser, David Frank. Tuesday and Friday she usually went to Kirkby Lonsdale shopping.

Mill Lodge soon looked a different place. It was good to see and easy to see there was a woman in the house not afraid of work, even at 72. In Mill Lodge, Joan had the double bedroom, which faced north. I had the single bedroom

'The Bothy', 1981.

facing east. The large living room faced west and another L-shaped lounge or dining room faced west and north.

We had a very good lean-to greenhouse along the south side and a large cellar under most of the rooms, where we had the heating installation and laundry washer, it was a very useful store provided everything was about two feet above the floor. The reason for this was that the cellar floor was about three feet below the flood level of the River Lune which was only about 25 yards away. When the river was in high flood the water used to seep through the concrete floor joints depending on how high the river rose and how long it stayed at high flood level; this could be once or twice a year or perhaps miss a year. This all depended on the rainfall higher up the Lune Valley and the catchment area which drained into the River Lune. The cellar floor was laid to drain to one corner nearest the river where we had a small tank below floor level and a float controlled Alcon electric pump, which pumped the water out of the tank into the drain to the river, and so while the cellar floor had water running all over it, the Alcon pump could always handle it, except in 1968 when in a heavy storm we had a power cut due to flooding at the local power substation, and we had three feet of water in the cellar, not so bad really once in now 28 years.

We had some very substantial stone built outbuildings which we had built in the 1960s where we stored all the fishing tackle, lawn mowers, tools, etc., and during early 1979 I had the idea the main building which we called 'The Bothy' would with extensions convert into a very nice small residence.

I had my architect, Arnold England, who had been a shooting and fishing friend for about 30 years, to look at my suggestions and he agreed it was a sensible project with no problems except getting planning permission for the conversion and extensions. After a bit of a battle with the planners we got the go ahead, cut down two very large sycamore trees, dug out a few hundred cubic yards of earth and extended 'The Bothy' just as I had visualised. We took out all the wooden windows and replaced with Croft Roplasto PVC and the extensions were PVC double glazed all round. We ended up with a lounge or living room facing west across the Lune Valley with a stone built fireplace, one single and one double bedroom, a study or office for me, a lovely modern Kitchen, bathroom, toilets, etc. all with which Joan and I were very pleased. It was all stone built, as at Mill Lodge. Almost all the stone we took out of the River Lune and Leck Beck; the Beck was about 100 yards from 'The Bothy' and was part of the land purchase from Stowe Trust Ltd.

In 1962 I had bought a 30 cwt Benford dumper truck, and with this we carted hundreds of tons of stone and gravel out of the Lune and Leck Beck. The only stone we imported came from Fulwood Barracks, Preston, during alterations there and from a stone building in Lancaster Road, Preston, which Thos. Croft & Son Ltd. were demolishing. This was dressed corner stone, window cills and door lintels, and some wall top flagstones from Crofts.

Included in the extension was a stone and PVC porch or small conservatory over the front door. Joan saw to the curtains, carpets, etc. and we moved into The Bothy just before Christmas 1979.

On the advice of the Group chartered accountants, Moore & Smalley, in 1973 a holding company Grommet (Holdings) Ltd. was registered on 17th December 1973, and all the shares in Dixon Bros., T. Kirkham & Co., T. C. Holden and Messhams were acquired by Grommet (Holdings) Ltd. from Nancy, Duncan, Alice and I either for cash or issue of Grommet (Holdings) Ltd. shares. I was appointed Chairman Director, Duncan and Nancy as Directors, and we all retained our positions as before in the subsidiaries. It was purely an accountancy change and did not make any difference to the day to day running of the business.

When Alice's estate was cleared up in 1978 her shares in Grommet (Holdings) Ltd. were sold by the executors to Nancy's daughters, Heather and Alison. These changes meant that early in 1979 I had only a small minority holding in Grommet. After consulting the accountants for advice I sold my shares to Alison and Heather.

I realised when I was selling my shares that I would no longer have any say at all in the running or future of the four companies or of Grommet (Holdings) Ltd. through not being a shareholder. This was early in 1979. I had long intended and expressed my wish to retire from all business interests on my 80th birthday, 11th May 1980, and that naturally from that date the £10,000 a year I received from Grommet (Holdings) Ltd. would cease.

However, much to my surprise I was informed later that at a meeting in October 1979 my son-in-law Duncan Milne had taken over the position of Chairman of Grommet Holdings and the four subsidiaries and that my salary ceased as and from the date of the meeting; so ended on a sad note my 32 years as Chairman of Dixon Bros. and Chairman of T. Kirham Ltd., T. C. Holden Ltd. and Messhams for roughly 10 years each, 62 years in all, and the end of my business career, 7 months before my 80th birthday.

During Alice's illness from 1974 to 1977 I had done very little fishing or shooting, the fishing in the River Lune, which like most UK rivers had not fully recovered from the disease of the late 1960s and early 1970s and I decided to sell the top section, about one third of the whole. This was on the other side of Leck Beck and the farthest away from The Bothy. R. Turner & Son, Bentham, handled the advertising and sale by auction at the Royal Hotel, Kirkby Lonsdale. Lively interest and bidding was shown, and it was knocked down at £21,000 to a party from Canterbury, quite a long way to come fishing.

I was quite happy. I had got back what I paid for 2,200 yards in 1961 and I still had ⅔ left. The remainder of the fishing I sold privately in 1980 and 1981. Splitting the sales into three tax years avoided quite a lot of Capital Gains Tax, quite legally, as I had the benefit of three years exemption limit. The sales in 1980 and 1981 were to a local landowner who had the fishing rights on the opposite bank of the river, and the total final outcome was I had sold for three times as much as I had paid in 1961, so that was a good hedge against inflation. It was quite interesting to note that when I bought the rights in 1961 the General Rate levied by Lancaster City Council for the sporting rights on the 2,200 yards was £243 per annum. In 1981 when I sold the third and last length the rate was over £1,400 paid, six times up.

In September 1979 Joan and I had 14 days holiday with her sisters in Clovelly, the first holiday I had been able to take since 1972 and very enjoyable. So passed 1979. I was very pleased and happy with my house-keeper, Joan for the past year. She was a splendid cook, looked after me and Mill Lodge perfectly and was a very competent flower arranger, having won many prizes at local shows for her efforts. All members of my family came to see us at The Bothy from time to time and seemed glad I was being looked after.

I now go back to 1978 when in May, six months after Alice died and was laid to rest at St. John's Church, Tunstall, I felt I would like to have a memorial stained glass window at the church, in her memory. There was a two panel plain glass lead light window immediately above Alice's grave which would be an ideal place.

I talked this over with the vicar, Reverend R. C. Riley and the previous vicar, Reverend R. Entwistle and many other people who had known Alice and me for many years. They all thought it would be a good idea and enhance the church which had very little stained glass in the main body of the church. Widespread enquiries were made and the stained glass artist, Jane Gray of Uxbridge was finally chosen to be invited to discuss my idea. On 3rd May 1978 she wrote me to say that due to pressure of work it would likely be June before she could come to look at the church and discuss designs. In the meantime I could make enquiries to the appropriate church authority for a faculty and the various procedures that had to be followed. It was a long drawn out procedure, through 1978 and 1979. Eventually all was agreed with all the parties concerned, the design approved and the window fixed, by J. Edmondson & Son, builders, of Burton-in-Lonsdale.

A memorial and dedication service was held on Sunday, 16th March 1980 by Reverend Canon Eric Rothwell, at one time Rural Dean of Tunstall. The church was almost full and the window much admired. Jane Gray had many of her windows installed in the church at Martindale in the Lake District. Following the Dedication of the window, Joan, always without fail, on the anniversary of Alice's birthday and also date of her death did a lovely flower arrangement which was placed in the memorial window recess inside the church. This continued without fail until November 30th, 1985, which was the last one before Joan's death on 23rd September 1986.

1980 was still a year of activity at the Bothy. The builder had one craftsman on the job on his own, when he could manage, sometimes I gave him a hand, I had not forgotten what I learned in 1920! And when required extra men were brought in.

One task was to build a dividing wall between Mill Lodge and The Bothy. Mill Lodge would be for sale and I thought it best to have an established wall to my liking. The country stonemason who had been on the job since early 1979 was Dick Willan. He was approaching retiring age, and a really good steady hard worker. The wall was built in two sections, total 90 yards long 2' 6" high and 18" wide. I carted all the stones out of Leck Beck with the dumper. There must have been over 100 tons in all. The wall was built as two with a cavity which we filled in with gravel and sand out of Leck Beck, and soil out of Leckfield.

When we finished it was planted with all kinds of bulbs, alpine and rock plants and is a very colourful picture all through spring and summer. So we called it Willans Wall in his memory.

1980 also saw the building and laying of a new drainage system and septic tank and further work on the river bank where there was a stream entering the Lune. The second length of Lune fishing was sold in 1980 to the owner of the fishing rights on the other bank. Joan and I went to Clovelly again in September 1980 for 14 days' holiday. She stayed with her younger sister, Thea, and I had my farmhouse bed and breakfast.

1981 saw the sale of the last of three lengths of River Lune fishing which I had bought in 1961, which I had enjoyed immensely and so many of my friends throughout the 20 years.

The alteration and extensions to The Bothy had included converting the two car single-storey garage into a large double bedroom. So in 1981 Dick Willan built a new double car garage, all stone built with a splendid airy dry storage loft over.

The joinery work in the roof and the slating were a very tricky job, due to the shape of the garage to fit in with the workshop and ground floor store already built. This meant the roof was five sided at the eaves, all different lengths and in consequence the roof had five different pitches. I carted all the stone out of Leck Beck and the wide sliding doors from the previous garage fitted to the new one.

Joan had now been separated from George Clough, her husband, for over two years, and was very happy with her new life so she commenced divorce proceedings to end her marriage; in due course all seemed to go smoothly and amicably and the *decree nisi* granted in 1981.

1981, another eventful year in which I seemed to be kept busy all the time. The amount of correspondence I had to deal with each year in connection with the Harold Bridges Foundation continued to increase and in many instances of appeals for donations I went to see the people and premises involved. The trustees' accounts for the year ending 5th April 1982 showed that 20 donations had been made totalling £25,950 and that to same date total donations made amounted to £588,390.

I usually attended four trustees' meetings each years, held at Moore & Smalley's offices in Preston. The trustees at this time were Williams & Glyns Bank Ltd., Trustee Division, Mosley Street, Manchester.

In mid summer 1981 Joan suggested we should have a different 14 days holiday, and after much pondering we agreed we would have 14 days in Tresco, Isles of Scilly. Joan had been once many years before and was sure I would enjoy it.

The journey to get there was a bit of a bind, it entailed nine hours train journey from Lancaster to Penzance, and two or maybe three changes on the way, helicopter flights Penzance to St. Mary's, Isle of Scilly and then motor launch from St. Mary's to Tresco about 30 minutes. Much the same in reverse order coming home. We stayed at the only hotel on Tresco, The Island Hotel, and it was very good indeed. The managers, John and Wendy Pyatt, were the most willing, efficient and homely couple I have ever met in the hotel business.

Tresco is an ideal island for anyone wanting a quiet, restful holiday, no cars, motorcycles or buses. The only mechanical vehicles are agricultural tractors used on the two farms on the island. Being about 40 miles out into the Atlantic Ocean from Lands End transport of goods and passengers is by normal standards expensive. I was told by a builder from Cornwall working on the island that it cost £80 a ton to bring building materials from Penzance to Tresco.

The M. V. Scillonian provides a regular weekday service between Penzance and St. Mary's, the main island. From St. Mary's to the other inhabited islands, Bryher, St. Martins, St. Agnes and Tresco, goods and passengers travel by motor launch. All this transhipping of cargo is what adds to the cost. I expect the same applies to any far off shore islands.

Joan and I enjoyed our holiday immensely. We had motor launch trips to the other islands, saw lots of seals on the rocks, and unusual sea birds. A longer trip, about four hours was to the Bishops Rock Lighthouse and we had lots of lovely interesting walks on the different islands. We were so pleased that we booked for 1982 and learned it was normal for the hotel to be almost fully booked before the New year. Wendy Pyatt was a very expert flower arranger, the hotel had lots of beautiful fresh flower arrangements and these interested Joan very much.

So back to Burrow, and the garden, grass mowing and the greenhouse in which I had 18 tomato plants, and they did very well.

Another activity I enjoyed was gathering wood for logs for our open fire, sawing and splitting it, and then during the winter enjoying a lovely blazing log fire in the open fireplace in the lounge.

I had several acres of woodland near The Bothy and there was usually a dead tree or two either blown down or which I cut down. The Range Rover and the trailer would go almost anywhere, in the carting process, and then during bad weather when it was not fit to be outside, I would get busy with my 12-inch circular saw electric drive or with one of my chain saws, one electric and one petrol. I also collected a lot of log wood along the river bank – one field I owned had about 500 yards of River Lune bank. When the river was in high flood it used to leave all manner of rubbish, including the log wood, along the top of the bank and the field, and it was quite easy to collect with the Range Rover and trailer.

Part of the arrangement I had with Joan as my housekeeper was that I would provide and maintain a small car for her own personal use or as required. Joan's car was an Austin Mini, past its best, so in 1981 Joan sold it to Lambs Hornby and I replaced it with a new 1981 Austin Metro, a grand little job.

Each year apart from correspondence and telephone calls I had at least one meeting with my accountants to discuss investments, taxation and sundry kindred matters and it was at such a meeting, when inheritance tax and Capital Gains Tax etc. were being discussed, it was mentioned that a man could transfer capital to his wife in trust as a marriage settlement and under current legislation could in certain circumstances, quite legally save considerable amounts of inheritance tax.

Joan and I talked this over many times in the following weeks. I was now 81, Joan was 75. She had been my housekeeper for three years and we got on together very well indeed, so why not get married, we were very fond of each other. Joan's son, John and his wife, Ingrid, and Joan's daughter Patricia came to see Joan on the rare occasions they were in England, and were made welcome and invited us to Paris and Bonn, Germany. My folks came to see us regularly and it appeared Joan was accepted by all as O.K. I saw George Clough frequently at Church and we were on quite good terms. Joan also would see George occasionally in Kirkby Lonsdale and there was no apparent animosity between them. However, Joan felt she would rather leave things as they were for the time being, and so came 1982. I was quite content with Joan's wish; after all, whatever tax might be to pay if I died would not bother me and all I wished for was Joan's happiness and wellbeing. I would never forget her great kindness to Alice in 1976/77.

Among my interests at Burrow was Robinson House Farm. The farmhouse and buildings, behind the Highwayman Inn, were about 500 yards from The Bothy and Mill Lodge. It was owned by the farmer occupier and his family until 1971. The farm itself was 127 acres and he rented a further 42 acres from the Stowe Trust Ltd., Burrow Hall. I bought the farm in 1971 and in 1975 bought 74 acres of agricultural land from Stowe Trust Ltd., Burrow Hall. This included 42 acres rented by my tenant and 27 acres tenanted by another local farmer.

My tenant expressed the wish several times in 1980/81 for me to sell the farm back to him at the current market price, there would be no doubt this would result in a handsome profit, but this would be considerably less than if it could be sold with vacant possession.

The tenant and his family held the tenancy on a lease drawn up in 1971 and provided he farmed the land reasonably well and paid the rent, there was no way in which I could offer the farm for sale with vacant possession.

Moreover he had a son who worked on the farm and if he wished to follow his father as tenant the lease and the tenancy would still apply. Legislation lays down or allows for a rent review each three years. The return to capital of rents on agricultural land was extremely low and in 1982 I decided to sell Robinson House Farm to the tenant. I retained two fields, North Field and River Field, and sold these in later tax years, with vacant possession, at a very much higher figure per acre. I was very pleased and happy with the result. It had been a very profitable investment and sale when farm land was at its peak.

The tenant did very well too. He sold all he had bought very shortly afterwards, and selling with vacant possession he made a good profit. This sale divided the land into several lots, the two main lots to local farmers. The farmhouse was sold separately and the stone built farm buildings were converted and extended into three nice dwellings and sold.

Joan and I had our 1982 holiday on Tresco and once again thoroughly enjoyed it, the only snag was the journey time, and we explored every possible alternative without success.

The builder had now finished at The Bothy. Dick Willan was approaching retirement age. He had worked at The Bothy on and off for about three years and often said he was looking forward to his retirement and his pension.

He finished work at The Bothy on Friday night, came on Monday morning with Edmondson's pick-up truck, took all the tools, concrete mixer etc. away and died 48 hours later from a heart attack at his home in Burton-in-Lonsdale – jolly hard lines for a really good country workman.

Towards the end of 1982 my meeting with my accountants again gave rise to the question of inheritance tax, and in consequence Joan and I went over the whole question again. I asked Joan, in view of our long and sincere friendship, and my earnest wish to secure her future, would it not be a good idea to get married in 1983.

Joan said she had thought about it quite a lot recently and she would be very happy to become Mrs. Bridges as early in 1983 as convenient.

All the legal and accountancy requirements were set in motion and Joan and I were married at the registry office in Lancaster a.m. 2nd February 1983. I was

82 to be 83 on 11th May, Joan was 76, to be 77 on 5th July 1983. It was a quiet family wedding. My sister, Rose, and her husband, Arthur Fryer, my brother, Frank and his wife, Doris, Mrs. I. Adams and J. W. Greenwood, accountants from Moore & Smalley, and R. N. Hardy, solicitor from Senior, Calveley and Hardy, Lytham. All went according to plan, brother Frank, a keen photographer, took photographs and most important I suppose apart from the actual marriage ceremony was the signing of the marriage settlement, witnessing and so forth. I had long decided on my own that apart from the Family Settlement for my eight grandchildren living in England, I would not leave any lump sums of capital above £1,000 to anyone but would put funds into trusts under control of independent trustees who would distribute the income only to the named beneficiaries and as the beneficiaries died the income and capital would go to the Harold Bridges Foundation.

In accordance with this plan of mine the Marriage Settlement was drawn up on the basis of my paying £250,000 into the Marriage Settlement Trust Fund. I would have no control in any way over it. Trustees would pay the income to Joan during her lifetime and on her death the whole of the funds capital and income would go to the Harold Bridges' Foundation.

The idea behind all this was that on my death there would be a considerable saving in inheritance tax. Joan was six years younger than me and it was always thought that females tended to live longer than males, so Joan would be financially secure for her lifetime.

I could not retract or alter the Trust Deed as I could my will and I was very happy indeed when it was all completed.

We had lunch in Morecambe and Joan and I went in the Range Rover to Kildwick Hall in Yorkshire for a few days. We had already decided we would have our honeymoon holiday 14 days on Tresco in May 1983 and our usual 14 days holiday also on Tresco in September 1983.

The day after we arrived at Kildwick Hall there was a fall of snow about six inches. It soon cleared away. We were not so favourably impressed with Kildwick Hall. I suppose the middle of winter is not the best time to holiday.

On our return home we received many messages of congratulations and both settled down very happily as a married couple at The Bothy.

May 1983 soon came along and we were very pleased that British International Helicopters had started a summer service of flights direct from Penzance to Tresco, which was a big improvement on the journey. The flight from Penzance to Tresco took about 20 minutes for the 40 miles and we were met at the Heliport on Tresco by the hotel bus which was a four wheel passenger trailer towed by a farm tractor. Quite a novelty ride, all the seats faced outwards and there were no side windows, the journey to the hotel was ten to fifteen minutes.

Our 1983 September holiday was another very happy one. We did seem to be very fortunate in that we had very few wet days, and everything went according to plan so we booked again for September 1984.

So far as I can remember the only event to record in 1984 is that I sold the land and building Spinney Barn which I had purchased in 1970 from the owners of the Highwayman Inn, Boddingtons Breweries Ltd. We had tidied up the whole site which had been the village garden refuse dump, built boundary walls and re-roofed the stone building.

R. Turner of Bentham handled the sale very well. We had obtained outline planning permission and all this was reflected in the sale price with which I was very pleased, another hunch of mine which came out very well. The purchaser made a very good job of the conversion into an all stone built residence, which is a credit to the village and him.

In 1984 and 1985 we tried an alternative route to Penzance on our way to Tresco. On one journey we took the train Lancaster to London, stayed with Joan's daughter, Patricia, two nights then early train Paddington to Penzance and caught the afternoon helicopter to Tresco. The other occasion we left Lancaster by train very early to Euston, London, taxi to Paddington and again were in Penzance for the afternoon helicopter to Tresco. On the return journeys the same problems of train changes arose, and we decided that in 1986 we would stay in Penzance overnight, which would enable us to take a through train from Lancaster to Penzance, and catch the morning helicopter to Tresco. On the return journey we would stay the night in Penzance and catch the only through train Penzance to Lancaster at 7.30 a.m. This would save all the hassle of train changes, worrying about missed connections and so forth, but so far as Joan an I were concerned it was not to be.

The early days of 1986 Joan began to complain of stomach upsets, lack of appetite etc. Her doctor gave her tablets, which did not do any good. Several times the tablets were changed without any improvement. We were due to go to Tresco in late May. We had booked our room at the Island Hotel for May 1986 in autumn 1985. Also we had booked a room at the Mount Prospect Hotel in Penzance for one night on the outward and return journey. I had also got the helicopter flight tickets.

I felt it would be unwise to carry on with our holiday arrangements without seeing Joan's doctor for the all clear. An appointment was made. When Joan went to the surgery she found the doctor whom she usually saw and had prescribed the various tablets over the past 4/5 months was away on holiday, so she had to see another doctor in the practice, whom Joan knew very well. The first comment of this doctor was, 'Goodness me, Mrs. Bridges, whatever is the matter'? Apparently Joan's features had so changed that it was immediately noticed by the doctor. Joan explained how she felt and about the tablets. The doctor then asked Joan a few questions, had her lie on the surgery couch and felt her tummy. In five minutes the doctor said, 'Well you can forget about

Tresco. You must go into hospital and very soon'.

Arrangements were made and I took Joan to The Lakeland & Nuffield Hospital in Lancaster where X-ray plates were taken. We waited till they were processed and took them to Joan's doctor the same day.

Next day the doctor rang to say arrangements had been made for a specialist surgeon to see Joan with the X-ray plates. Two days later when we attended we took the X-ray plates with us for the surgeon to see.

After a short chat with Joan about her condition he took the plates out of the envelope, held them up to his lamp, turned to me and said, 'Oh dear, what a mess'. Joan asked what he meant and told him she wanted the truth and to know no matter what it was.

The doctor replied, 'I fear, in fact, I am certain from these plates you have a very serious tumour problem at the base of your stomach.'

Arrangements were made for Joan to go into the Nuffield Hospital next day, and two days later she had major surgery which confirmed she had three malignant tumours at the base of her stomach, part had become attached to a main artery from the region of the stomach to the liver. It was too dangerous to attempt to remove or treat the tumours and all they had been able to do was bypass or isolate the lower part of the stomach which would possibly give some relief and enable some form of food to be taken.

Joan and I learned this awful news three or four days after the operation, and I cannot describe the shock to us both. Joan was very very brave, she insisted the surgeon explain it all in detail, and then said, 'Let me have it straight. How long have I to live?' The surgeon said, 'Possibly four to six months. It is very difficult to forecast.'

The surgeon was standing at the foot of Joan's bed. I sat at the side holding Joan's hands. We looked into each other's eyes for what seemed a long time. I gave Joan a kiss and we both shed a tear. The surgeon said, 'I am so sorry. The position of the tumours prevents any surgery'. Joan's courage in the face of this awful outcome of the operation was fantastic. The hospital matron, sisters and doctors all made comments at various times on Joan's bravery. Joan made a wonderful recovery from the actual operation, nine days later she was ready to go into a nursing home for convalescence. Arrangements had been made with Fairfield Hall Nursing Home, Westbourne Road, Lancaster, where full nursing care was provided. Matron at Nuffield applied to the Lancaster Royal Infirmary for an ambulance to move Joan which would be paid for if required, and was informed that as the movement was for a private patient, from a private hospital to a private nursing home, an ambulance could not be provided. Whether this decision was a N.H.S. ruling or union drivers I don't know. Matron said she could get an ambulance from a firm in Kendal who provided the service as a business.

Kendal is 30 miles from Lancaster and Joan's journey would be under one mile, what a farce, 60 miles for a two mile journey.

However, I recalled that the County Director of St. John's Ambulance Association, Captain T. N. Catlow, CBE RN (retd.) JP lived in Tunstall about two miles from Burrow. I gave him a ring and explained the problem. He said, 'St. John's will find Joan an ambulance and be very pleased to do so. I will get in touch with St. John's, Morecambe and they will contact Matron at the hospital.'

So, problem solved, Joan was moved very comfortably and efficiently to the nursing home. I saw Mr. Catlow at Church the following Sunday, and thanked him and St. John's from Joan and I for his help. He said, 'Look Harold, it was a pleasure to help. St. John's in Lancashire has to date received just over £60,000 from your Foundation and it was the very least we could do'.

Joan had a very nice room, very soon filled with flowers from our many friends and well wishers. Everyone at the nursing home was very kind, efficient and caring to a very high degree. For the remainder of June and all July 1986 I went to see Joan every afternoon from around 2.30 p.m. to 6.30 p.m. The staff nurse brought afternoon tea and it was heartbreaking to see the very few times Joan would have anything to eat or drink and I was told this applied at most meal times. Joan had no appetite at all and this, of course, led to a gradual increasing weakness and deterioration in her general condition.

At the end of July Joan said she now felt she had not long to live and would like to be at home at The Bothy when the end came. Joan had to use all her powers of persuasion to the doctors and nursing staff to get her way. So in early August I brought Joan home in the Range Rover. Arrangements had been made for day nursing care, and for three weeks Joan was much happier and brighter at The Bothy.

It was a very good month weatherwise and each afternoon Joan would sit in the front porch of The Bothy, where she could see all her lovely flowering pot plants, the birds in the garden and river and lovely views across and down the Lune Valley. Relatives and friends came to see her by arrangement and Patricia her daughter. All the time Joan was gradually getting weaker and by the end of August the doctor and nurses agreed the amount of nursing care Joan needed could no longer be provided at The Bothy and so I took Joan back to the nursing home in the Range Rover. Joan loved the Range Rover. I continued my daily visits to see Joan and we talked when she was not too tired of our happy memories: Clovelly, Tresco and our holiday in Norfolk with my sister, Rose, in late 1985, the last holiday we had, and in the Range Rover.

Joan was very strong in her Christian beliefs and principles, she knew I was not so firmly convinced of the life hereafter, and she said I was a free thinker and no worse for that. One day on this subject I said, 'Well Joan you are so firmly convinced what you believe is correct, and it may well be, your only brother Fred was drowned in Australia many years ago, and he will be waiting for you. Alice, my wife, your very good friend died in 1977 so she will be waiting for you, your sister Thea died a few years ago, she will be waiting for you and if I keep my good health I would like to live to be 100, but I will die some day and come along too'. Joan looked me straight in the eyes and said with a little smile, 'Yes my dear, don't be too long will you?' (What can you answer to that?) The way Joan made jokes and comments about her illness astounded everyone. I am sure it was her strong Christian belief that gave her the strength and the courage.

One day at afternoon tea the nurse persuaded Joan to have a little piece of cake and a drink of milk. A few minutes later nurse turned Joan over to be more comfortable, which resulted in a tummy rumble. Joan smiled and said, 'Listen to that, my three little devils are fighting for what I have just had'.

During the last two weeks the sisters on night duty 'phoned me three separate times in the small hours of the morning to say Joan was failing fast, would I come at once, which I did right away each time. It was usually 2.30 a.m. to 3.00 a.m. when I arrived, and each time after I arrived and sat beside the bed, Joan would open her eyes just once, smile, give my hand such a weak little squeeze and go to sleep. She knew I was there.

Before Joan went into hospital I had cancelled all our holiday arrangements for 1986. Joan said she hoped and wished that so long as I could make the journey I would go to Tresco each year in her memory, so I will while I can.

Inevitably came the last day. My dear Joan passed away peacefully late afternoon 23rd September 1986. Funeral arrangements were all according to Joan's wishes which she had recorded. Funeral service at St. John's, Tunstall, cremation at Lancaster and her ashes laid to rest next to Alice's, beneath the memorial window, where Joan and I had attended early communion at 8.00 a.m. regularly for over seven years.

Up to knowing she was dying of cancer Joan had always been most insistent on having what she called a proper Christian burial and no cremation, when she knew the inevitable she said, 'My three little devils are going to kill me but I will win in the end. I'll burn the little devils, I WILL be cremated, so I will win'. What a brave little lady. God Bless Her.

The church was almost full at the funeral service and donations to North West Cancer Research in lieu of flowers raised several hundred pounds. Joan's daughter, Patricia, came from Germany and son, John, from Paris, and stayed with their father, George Clough, at Keepers Cottage, Burrow.

I received very many letters and messages of sympathy, everyone was very kind, helpful and very sad. Joan was such a cheerful, optimistic loving person and in consequence was sadly missed.

Chapter Thirteen

Life Goes On

S O HERE I was, on my own again, 86 years of age, and to think about my future plans was my first thought. I had lived in the Lune Valley 22 years, my two wives laid to rest in St. John's Tunstall, and my many friends in the valley, made me feel I must and would stay at The Bothy.

My eldest son, Charles and his wife, Ann, were very kind in coming to Burrow most weekends, arriving Sunday morning and returning to Bolton Sunday evening. Ann would cook Sunday dinner, wash and iron my laundry and between them leave everywhere spick and span for another week.

At Christmas 1986 Ann and Charles stayed at The Bothy over the Christmas holiday and we all went to my sister Rose at Grimsargh for dinner on Christmas day 1986. During general conversation I learned that Charles and Ann had been thinking about a move from Bolton, and I more in a joke than anything said, 'Why not come to Burrow and look after me?' This set us all thinking about what sort of arrangements could be made. Ann was working full time at Littlewoods Store in Manchester, she had been there about 12 years and was departmental manager in the textiles department. Before that she had been at Marks & Spencer and Debenham stores. Charles was working for a road transport operator, where he had been about 10 years. Eventually we sorted out what would need to be done, so that everyone was happy and willing to plan our future together.

The first requirement was accommodation at The Bothy. After a lot of thought and scheming we decided on alteration to The Bothy and adjoining outbuildings that would enable Ann and Charles to have a nice size lounge and double bedroom with w.c., washbasin and shower all *ensuite*, as their own private rooms. This plan required the demolition of a concrete block wall about 14 ft long and 7 ft high between my office/study and an outbuilding.

My builder, John Edmondson, could not start on the alterations for two weeks, so I set about it myself. It was winter, bad weather and it was an inside job. All went well, I had the wall down, carted away in my dumper and all cleaned, ready for the builder to start. I had the local joiner from Cowan Bridge, G. Huggonson, decorator, W. Denninson from Casterton and my gardener/handyman, Michael Reakes, part-timer, did all the plumbing. They all worked very well together, did a first class job, and so Charles and Ann moved into The Bothy on 21st March 1987. Ann chose and arranged for carpets, curtains etc. and named the extension 'The Blue Suite', which was the colour scheme.

Ann did not want to take full-time job for a start, so she was able to arrange for part-time on five days a week by transfer to Littlewood's store in Lancaster. Charles was to carry on at Bolton for the time being, and seek employment locally. At 61 years of age in a country district this would likely not be easy.

However, all went very well. I had 10 or 12 laying hens and Ann took charge of these. She soon had them feeding out of her hand, and when spring came began taking an interest in the flower borders. Charles mowed the lawns, about 3/4 of an acre, and I looked after the kitchen garden, where I grew most ordinary vegetables, salads and soft fruit.

This was all a great relief and pleasure to me. It had been nine months from Joan going into hospital in June 1986 to 21st March 1987 when they came to The Bothy and was a very satisfactory solution to my problems. We all settled down together most amicably. Ann is an excellent cook, very clean and houseproud, just another Alice and Joan. I often reflect and realise how very, very fortunate I have been to be looked after so well for the 63 years since I married Alice.

Came holiday time, and I went for my 14 days to Tresco, Isles of Scilly in spring and autumn 1987. Charles and Ann had a very nice BMW car. I had the Range Rover and the Austin Metro, which I told Ann to use anytime just as she wished to get to work, etc.

April 1987 – the train times Lancaster to Penzance had been changed. The through train I wished to go on did not stop at Lancaster now, so Ann took me to Preston 2.30 a.m. to catch it. Charles and Ann had their 14 days holiday in June, and as usual went to Torquay for a well deserved rest and change.

So passed 1987, not very exciting in the latter half, certainly there was plenty going on in the first half. We had a quiet peaceful Christmas period at The Bothy, not too many visitors and Father Christmas arrived on time!

Early on in Joan's illness she had expressed a wish that anything in connection with a memorial to her should take the form of a new altar curtain at the church. Attempts had been made to find out how long the present one had been in use. It was literally falling to pieces. No one attending the church or on the Parochial Church Council could recall or say how old it was and there was no written record. I mentioned this to the Vicar, Reverend R. C. Riley. He put the matter before the Parochial Church Council and the ladies set things in motion to fulfil Joan's wish. In due course in 1988 the new curtain was installed and I arranged for the cost to be met. It has been greatly admired and a fitting memorial to a wonderful and very brave lady, who had attended the Church for over 20 years, my dear Joan. Part of the land I had bought from Stowe Trust Ltd. was a 27-acre area between the main road, A653, and the River Lune. It included several acres of woodlands, gravel beds and Leck Beck and was known as Burrow Holme. When I bought it in November 1975 it was subject to the usual agricultural agreement dated 23rd May 1955 between Stowe Trust Ltd. and a local farmer.

Burrow Holme had a bank of the River Lune about 400 yards as the west boundary; when I sold the fishing rights I agreed verbally with the purchaser that if ever Burrow Holme was for sale, I would let him know.

This led to negotiations starting on 23rd March 1988. The negotiations were very amicable but long drawn out, as the intending purchaser only wished to purchase a strip of land about average 15 yards wide, which he would fence off and maintain. The deal, as eventually agreed, also included two small sections of land and river bank which I had bought in 1961 and later there were, therefore, three separate conveyances involved.

However, eventually all problems were solved and I sold the strip 500 yards long by about 15 yards wide including 500 yards of River Lune bank. Contracts were signed on 4th April 1989 so the deal had taken just over 12 months to complete. I was very happy with the outcome, as this part of the River Lune is subject to severe bank erosion and I had got rid of a 500-yard responsibility of river bank.

Late in 1988 our neighbour, who had bought Mill Lodge from me in 1981, expressed a wish to buy a small plot of land next to his land, which I had bought in 1970 together with the private road and the old mill stream from the then local owner.

This small plot was subject to a right to park two cars for fishermen, which I had granted to the purchaser of the fishing rights in 1981. I could not, therefore, sell it with clear vacant possession, unless I could get agreement to vary the parking area to another space along the private road. Luckily I owned the land along the side of the road, and the fishing rights owners agreed to the variation, it was the same people with whom I was negotiating to sell the strip of Burrow Holme river bank.

While this was proceeding I realised I still owned the river bank in front of Mill Lodge. When I bought the fishing rights in 1961 it included the river bed, the river bank and about an acre of land, the site of Mill Lodge. About 1975 in order to preserve the river bank in front of Mill Lodge we had built a concrete wall to a height above flood level. When I sold Mill Lodge in 1981 the concrete wall was the river side boundary; when I sold the fishing rights in 1981 it included the river bed, so this left the river bank in front of Mill Lodge, 75 yards by 8 yards still owned by me.

I offered this to our neighbour with the parking area site and very wisely, I think, he agreed to buy. I was suited, I had now sold all my river bank and its erosion liability was no longer mine. Contracts were signed, 4th April 1989, another good deal. This now left me with Burrow Holme, now 25 acres or thereabouts, which was, of course, subject to the tenancy agreement of 1955. The tenant had on occasions expressed a willingness to negotiate to purchase Burrow Holme, he had two sons active on his farm, and was a near neighbour and had bought a large part of Robinson House Farm. We agreed a price and Burrow Holme was sold on 21st August 1989.

The private road, Mill Lane, is about 300 yards long from the main road, the A653 to the bank of the River Lune where Burrow Mill before 1936 was a water wheel driven saw mill on the Fenwicks Burrow Hall estate.

The water to drive the wheel was taken out of Leck Beck about half a mile from the mill, and passed under the main road then in an open stream behind the village and down the side of Mill Lane to the mill, over the wheel and then into the River Lune. The road and stream were not fenced off from the open agricultural pasture land to the south. The road edge and the stream edge were very close, the stream about 6 feet wide average and the road 9 feet.

During the building and road making at Mill Lodge we were having stone, sand and gravel delivered by Bradshaws Hauliers, Cowan Bridge. This usually came in 8-ton loads, and one day a tipper coming down the road must have got a bit too near the edge of the or road and stream. The stream bank gave way and the tipper with 8 tons of gravel ended up on its side in the stream, although the driver was O.K.

This gave me the idea of piping the stream with 12" concrete pipes, filling it in level with the field and road, sowing it with grass seeds and so make about ¼ acre more pasture and make the road safe for the future. This was completed and as the stream could be diverted into another stream behind Mill Farm, the 12" pipe was adequate to take the normal water flow, very much reduced after non-use of the water wheel.

All this meant that cattle and sheep had now unhindered access onto the road along its full length. The side of the road opposite the stream had a high hawthorn hedge and there were a few alder trees on the roadside. On wet, windy days and nights the cattle and sheep sheltered along the hedge and under the trees and did not want to move when traffic came down the road day or night; cattle, sheep, lambs in the spring, and when they had gone, barrow loads of dung to clear up.

The farmer who owned the field had two sons working on the farm with him. They were all very hard workers, he acquired extra suitable land if it became available near the farm, including some of Robinson House farm in 1982.

This progress, which I was glad to see as he was a near neighbour, meant that his cattle and sheep herd kept increasing in numbers. The owner of Mill Lodge, rightly, kept complaining about the state of the road at times before we had time to clean it up and the cattle on the road, suggesting it should be fenced off. I agreed and pointed out that the field owner had the right to use the road as he wished and that the purchase agreement did not mention fencing. He and the farmer had to join with me in the cleaning and maintenance of the road.

However, I said I would see what could be done about it. I wrote to the farmer on 4th May 1985 and, to cut a long story short and scores of letters later, legal and otherwise, the fence was erected, gates in agreed positions and the whole scheme completed on . . . wait for it . . . August 21, 1989. Over four years of tough negotiations, everyone happy, especially the solicitors, 'nuff said!

Charles and Ann had their annual 14 days holiday at Torquay in June 1989 and I went to Tresco in April and September 1989, staying in Penzance one night each way, so I could have a through train each way without any changes.

In September I had to come home two days early due to having caught a bad head and chest cold which was soon put right when I saw my own doctor, and had antibiotics. During 1989 I had begun to feel my age, 88½ and still willing to keep very active. I kept battling on. I used to feel more tired sooner than usual and began to lose my appetite.

While Ann and Charles were away in June this weakness increased rapidly, so the day they returned home Ann sent for the doctor. He called a few hours later, pulled my eyelids down and said, 'How long have you been like this, you're very anaemic'. I said, 'Rubbish. I'm not anaemic'. Clever me. The doctor took a sample of blood from my arm which he would send to Lancaster for tests and I had to stay indoors.

A day or two later, doctor 'phoned to say my blood count was 7.4. Normal would be between 12 and 14 and by all the rules I should be dead, 'Very cheerful', thought I! He had made arrangements at Lancaster and Lakeland Nuffield Hospital for a bed and I was to get there as soon as possible. This would be late afternoon. Nancy, my daughter, had come to see me so Ann, Nancy and I arrived at the hospital about five o'clock. In about ten minutes they had taken another blood sample, got me into bed and I was on a saline drip for about an hour. I expect this was while they did another blood test. Next thing I was on a blood drip for 12 hours, and by six o'clock next morning I had been given three pints of blood at £29.29 a pint. I said to the sister, 'If you carry on much longer blood will be running out of my ears, where does it all go?'

However, I certainly felt very much better very soon. A stomach check showed I had a very small bleeding ulcer above my stomach which might have been caused by tablets my previous doctor had prescribed for me for arthritis. All went well and I was home in five days feeling my old self again.

The medico's did not know whether the blood came from a white, black, yellow or brown donor, but it did the trick for me; another medical wonder I experienced and a life saved. Ann's mother had lived in or near Chester and Wrexham for most of her life. Ann and Charles went to see her at weekends occasionally to Rossett. During 1989 she began to have chest and breathing problems which worsened quickly by autumn, and Ann decided to have her mother nearer so she could see her everyday if possible. On Friday, 8th December, Ann's mother was brought from Rossett to Lancaster by Ann and Charles in the BMW and entered the Fairfield Hall Nursing Home, Lancaster, where she could have full nursing care. This was all that could be done. The surgeon specialist diagnosed lung cancer which could not be treated by an operation and it was, unfortunately, only a matter of time – weeks, perhaps days; all they could do was relieve the pain. Ann's mother died nine days later,

'What are his thoughts?' – my ninetieth birthday celebrations at Gibbon Bridge.

'A happy day' – my ninetieth birthday party. From left: John, myself, Charles and Nancy.

Sunday, 17th December 1989, in the morning and the funeral was arranged for Friday, 22nd December; a very sad Christmas for all of us.

The funeral was very simple as Ann and her mother wished, nine mourners – Ann and Charles, Nancy and I, Rose and Arthur and three from Rossett. It was a bitterly cold windy day, typical December. Our vicar, Reverend R. D. Riley, took the service at Lancaster Crematorium, the ashes to be laid to rest at our local church, St. John's, Tunstall, later.

So 1989 drew to a close on a very sad note, what would 1990 hold for us all? Who knows? Not me! Certainly the whole world seemed to be in turmoil – Panama, Eastern Europe, China, Hong Kong, The Phillipines and still the Irish problem. Which reminds me of 1921, the 'Black & Tans' and what might have been but for the RAMC Captain at Fulwood Barracks and his advice to me, 'Get into Road Transport'. How right he was. At home the industrial situation seemed beset by the annual round of pay talks, no one seemed to be prepared to be tolerant in their demands for more money and less work.

The first event of purely local interest in 1990 was the retirement of our vicar, Reverend R. C. Riley, after 17 years as our parson. Unmarried, his mother was 93 and his sister, Barbara, 68, lived with the vicar at the vicarage in Church Lane, Tunstall. The farewell presentation and party held at the Village Hall, Tunstall on Sunday 14th January 1990 was very well attended. The vicar was presented with a painting of the church and a cheque for £1,200. I expect it will be some time before we have another vicar, the present vicarage is far too big by present standards, needs modernising and has a very big garden.

The old school next to the church is being converted to a modern vicarage, and at the same time the three parishes of Leck, Tunstall and Melling are to be merged, to have one vicar at the new vicarage. Mr. Riley, our recent vicar, has not found a house to retire to so is staying at the old vicarage as tenant for the time being. Early 1990 was on the whole a mild uneventful period, no snow, and only two morning frosts which enabled me to press ahead with my kitchen garden and greenhouse, early spring works.

A letter from the trustees of The Harold Bridges' Foundation showing the total donations made to date.

I have nearly 200 square yards to manure and dig. I had this completed, broad beans sown and tomato plants in the greenhouse, planted cauliflower, brussels sprouts out and onion sets, and a few early potatoes before I left home for my spring holiday, 14 days on Tresco, Isles of Scilly from 11th April to 25th April 1990. I had very good weather, and my through train Lancaster to Penzance, nine hours, was spot on time on arrival.

The early gales of 1990 had caused a great deal of damage to trees on Tresco. I was informed around 200 mature trees had been lost. A temporary wooden school extra classroom, about 20 feet by 10 feet,, had been lifted by the gale and dropped on the beach, 150 yards away. The church roof was also badly damaged and needed urgent and costly repairs, a rather daunting task for a small island community.

```
H Bridges Esq Comm St J OBE
A.I.R. 90
Luneside
Burrow
Via Carnforth
LA2 2RJ


12 May 1992

Dear Mr Bridges

Trustees of The Harold Bridges' Foundation

We thought you would like to know that with dona-
tions made this year, the total donations made
by the Foundation to date amount to £1,083,290
(One million and eighty three thousand two hun-
dred and ninety pounds). We felt you would
appreciate this formal letter signed by the
Trustees to mark this achievement.


Yours sincerely

G. Gell on behalf of The Royal Bank of Scotland
plc
Richard Hardy, Jeffrey Greenwood
Trustees of The Harold Bridges' Foundation
```

Arrived home safely, 25th April 1990, my 13th trip by British Rail, nine hours each way, 234 hours, and on only one occasion was my train late due to diesel engine failure on a return journey when approaching Birmingham. Well done British Rail. The train is the 'Cornish Scot', Edinburgh to Penzance and I have always found I had no fault to find with the condition of the carriages. It is said comparisons can be odious. The rail fare spring 1990 Lancaster – Penzance return, standard class, senior citizen blue saver was £36.65, near enough to £2 per hour; the helicopter fare from Penzance to Tresco or Tresco to Penzance takes 20 minutes and costs £33 which is £99 an hour, so much for modern travel.

May and a lovely spring, very soon my daughter Nancy and daughter-in-law, Ann, were busy making preparations for my 90th birthday on 11th May 1990. They did a really wonderful job. Ann did a very good notice which was on the notice board at St. John's Church, Tunstall, for two Sundays and on the village of Burrow notice board all one week, to let all our friends in and around the two villages know that I would be AT HOME 2.00 p.m. to 5.00 p.m. Friday, 11th May 1990 to celebrate my 90th birthday and all would be welcome.

It was a lovely sunny day. Nancy and Ann had made very good ample catering for food and drink. Around thirty of our friends joined us for the afternoon and everyone felt it was a great success and occasion to be remembered. I received all manner of presents and 54 birthday greetings cards. My two grandsons, John and Steven, 'phoned from South Africa and in all it was a day to be remembered.

On Sunday, 13th May we had the family get together and celebrations at The Gibbon Bridge Hotel, Chipping, Nr. Preston. In all around 30 had a jolly good meal and afternoon. I have eight grandchildren in England, the only one absent was John's elder son, Michael, who had got married on 28th April and was away on honeymoon. Five great grandchildren, 7 grandchildren, wives, husbands and fiancés, with my own two sons, their wives and Nancy, my only daughter, made up a real family do, which everyone enjoyed. So passed a very memorable occasion, the like of which not many people are fortunate enough to attain with generally such really good health that I enjoy. Good health is without any shadow of doubt the greatest blessing anyone can have, and for my good health, I am most sincerely and gratefully thankful.

Next on the list of events in 1991 was a meeting of trustees of the Harold Bridges' Foundation on 5th June. Normally a trustees' meeting is held roughly every three months when Nancy and I attend, together with The Royal Bank of Scotland Trustees Division, Preston Manager, and J. W. Greenwood and R. N. Hardy, the other trustees. The early part of the meeting is also attended by an investment officer from the bank to advise and discuss the investment portfolio results and any changes considered.

The first meeting after 5th April is also the annual general meeting when the annual accounts, balance sheet and matters related to donations are considered. The accounts to 5th April 1991 showed assets at approaching one and a quarter million pounds, donations made for year end 5th April 1991, £106,200 and total donations to same date £1,005,140. Yes – one million, five thousand one hundred and forty pounds. Yes – and he left school on his thirteenth birthday!

While I am sure my family and certainly myself are very proud of the Foundation's achievements we have always tried to keep a very low profile and very rarely are donations mentioned in the press or other media.

In case anyone who left school as I did on my *thirteenth* birthday, or later, and having made the progress I did, feels inclined to do likewise, the prelude to the Foundations Annual Accounts is as follows:

Trustees Of The Harold Bridges' Foundation
Capital And Income Accounts
For The Year Ended
5 April 1991
And Balance Sheet
As At
5 April 1991
Date of Settlement: 14 October 1963 (established as The Harold and Alice Bridges' Charity) and registered with the Charity Commission under Number 236654. For day-to-day operations, the Settlement is known as The Harold Bridges' Foundation.

Terms of the Trust: The income and capital is to be applied for Charitable purposes and objects as the Trustees may think fit.

Investment: The Trustees have wide power of investment in relation to the Trust monies but their policy is generally to avoid companies having interest in breweries or tobacco. The Trustees' investment objectives are:

   a)   to achieve an income return 40% higher than that indicated by the FT A11 Shares Index, and

   b)   to achieve an annual rate of dividend growth and capital growth in excess of the rate of inflation.

Present Trustees:
The Royal Bank of Scotland Plc.
Mr. Richard Newell Hardy (solicitor) and
Mr. Jeffrey Wyndham Greenwood (Chartered Accountant)

Looking back over the many years of the Foundation's activities, I very often recall when on 11 May 1936 Alice for my 36th birthday gave me a framed floral card, very nicely and tastefully printed which for the next 30 years was hung in my office over my desk and for the following 24 years has been hung in Mill Lodge and The Bothy. It reads as follows:

I Shall Pass Through This World But Once.
Any good thing therefore that I can do,
or any kindness that I can show to any fellow creature
Let me do it now
Let me not defer or neglect it,
for I shall not pass this way again.
(Anon)

Twenty seven years later events which I have told led to the formation of The Foundation in 1963, another instance of seemingly trivial incidents which can influence happenings many years later.

'Cast thy bread upon the water
And it shall return after many days'

and I add – *'With ham between it if you're lucky!'*

So much for what I remember of the past; 90 years 11th May 1900 – 11th May 1990, two world wars, near enough to ten years at war, followed by 45 years comparative peace. Looking back again and taking everything into account, I have no regrets for actions I took at various times, and would not have wished for anything different or better, even if that had been possible.

I have had a wonderful, exciting and successful life, and have been blessed by being able so far to have enjoyed over 20 years healthy retirement from active business, following 53 years of happy, oh so happy married life with my dear Alice. My success in business could never have been achieved without the support of hard working, loyal and happy employees for forty four years, encouraged no doubt by the personal interest Alice and I always took in our employees in all grades, and the non-contribution pension and profit sharing schemes we operated in the transport companies.

I am sure it would also be correct to say how over so many long years since 1926 the services, wise counsel and advice given to me by the transport companies' accountants and solicitors, played a considerable part in our success. When I started in business in 1921 there were no PAYE, tax deductions; employers supplied information to the Inland Revenue and the employee sent in his own tax return and received a demand note where applicable. In consequence, as I was self-employed, I was not asked for an income return till 1927 when in consequence of buying 137 Warton Street, Lytham, the Inland Revenue got a line on me (after six years). A friend suggested I see William

Latham, who had recently opened an office in Park Street, Lytham. Mr. Latham had been in H. M. Forces, qualified as a chartered accountant on demobilisation and on his death at a comparatively young age he was succeeded by Frank Greathead as senior partner and on his retirement by David Denton. All these served us well over so many long exciting years, and it was only on the sale of Bridges Transport Ltd. to Tayforth in 1966 that William Latham & Co. ceased as accountants to the transport company.

I have mentioned earlier it was on the purchase of 137 Warton Street that I met Mr. Robson Byers, who like Mr. Latham had set up a solicitor's office in Market Square, Lytham, later moved to 8 Hastings Place. Over the years, Mr. Byers was followed by Mr. Fred Senior, and on his death by Mr. Calveley and on his retirement by Mr. R. N. Hardy as senior partners. At the time of writing Mr. R. N. Hardy is still the family solicitor and a trustee of The Foundation and ten family settlements. Sixty-four years is a long time to have such a close relationship and I am deeply grateful for all the wise counsel and advice I had for sixty-four years from the original, succeeding and present partners and staff of the now Senior, Calveley & Hardy solicitors.

One other professional service is worthy of mention. In 1927 we insured the property in Victoria Street, Lytham, and 137 Warton Street through insurance brokers Donald Moores Ltd., St. Annes, soon afterwards taken over by the senior active partner, J. I. Badger, who was a big strapping young chap who played rugby for Fylde R. F. Club, Ansdell. James Ingham Badger or, as we called him Jimmy Badger, formed the business into Ingham Badger Ltd and from 1927 to 1966 when we sold the transport business to Tayforth Ltd. Ingham Badger Ltd. acted as insurance brokers for the whole of our insurances, and always all those years did a really good job. Jim Badger was always most meticulous in all his duties as our broker and I felt a great sense of loss when Jim died, found dead in his car parked at the roadside on the outskirts of Blackpool from a sudden heart failure.

5th June 1992

I see it is well over three years since I first put pen to paper to record for posterity some of the events and incidents of ninety years as I remember them. The story I have told is to my knowledge and belief all the truth as I remember it. There is no doubt many events and incidents have gone from my memory, and also no doubt I shall remember many more which have not been recorded. The story is all from memory as I remember it; some events are supported by documents, and a few by old faded photographs, and papers.

I will repeat what I said at the start of my story, that it is dedicated to my dear wife, Alice, without whom none of what I have told since 1921 would have been possible.

To those who read my story, particularly those at the start of careers, and to those who have made it to the top or anywhere in between, I would say remember the picture Alice gave me in 1936:

'I Shall Pass Through this World But Once'
Any good thing therefore that I can do
or any kindness I can show to any fellow creature
Let me do it now
Let me not defer or neglect it,
For I shall not pass this way again.'

and my final words: *'Go Thou and do likewise'*

HAROLD BRIDGES, O.B.E., K. St. J.
A.I.R. 90
Luneside
Burrow
Via Carnforth
LA6 2RJ